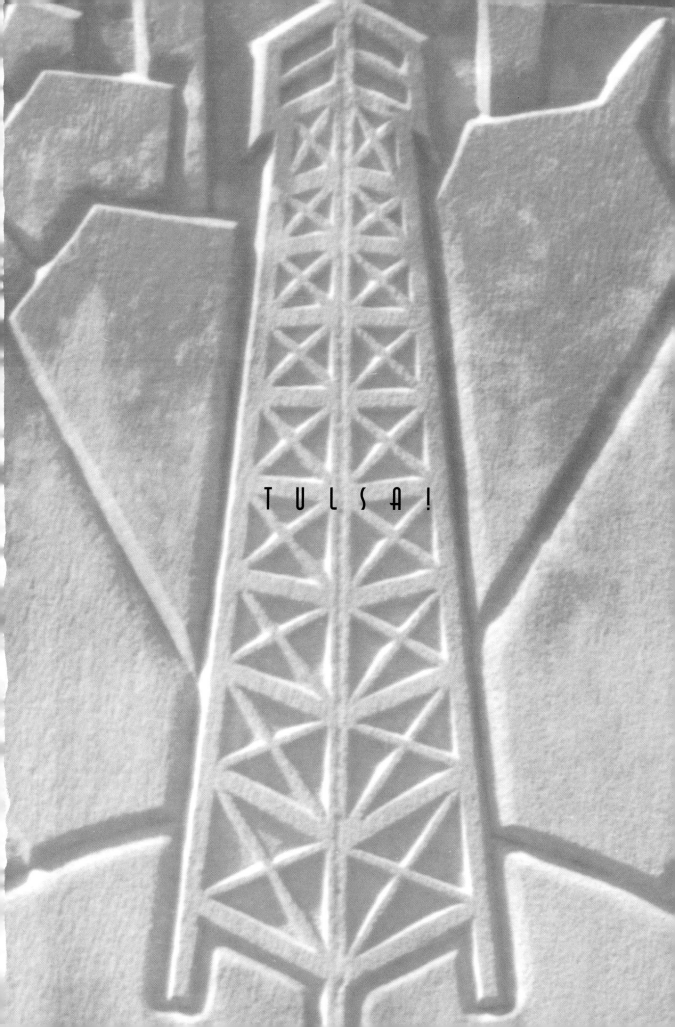

TULSA!

TULSA!

BIOGRAPHY OF THE AMERICAN CITY

Danney Goble, Ph.D.

Council Oak Books, Tulsa

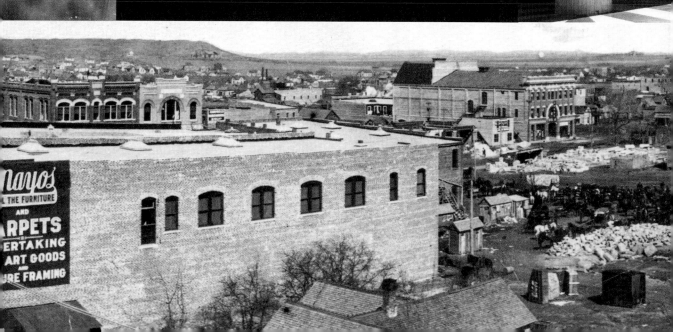

PUBLICATION OF *TULSA!* WAS MADE POSSIBLE BY THE GENEROSITY OF

    THE HELMERICH FOUNDATION

    THE ZARROW FAMILIES, SOONER PIPE & SUPPLY

SPONSORS OF THE TULSA CENTENNIAL CELEBRATION:

    THE DEPARTMENT OF TOURISM, STATE OF OKLAHOMA

    PEPSI CORPORATION

    CITY OF TULSA

COUNCIL OAK BOOKS

1350 East 15th Street

Tulsa, Oklahoma 74120

Tel. (918) 587-6454

LIBRARY OF CONGRESS CATALOGING-IN-PUBLICATION DATA

Goble, Danney, 1946–
    Tulsa! : biography of the American city / Danney Goble.
        p. cm.
    Includes bibliographical references and index.
    ISBN 1-57178-051-3 (cloth)
    1. Tulsa (Okla.)—History. 2. Tulsa (Okla.)—Economic conditions.
I. Title.
F704.T92G63 1997
976.6'86—DC21   97-34094
                                CIP

DESIGN   Carol Haralson

PHOTO RESEARCH   Robert Powers, with assistance from Jeff Kauffman

PROOFREADING   Hazel Rowena Mills and Michael Hightower

OBJECT AND COVER PHOTOGRAPHY   Don Wheeler

*All historical photographs unless otherwise designated
are from the collection of the Tulsa Historical Society
and are published courtesy of THS.*

Printed in Canada

BOOK COMMITTEE

Sharon King Davis, *General Chairman,*
Eddie Faye Gates, Ann Patton, Robert
Powers, Ron Ricketts, Larry Silvey,
Suzann Stewart

TULSA CENTENNIAL
STEERING COMMITTEE

Mayor M. Susan Savage, *Honorary
Chair,* Sharon King Davis, *Chair,*
Councilor Vickie Cleveland, Barbara J.
Gardner, Eddie Faye Gates, Walter M.
Helmerich III, Senator Maxine
Horner, Ed Keller, Paula Moore, Dean
Sims, George A. Singer, Paula Hale,
Centennial Coordinator, Peter and
Nancy Meinig, *Book Premier Chairs*

Tulsa
Celebrating
100 Years.

T U L S A !

Preface

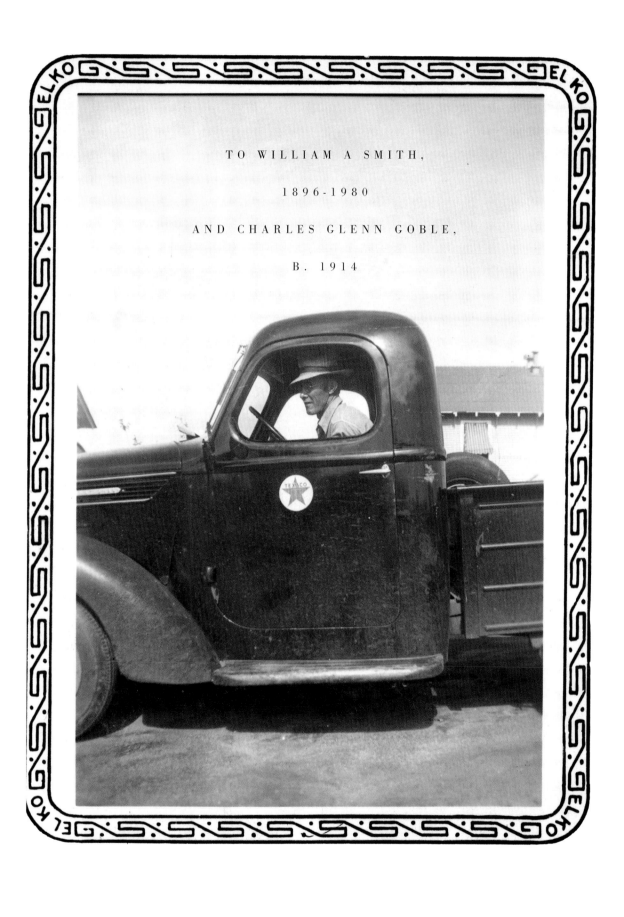

TO WILLIAM A SMITH,

1896-1980

AND CHARLES GLENN GOBLE,

B. 1914

"*f making many books there is no end*" (ECCLESIASTES 12:12, RSV). The words are those of the Old Testament writer known only as the Preacher. As is true of many bits of Scripture, I have never been entirely sure just what they mean, since they admit to at least two different readings. One bemoans the number of books to be read; the other laments the difficulties of writing them.

Either interpretation accurately fits my experience with this book. Before the writing even began, there was much reading to do, quite enough to affirm the verse's final words: "much study is a weariness of the flesh." Flesh did grow weary as it labored through some ten thousand or more pages of books, articles, theses, dissertations, and research notes. I confess that the spirit (to make another biblical allusion) sometimes faded to less than strong. Nonetheless, flesh and spirit combined to make this book, and its readers should know that it is both a work and a statement.

As a work, it is a history of Tulsa, Oklahoma, as it observes the centennial of its incorporation as a city ("of the second class") on January 18, 1898. Commissioned to become part of the official Tulsa centennial celebration, it has a purpose to record, as accurately and faithfully as possible, the major events and personalities that shaped Tulsa's history during its first century as a city. In fact, it covers more than a century, since it (like Tulsa) begins with the first permanent human settlement of the land that gently undulates away from the sandy banks of the Arkansas River. Thus, the book is a history of Tulsa—as well as Tulsee Town, Tulsi, and Tallasi, names favored by its first residents, the ones others called Creeks.

This book also is a statement, and its readers deserve to know that up front. In some measure, any work of history must be one. However objective or however dispassionate a historian might fancy himself or herself, the fact is that (appearances sometimes to the contrary) all historians started as human beings. They remained human even while and after receiving their graduate training. As human beings, they have their biases and their preferences. I do, and I intend to make them explicit in a moment. But even a perfectly rational, perfectly impartial, perfectly detached historian (which is to say, a non-human historian) would still have the problem of selectivity. Not every fact can be included, not every name mentioned, not every event discussed—particularly not in a book that was understood to cover more than one hundred years in approximately three hundred manuscript pages. How, then, does one choose what to include and what to omit?

Enter this book as a statement, guided in part by its writer's predilections. Before I had collected even one of the final ten thousand pages of research, I had a distinct vision of the final book's shape. I saw a book that was chronological, narrative, inclusive, and readable. Each adjective guided everything that followed.

Chronological, it would recount Tulsa's long history as it happened, year by year or, at least, decade by decade. Because I made that choice, readers interested chiefly in Tulsa's social history will find themselves skipping from chapter to chapter. Readers interested in its economic history will dip into a few pages here and a few more there. Should that be cumbersome, they might take solace in the fact that the Tulsans who made its economic history, its social history, and its every other kind of history found themselves making a life even while they were also making a living and making a city.

Narrative, the book would be built around a series of stories. Academic historians often forget that the historian began as a storyteller. This historian (although an academic) not only remembers that but rejoices in it. Readers will find here stories about desperate Native Americans—and white desperadoes. Down-and-out wildcatters—as well as up-and-coming millionaires. Along the way, they will discover the legend of a particular hotel, the businesses along certain streets, and such Tulsa personalities as a thirty-year-old millionaire and an eighty-seven-year-old madam.

They will not find all of the Native Americans, all of the desperadoes, all of the buildings, all of the businesses, or—for that matter—all of the madams. This book is inclusive only in the sense that it strives to represent, as much as possible, the people who have made Tulsa their homes and have made Tulsa's history theirs too.

Tulsa is a city of many histories, not all of which could be included. Its record of generous philanthropy, whether expressed in the singular gifts of a man like W. K. Warren or from families like the Helmerichs and Zarrows, is untold in these pages. Its citizens' remarkable support for the United Way and other, nonaffiliated social agencies is suggested but not fully developed. The best work of innumerable public servants—one thinks of J. D. Metcalf's untiring efforts at managing the city's floodplain—is unacknowledged, even though they have benefited countless Tulsans.

Overall readability, not any one author's bias, is what closes these pages to such stories. I do hope that readers find it readable. Every page, every sentence, nearly every word has gone through at least twenty revisions, some by myself, others by generous coworkers. If the text flows, if it is clear, if it is dramatic, if it is (at spots) funny and (at other spots) sad, all of us, working together, will have succeeded. If not, I alone have failed. After all, statements unread are no statements at all.

As mentioned, this book is a statement. Whatever its origins, it is not really (or, more accurately, not *merely*) a celebration of Tulsa's history as a city. It is not even (just) an observance. What it seeks is a consideration more than a celebration, an observation more than an observance. Looming behind every story and every chapter is the sense that Tulsa is really a representative American city, one with some unique features, but mostly one that has wrestled with problems universal to all our nation's cities. As is true in the others, Tulsans have sometimes achieved mightily, but they also sometimes have failed miserably. This book's readers will find many of both the successes and the failures in its pages. Should they judge there to be too much of the latter, my answer is this: It really did happen, it really was important, and it really must be remembered. How else might we better assure that it does not happen again?

I assure everyone that, if I ever have to write again, I want to have the kind of resources available to me on this book. Sharon King Davis, Paula Hale, and the others who work so hard to commemorate the city's centennial have been indispensable on this, just one of the projects they oversee. The centennial's special book committee—consisting of Eddie Faye Gates, Ann Patton, Larry Silvey, Ron Ricketts, Suzann Stewart, and Robert Powers—has been good enough to trust me and wise enough to correct me. Robert Powers also heads the Tulsa Historical Society. Without his interest, his work, and his resources, there might be no book at all. If there were, it would not be a very good one.

I sometimes say that my job in the project's earliest stages was to recruit and command a small army of research assistants. I was lucky to recruit an excellent army and luckier still to discover that they needed little command. All were as imaginative as they were thorough. Most served without rank and, for that reason, are listed here in alphabetical order: Melanie Black, Olivia Cunningham, Alisa Dougless, Mary Alice Ingham, David Schumacher, Jane Spake, Brent Townsend, and Sarah Passmore.

One assistant did have rank: Sharon Vaughan Goble, my wife and faithful helpmate through this entire project. I can truly say that without her skills and her patience there never would have been this book. She created the twenty-five-page annotated bibliography that made possible the research. She maintained the order and comfort that made possible its writing. She also did much of the editing that made the writing better.

The book's dedication is to two men. William A. Smith was my maternal grandfather. He left a sharecropper's farm in Sequoyah County in 1920 to work in Tulsa-area oil fields. Men like him made a lot of Tulsa's history possible, and he, in particular, made it possible for me to write it. Charles Glenn Goble is my father. Although he has never lived in Tulsa, he is a man good enough that the loss is Tulsa's, not his. He also worked in oil and carried the mail, the two jobs interrupted by service in the Second Division, United States Marine Corps, 1942-1945. Men like him made a lot of things possible.

DANNEY GOBLE
Rogers University, January 31, 1997

A blending of many cultures, modern Tulsa proudly traces its roots to the days of Indian Territory and its first Tulsans to the First Americans. Above, U. S. Indian Band, ca. 1900. Below, early promotional booklet.

THE JOURNEY OF THE PEOPLE WHO BURNED THE SAME FIRE

Had he been fluent in the whites' tongue, he might have said that it was "unavoidable necessity" that forced him to repeat the pledge he first had made at the other village in the previous March. But Opothle Yahola owed his primacy to more than rhetorical eloquence in either the whites' or his own people's language. The *Yahola* of his name was less a surname than an honorific that served to identify him with a supernatural being of awesome power, one to whom all his fellow Creeks paid reverence and respect. In many years' battles and councils, Opothle Yahola had earned something of the same.

This time, though, he knew that no merely human honors would protect either him or his people from their certain fate. And so he rose to repeat his pledge. The people of his town and of many others, including the earlier village, "all burn the same fire and talk with the same tongue." Within a month, he promised, "we shall . . . take our last black drink in this nation, rub up our tradition plates, and commence our march." One of the anxious white men present was relieved when the great warrior added that he already had prepared "his marching physic" and that he was "preparing his traveling clothes, and will put out his old fire and never make or kindle it again until he reaches west of the Mississippi, there never to quench it again."

Surely the white recorder of Opothle Yahola's thoughts must have known the words "unavoidable necessity"; it was his people and his politicians that had made it so. For years, federal authorities had forced successive, solemn treaties upon the Creek people. Nearly all had required land cessions, and each had pledged that this one would be the last. The repeated promises had become repeated betrayals. Opothle Yahola himself had been one of the delegates who had traveled to Washington in 1832 to protest the federal refusal to enforce earlier agreements, only to be handed another one. Under this one, the Creeks would surrender all of their remaining lands, roughly 5,200,000 acres in Alabama, to the United States. Heads of families could first select a half-section (320 acres) of land to provide their homes. After the sites were surveyed and deeded, the owners would have to sell their land and its improvements within five years. The proceeds would be their individual recompenses for the loss of their nation. That completed, all Creeks were to be removed to the West, the United States paying the costs and providing a year's subsistence upon their arrival. The western lands were to be solemnly guaranteed to the emigrants and their descendants forever. In words that some, at least, would remember, the United States further pledged that no "state or Territory [shall] ever have a right to pass laws for the government of such Indians, but they shall be allowed to govern themselves."

No agreement could have looked more reasonable—nor have been more disastrous. As Grant Foreman, the most careful student of the entire process, would write a full century later,

> If the government had deliberately sought to accomplish the complete ruin and demoralization of the Creeks, a more vicious measure could hardly have been devised than the provision of the treaty permitting them to sell their selections under the influence that existed.

The "influence that existed" was mainly white Alabamians' insistence upon defrauding the Indians of as much as possible as soon as possible. Even before surveyors could set their stakes and unpack their instruments, swarms of whites descended upon Creek lands. They brazenly seized fields, crops, and livestock, driving their owners into the swamps or woods. They occupied the best of the abandoned homes and burned the rest. Many—no one knows how many—they killed. Neither threat of law nor pang of conscience stayed their bloody hands. Even among the more honorable, few bothered to make more than token payment for Indian property. The little money that changed hands often passed back again, exchanged for the whites' liquor. State officials only promoted the orgy. The Alabama legislature immediately designated the state's Indian country as eight new counties, and the governor referred aggrieved Indians to the courts of those counties as their only avenue of redress. He had to know it was a dead-end avenue: Alabama law disallowed Indian testimony in court proceedings involving whites.

Thus it was that Opothle Yahola had agreed to meet with federal agents at the village that his people called Lochapoka on March 28, 1836. Lochapoka—the word meant "place of turtles"—was a small and rather undistinguished Creek town that recognized its kinship to a much older and more honored town. The mother town's name was Tallasi, meaning "old town," a word that whites would eventually turn into several place names, one being Florida's capital, Tallahassee. Five hundred sixty-five people resided in Lochapoka in 1836, and surely all of them were present for the occasion.

No description of the site and no account of the assembly survives, but Lochapoka must have been like the many Creek towns of the day. Like nearby Coweta, Broken Arrow, and others, it would have been ringed with family dwellings, each constructed of upright timbers, the gaps filled with twigs and bark, the entire surface carefully plastered with clay. Behind each lay fields planted with corn and other vegetables, until then tended by the women. At the town's center was an elaborate square defined by four public buildings, each reserved for a specific community purpose. These opened upon land worn smooth by generations in countless ceremonies and elaborate rituals.

None had been more important than the annual boosketah, or busk. Generally falling in late July or early August, the festival was the high point of both the Creeks' calendar and their moral universe. With sacred observances that carried the deepest social and religious significance, the many ceremonies marked the end of the old year and the beginning of the new.

The men would clean the square before piling it with all the rubbish, old clothing, broken pottery, and stored food from the previous harvest. Once these had been burned and the ashes of the old fire removed, they would ceremoniously lay four new logs and kindle at their axis a new fire.

Four to eight days of fasting followed, interrupted with proscribed bathings and ceremonial handling of ashes, corn, and the small, sacred tobacco flower. Ritualistic dances recreated in intricate rhythmic movement the entire town's collective experience—wars fought, hunts conducted, groups befriended, and the mystic relationship maintained between humanity and nature. In ancient style, men took the "black drink." The drink was brewed from the yaupon holly and was the deity's peculiar blessing bestowed upon the Creeks as his special people. In this deeply religious rite, its consumption purified the imbiber of all sin, leaving him in a state of perfect innocence, invincible in war and unequaled in benevolence. The collective fasting broke only with the festival's end, when the people carefully unpacked and rubbed their tradition plates before loading them heavy with the new year's first crop of green corn.

And so it is likely that Opothle Yahola's unrecorded words at Lochapoka were similar to those transcribed later. Surely his conclusion was, for he told the silent, gathered people of Lochapoka that neither he nor they had a choice. They must soon take up their last black drink in their own nation. All must leave their towns and their country. All of the people of one fire would have to put out the old fire and kindle it again west of the Mississippi. They must do it, he said, by the end of April 1836. It was an unavoidable necessity.

As it turned out, his listeners did not have even that long. Seizing upon the opportunity afforded them by small-scale resistance from a band of Euchees, whites proclaimed there to be a "Creek Uprising." A mob descended upon Lochapoka, drove its frightened inhabitants into nearby swamps, and torched the village. Other such episodes provoked the United States War Department to order General Thomas S. Jessup to seize all resisting Indians as "hostiles" and remove all Creeks by force.

As Jessup and his men went about ethnic cleansing, some whites seized what little Creek property remained, and the government hired others as blacksmiths to forge handcuffs, chains, and shackles. The pitiable uprising hardly amounted to much; official force had broken all resistance by July. Dragging rebels from swamps, timber stands, and other hideaways, the government placed the men in fresh irons.

Accompanied by their wailing women and children, those prisoners—a total of 2,495 human beings—were forcibly removed to the West. Among the manacled and chained was Eneah Emarthla. Then eighty-four, he impressed even his captors as "a noble, fine looking fellow . . . [who] has been, and ever will be, the enemy of the whites; this he declares openly, and who can but respect him for it?"

Right behind them came the nonrebellious. If any of the 21,792 Creek Indians that the government had carefully enumerated in 1832 escaped the deportation, they were few—and not necessarily fortunate. Sweeping across the vacated lands, Alabama authorities and vigilantes hanged several and sold others into slavery. About a hundred were still being held as slaves right up until 1865, when the state of Alabama would have to pay for its own rebellion.

Although numerous written accounts survive to document the horrors of the forced emigration, none speaks directly of the Lochapoka people. Surely their experience must have been like others'. Entrusted to private, profit-seeking contractors who were overseen by military officers, the band would have marched westward partway and traveled by boat in places. At Little Rock, they would have followed the Arkansas River to its confluence with the Grand and Verdigris Rivers. Known as Three Forks, that site lay near the recently established Fort Gibson and had been settled by an earlier band of Creeks, generally mixed-bloods, in the previous decade. Death would have been the Creeks' constant companion. Disease, exposure, and exhaustion took an almost daily toll. The best estimate is that not even half of the Creeks who left Alabama reached the West alive.

In this regard, the Lochapoka community was thoroughly and tragically typical. A federal census taken in 1857, after twenty-one years had passed to recover from its losses, set Lochapoka's population at 274. New births included, the figure was barely half of the pre-exile number.

Such is about all that the surviving written record tells of the community. There is, however, an oral tradition that still survives among its descendants. It maintains that the Lochapoka people returned to their devastated town as soon as the Alabama marauders had left. There, they carefully assembled its most sacred treasures, none more priceless than the ashes from the old fire that had burned in their ceremonial square since the previous summer. Carrying those ashes, they crossed Alabama, Mississippi, and Arkansas as a single band under the leadership of Achee Yahola. The *Yahola* denoted not a physical kinship to the great Creek leader but a sharing of popular respect. The people of Lochapoka recognized him as their leader both for his physical prowess and his keen intelligence, and Achee Yahola saw to it that the entire community preserved itself by the frequent exercise of their oldest rituals and ceremonies.

Upon reaching Three Forks, the people resolved to travel farther up the Arkansas as it meandered its way across about forty miles of uninhabited country. At a point just before the river made its great bend to the west, they stopped. Achee

THE CREEK COUNCIL OAK

Yahola and other leading men climbed a slight hill that rose from the river's sandy banks. At its crest, they gathered beneath a large oak tree that towered mightily above the lesser willows, sycamores, and birches nearby. With the oak defining a southeastern corner, the people of Lochapoka proceeded to lay out, with painstaking exactness, a new square for their new home. When it was complete, they solemnly scattered the ashes so carefully carried with them, lit a new fire, and began the many ceremonies that marked the end of the old life and the beginning of the new.

And so it was that the people of Lochapoka, a daughter town of Tallasi, came to the Indian Territory to begin a new life. Not one of them could have foreseen just how much that new life would contain. As the new life ran its course, the first buildings would grow old and then decay, the community would scatter, not once but many times, and the ceremonial grounds would, in time, provide lawns for buccaneering tycoons.

The oak that provided them their first council site would, however, survive. Now much older and even more stately, it stands between Seventeenth and Eighteenth Streets and Cheyenne and Denver Avenues in Tulsa, Oklahoma. For that is where that life would lead. And this book is the story of that particular journey.

"Boost your city, boost your friend, Boost the lodge that you attend, Boost the street on which you're dwelling, Boost the goods that you are selling . . ."

THE
MAGIC
CITY

SOME-
THING
THAT
CALLED
ITSELF
A CITY

MAIN STREET SOUTH, TULSA, OKLA.

Moonlight over Tulsa,
postcard, 1908.

Previous page: Tulsa
boosters arrived in
Washington, D. C., in
1908. All had
memorized the
Booster Yell:
"Come, everybody!
Get off the grass! /
We're from the town
of natural gas. /
From Indian
Territory and don't
give a rap. / Move to
Tulsa and get on the
map!"

Tulsa's first visitors were tough, hardy, and imminently practical men. Thoroughly prosaic, they were not given to poetic flights of fancy. They were railroad workers who got there by hammering sections of bright, glimmering steel into freshly hewed timbers as they made their way southwest from Vinita foot by foot and mile by mile. The grading crews that had preceded them had told them what to expect at the end of the last stretch: nothing. There was nothing out there, they had said, nothing, that is, but some trees, a lot of prairie, and one or two passing Indians.

The steel-driving men had seen the trees, and they were impressed. In the last ten miles or so, they had enjoyed the shade of rich, thick walnuts and towering, ancient oaks. They must have admired the interspersed prairies that seemed so fertile. Thick carpets of bluestem reached as high as a rider's saddle. And they could not have missed the Indians. They were about the only locals out there. All were peaceable enough. Some spoke English, a few of them better than the immigrants with the railroad gang.

Still, the gandy dancers and track layers must have been surprised when they topped the final hill. Sitting there below them, already laid out and waiting, was something that called itself a city. It was a title that none of the matter-of-fact men would have granted it. After all, the "city" was really nothing more than a few tents scattered here and there along a path of barely worn grass that ran into the line defined by the earlier grading crew's stakes. Any fool who would call the place a city probably would call that path Main Street.

Sure enough, that was its name. The men laid their last seven-hundred-pound section of track, wiped the sweat off their tired faces, and headed over to Main Street's largest tent, the one that styled itself a "boardinghouse." There they were greeted by the proprietor, a white man, and served by his wife, an Indian woman who introduced herself as Aunt Jane. One presumes that they found the food good, but the city? If that is what it was? All they really knew was that they were getting their first home-cooked meal in months and that they were getting it in a "city" called Tulsa, located in the extreme northeastern corner of what their bosses had told them was the Creek nation.

The rough construction workers would have had no reason to know this city's history. It was so young and so fresh and so hastily thrown together that it appeared to have no history at all. Neither did it seem to have much of a future. A good, strong wind could have blown most of it away at any moment. With neither perceptible past nor predictable prospects, Tulsa did not look like much of anything at all to these, its first visitors, in August of 1882.

It did, however, have a past, and that past stretched backward in time and eastward in geography. Before the grading crew had arrived, before men had laid the heavy rails, before the tents had sprouted, it had been the place where the Lochapoka people had finished their journey and laid out their square. As such, it was a direct descendant of Tallasi, a Creek town already old in 1540, when Hernando de Soto had been the first European to see it. The relocated community occupied land long since explored by other Europeans and (some say) Africans as well. For nearly a half-century already, people that whites knew as Creeks had called the place home—even if some of them had called that home Lochapoka, some Tallasi, and others Tulsi.

Its first permanent residents had not come from choice, and much that had happened to them since had not been of their own choosing either. Nonetheless, many had prospered, some fabulously so. Many had changed, some strikingly so. Others had resisted both prosperity and change, all stubbornly so. All had endured what history had handed them. More than that, they had triumphed over it with the history they had made. Their endurance and their triumph were the past hidden from the visitors who called the place Tulsa.

Tulsa's future was no more visible and even less predictable. Those who smirked at its calling itself a city likely would have guffawed had they heard some of the titles it would later bestow upon itself. There would be many in the century or more to follow, and somehow each would manage to be more boastful than the others. None, however, would seem grander or be more accurate than its first. In a few years, some of the very men who occupied those flimsy tents in 1882 would be calling it "the Magic City." Later settlers would brag that their new hometown was a city captivated—even transformed—by magic. Business leaders would never tire of recounting the magic of its singular growth. Neither homeowners nor boosters would be alone, however, for Tulsa swiftly had outgrown its canvas tents and grassy single street to become a city known across the state, the region, the nation, and the globe.

What it had not outgrown, however, was its own history. Most assuredly, it would never outgrow the history of its earliest years, for these were the years that directed every one of the many still to come. These first ones were years of disaster and of hope, of war and of restoration, of Indians and of cowboys, of bankers and of roughnecks, of men, of women, of grass, and of oil. All came together in those years long ago to brew the potion that would conjure modern Tulsa, "the Magic City."

Early public relations: An advertising card from Brady Martin's Red Front Store, ca. 1890, and a promotional booklet from the 1930s when "the Magic City" had become an "empire."

THE *End* of the Line

THE UNITED STATES designated the land set aside for the exiled Native Americans, including those of the Lochapoka settlement, the Indian Territory. Its nearly seventy thousand square miles provided new homes for the Creeks and for other major tribes native to the American Southeast. These included the Seminoles, who earlier had separated from the Creeks to take up homes in Florida. They too were rooted out and driven west by American troops. Three other fellow exile tribes heretofore had been traditional Creek enemies. These were the Choctaws and Chickasaws, whose homelands bordered theirs to the east, and the Cherokees, natives to the east and north. Common experiences erased old enmities, however. Each tribe's homes had fallen prey to American land hunger. Each had traveled its version of what one tribe so memorably called the "Trail of Tears." Having put them out of sight, most whites also put them out of mind. They would have to make their own way, way out yonder in the Indian nations.

Sharing with their Seminole kinsmen a crescent-shaped section between the South Canadian and Cimarron Rivers, the Creeks began the painful process of rebuilding. Tragedy had defined their lot, but demoralization was not its consequence. Instead, the Indians restored their communities and rebuilt their lives. In the new lands, the Creeks recreated their traditional towns, usually under names that honored their ancient origins. In that way, the little settlement on the Arkansas came to be commonly referred to as Tallasi, the name paying homage to its still-honored mother town in Alabama. Two other restored communities took the same name for the same reason. The new geography of western rivers distinguished them as Tallasi on the Canadian and Tallasi on the Little River. Unaccustomed to the Creek tongue and unenlightened by what they venerated, the few whites who took note of them often began to pronounce the unfamiliar names as Tulsi, Tulsee, or Tulsa.

Very few whites, however, did take notice. From time to time, federally licensed contractors ascended the Arkansas from the Three Forks area to deliver goods promised under the removal or subsequent treaties. Occasionally they even kept honest records of their deliveries for government reimbursement. Much more common was the practice of defrauding both the Indians and the taxpayers with phony accounts for goods never dispensed. Every so often, a well-meaning missionary would pass through, Bible in hand and heart hungry for converts. "Tulsee town" turned out to be rather rocky soil, however, one describing it as "a remote part of this nation . . . where the people are yet very wild and superstitious."

The would-be converts thought themselves neither wild nor superstitious. After rebuilding their ceremonial square, they cleared nearby land for small but generally self-sufficient farms, always within easy distance of the restored center of the community. Several families moved past the Arkansas's westward bend to establish a small settlement where the river took on the Sand Springs. The stern and thrifty full-blood Sapulpa similarly went downstream and east to Rock Creek. Achee Yahola, the revered figure who had led and preserved the Lochapokas as a people, cleared timber and erected a small cabin not two miles north of the square before moving to a second site even closer. The United States agent appointed to oversee Creek affairs duly noted that Achee Yahola remained the community's leader until he died during the smallpox epidemic of 1850. His brother, Chiaha, then assumed the role until his own death later in the decade. Town leadership thereupon fell to Tulsee Fixico, *Fixico* being Creek for "heartless."

During the same time, Creeks from other regions moved into the area. The most notable of these was the Perryman family. Long prominent (one, Benjamin Perryman, had sat for a famed portrait by George Catlin), the Perrymans were true mixed-bloods who combined European, African, and Native American ancestry. Many of them had taken up the practice of slaveholding and plantation agriculture back in the Southeast. The family was one of those which had voluntarily resettled in the 1820s in the Three Forks area, where many newcomers continued to hold black slaves and farm commercially. In 1839, Lewis Perryman relocated his branch of the family to the Big Spring community on the Verdigris River, about eighteen miles east of the Lochapoka square. According to family tradition, Lewis Perryman and his large brood, which included five sons (Legus, Sanford, Thomas, George, and Josiah), left Big Spring in 1848 to settle near the Lochapoka square. There he built what passed for a mansion: a story-and-a-half home of hewed timbers, surrounded by numerous out-buildings, including slave quarters.

The Perrymans and those like them—generally mixed-bloods of commercial bent—provided more fertile soil for proselytizing than did the "wild and superstitious" folk of places like Lochapoka. In 1850, the Presbyterians (*Weofeska*, or "water sprinklers") established a large boarding school under the direction of young Robert Loughridge and his bride. It was at Tullahassee, a community thirty miles or so south, downriver from the Lochapoka settlement. Several of the young Perrymans and their kin from Big Spring attended and became active converts. Already, the Baptists (*Weaksumkulke*, or "water divers") had established churches at Broken Arrow and Big Spring, both under the pastorate of James Perryman, Lewis's brother.

The conservative and traditional folk of Lochapoka neither sprinkled nor dived. Instead, they gathered for ancient ceremonies and festivals at their square, where they sipped the black drink and celebrated the feast of green corn. The place was new and different, but the spirit illuminated by the annually rekindled fire remained both ancient and familiar. In time, that spirit transformed even the people's sense of place, for holy men reminded them that this fire arose from the one that had burned in Alabama. Pointing westward across the Arkansas, they declared that "the mountains and hills that you see are your backbone, and the gullies and the creeks which are between the hills and mountains are your heart veins!"

If Indian communities like Tallasi were able to isolate themselves and their faith from white presence, they were not able to escape the consequence of white politics. What white southerners insisted upon calling the "War Between the States" became, for the Indians they had dispossessed, a war within the nations. With more or less enthusiasm (in some cases, none at all), the leaders of every tribe entered into formal treaties allying their nations with the Confederacy. Among the Creeks, this was primarily the work of mixed-blood slaveholders, men of obvious southern interest who, moreover, were persuaded that federal dissolution was an accomplished fact. Although no Perryman affixed his name to the formal agreement, the five sons of Lewis Perryman left their home on the Arkansas to enlist in Company H of the First Creek Mounted Volunteer (Confederate) Regiment.

Because they believed themselves morally bound by the old treaties with Washington and because they distrusted southern representatives, many full-bloods rebelled and allied themselves as Unionists (or Neutrals) under the leadership of their most trusted figure. Opothle Yahola left his little cabin north of Brushhill. Traveling north and west, he assembled a band of seven thousand to nine thousand men, women, and children; collected their belongings in 150 or so wagons; and took them northward toward the protection of Union guns in Kansas. As the refugees reached the Cimarron near present Keystone on November 19, 1861, a force of Texas cavalry and Confederate Indians commanded by Colonel Douglas H. Cooper attacked the column in what came to be known as the Battle of Round Mountain. Repelling the assault, Opothle Yahola then crossed the Arkansas and passed through Sand Springs to reach Tallasi. The Lochapokas fed the retreating Indians, gathered up what property they could carry, and joined the exodus. All headed north, and they were joined by other Creeks and Skiatooka's band of pro-Union Cherokees. At a horseshoe bend in Bird Creek, they again fought off Cooper's forces and slipped away to the west on December 9.

December 26 found them camped on Hominy Creek. Then and there, a much stronger and better armed force of Texas and Arkansas cavalry under Colonel James McIntosh fell on them. Fighting until they had exhausted their small store of ammunition, Opothle Yahola's forces abandoned their provisions and fled northward. The orderly exodus thereupon became a terror-stricken rout. Adding to the sizable death toll from the three battles, Confederate forces—now augmented by Stand Watie's Cherokees—rounded up and hunted down noncombatants. Creek tradition maintains that they took hundreds of prisoners back to a sandbar on the Arkansas near Tallasi, where they executed them all, men, women, and children.

Those who escaped continued their flight north through howling winds and across snow-blanketed soil littered with the bodies of those who had fallen ahead of them. Group by group and person by person, they reached the Verdigris in southern Kansas. Federal officials from the Indian service and army found them there, some literally naked, others starving, many racked by pneumonia or helpless with frozen limbs. With warmer weather, the reassembled band gathered in a refugee camp on the Neosho (or Grand) River. Most of the exiles remained there for nearly three years under miserable conditions. In July 1862, some of the men enlisted in the Northern army as the First Regiment of Indian Home Guards, invaded Indian Territory, and struck for Fort Gibson. Their effort was unavailing, but it may have been what led Lewis Perryman and his family to redirect their allegiance to the Union. In November, the family abandoned its home on the Arkansas to join the refugees in Kansas, where the five Perryman sons left the Confederate service and enlisted in the Federal army.

Throughout their exile, the Lochapoka people maintained their town organization and religiously observed their ancient ceremonies. Their leader, Tulsee Fixico, died in battle in 1862, and their neighbor, Lewis Perryman, later perished in the Kansas camp. It was the summer of 1864 before they and the other exiles were able to return to their country. Even then, they had to cluster under the shadows of Union guns at Fort Gibson. There they stayed even after the war ended, for the last Confederate forces (Stand Watie's Cherokees) did not surrender until June 23, 1865, too late to plant any crops. Moreover, the victorious federal government was demanding

that the Creeks and the other nations surrender nearly half of their estates. It was the penalty for their governments' ill-fated Confederate treaties. There was no reward for Opothle Yahola and his suffering Unionists, including the people from Tallasi. New treaties of early 1866 freed the Indians' slaves (nearly all of whom had long since freed themselves) and penalized all of the Creeks, loyal and disloyal alike, by seizing the western half of their nation to be used to relocate other tribes then living in Kansas and the rest of the southern plains.

If the formal peace preserved Tallasi for its people, the war had nearly destroyed it. Stench from four years of slaughter greeted them when they returned to the Arkansas in early spring. What marauders of one side had not stolen or burned, those of the other had. Gone were the cattle and swine. Ruined were the public buildings and modest cabins. Overgrown were the fields and the old ceremonial square. And so the people did what they had learned to do best. They rebuilt.

This time, the result was less a town in the whites' sense than an open facility devoted to scheduled events and public celebrations. Rather than cluster their homes nearby, the people tended to scatter across the surrounding area. Sapulpa returned to his home on Rock Creek. Noah Partridge built a little log house for wife and stepson in the timber north of the old square. Just south of Noah Partridge's place, Tuckabatchee constructed a cabin, from which he and his pack of dogs hunted deer all along the river. Noah's son, Kipsee Partridge, crossed the river to build opposite the Arkansas's western bend.

In all such cases, each dwelling lay near a little patch of corn enclosed by the owner's rail fence. Ponies, cattle, and hogs belonging to all ranged freely through the woods. Like the trees that sheltered them, the fish that swam in nearby streams, and the wildlife with which they shared the hills and valleys, their partly domesticated animals were less commercial property than nature's bounty given for personal subsistence.

Lewis Perryman's sons returned, each the veteran and the victim of both armies. Thomas served the Coweta settlement as a Presbyterian minister. Josiah built a ranch about three miles east of the Arkansas, where Legus soon joined him to ranch and plant a much-admired fruit orchard. George Perryman returned to the old home place and married a full-blooded woman of Lochapoka. In a few years, the two left the old log place for a new home built of lumber freighted in by wagon from Coffeyville, Kansas. Locally known as the "White House," the new home was the region's showplace, generally crowded with visitors and usually providing shelter and comfort for one or several of the community's many orphans. In March 1879, the United States designated the home as the first post office to serve what it referred to as "Tulsa." It was the first official use of that particular form. Josiah Perryman became Tulsa's original postmaster and dutifully posted what little mail that came in by horseback on a four-day route from Coffeyville through Tulsa to the Sac and Fox agency and back.

Beginning in the 1870s, a noticeable number of white people began to take homes among the Creeks. In 1874, William P. Moore bought a federal trader's license and established a store near the Broken Arrow community. The store also briefly served as a post office, with Thomas Perryman its assistant postmaster. Because his wife, already known as Aunt Jane, was Creek, Chauncey A. Owen was an intermarried citizen of the nation, and he took control of several thousand acres of the national domain. Some he ranched; the remainder he farmed, the labor supplied by imported white workers. In 1879, Antoine (also spelled—and pronounced—Antwine) Gillis leased land near Broken Arrow from Owen. As white noncitizens, Gillis and the others were required to buy annual permits from the Creek government; most never bothered. The Creeks protested and duly reported the "intruders" to the United States agent, but they remained in open defiance of Creek law. Year by year, their numbers increased, but the defiance held constant.

No tribal law could stop or even slow what was destined to change Indian Territory forever—in fact, to end it. The postwar treaties of 1866 had required the nations to permit the right-of-way for at least one north-south and one east-west railroad through their lands. The Missouri, Kansas, and Texas (M. K. T., or Katy) Railroad earned one franchise and laid track from the Kansas border southward to a new station near the historic Three Forks: Muskogee. The line passed about thirty miles east of Tulsa.

The east-west franchise went to the Atlantic and Pacific, soon to be reorganized as the Saint Louis and San Francisco (Frisco) Railroad. Entering the Indian Territory in its northeast at the tiny Quapaw reservation, the Frisco crossed Cherokee lands until intersecting with the Katy, where an enterprising Cherokee named E. C. Boudinot hastily laid out a townsite and called it Vinita. There, construction stopped until January 1882.

In that month, the construction company sent a grading outfit, sixty-five mule teams, hay, corn, and oats to the Vinita terminus. About seventy-five ragged, hungry men also arrived and bedded down in the hay. This was the construction crew, overseen by a small handful of supervisors, including two Tennessee-born brothers, Harry C. and James Monroe Hall. The first maintained the payroll. Because there were no towns or even stores between Vinita and the Arkansas River, the second brother kept a small company store in a tent that would move westward with the crew.

Grading and construction proceeded rapidly across the Cherokee lands to the bank of the Verdigris River, where the crew paused to build a bridge. "Fort Spunkey" served as a temporary terminal and resting place until the bridge was up and a station (Catoosa) was placed on the river's east bank. The pace then quickened until it reached its expected end, and the chief engineer prepared to lay a sidetrack and set up a townsite. At Harry Hall's urging, the engineer agreed to move both two-and-one-half miles west from his original choice. Like the first, the relocated terminus could tap what the railroad men regarded as prime commercial resources: virgin forests, fish, and furbearing animals. Now that the buffalo had been "harvested," both sites were perfect cow country. The difference was that the relocation placed the terminus just across the Cherokees' boundary line into the extreme northeastern corner of the Creeks' domain; and, as J. M. Hall so innocently put it, "their land leasing relations with whites were liberal."

On August 7, 1882, the tracks and crew reached the new site, where a fledgling city constructed entirely of tents awaited them. Their work done, the exhausted men walked or rode over to the big one that sheltered Chauncey Owen's hastily located boardinghouse, if one could so consider a wooden-sided tent. Those seeking medical attention could go to Dr. W. P. Booker's tent, but only if they needed it badly. The Gillis family's tent was nearby, as was one housing George Bullette, an educated Delaware Indian, and his white wife. Jeff Archer, a Cherokee mixed-blood, occupied another tent, which he styled a general store. The Hall brothers immediately offered competition with their own canvas-clad store. The only permanent lodging in sight was Noah Partridge's little cabin. Obscured by about two miles of woods and hills was the Lochapokas' ceremonial square, which had hosted Tallasi's boosketah just a few weeks earlier.

In a few days, the first Frisco train headed east—there being no other direction to go. Its "passengers" were sixty-five exhausted mule teams. The mules safely reached Vinita, having left behind a crude depot bearing a freshly painted sign ready to tell any future westbound travelers that they had arrived in Tulsa. It was the end of the line. And it was the start of the modern city.

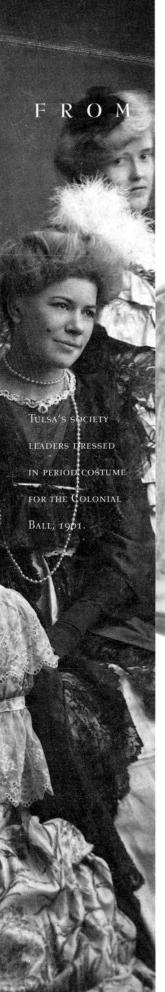

From *Tallasi* TO Tulsa

JAMES MONROE HALL'S expectation turned out right. The Creeks—or, at least, their tribal government—proved to be very "liberal" in leasing arrangements. Because the new village was in the Creek nation, not one person in it, not even full-blooded Noah Partridge, held title to his or her landed property. Every tent, every cabin, every business, and every farm occupied land owned collectively by the Creek nation. Like other tribes in the Indian Territory, the Creeks allowed any citizen to use as much land as he or she might need. Citizens also could own, even convey, any improvements made to it. But no citizen—and, assuredly, no noncitizen—could claim legal title to as much as one square inch of land. Traditional Creeks had learned well what legal deeds and paper titles foretold.

Others learned how to get around such circumstances. Those who claimed any degree of Creek ancestry also could claim every right of citizenship, none more valuable than unlimited access to the tribal estate. Creek freedmen and their descendants had the same rights, since they were adopted citizens under the guarantees of the 1866 treaty. People married to Creeks had the same rights, since the tribe recognized them as intermarried tribal citizens. As an unwritten mutual courtesy, members of other Indian nations freely exercised the same privileges. In time, there were many whose claim rested upon no such circumstances and no privilege at all except the brutal equation of right with might.

The railroad builders were correct about something else. Tulsa sat in the middle of some of the best cow country on earth. Because it made it possible to ship entire herds, the railroad permitted the swift exploitation of that richness. Creek mixed-bloods were particularly active. They helped turn the land to Tulsa's east and southwest into an unbroken string of massive ranches. Daniel Childers built a ranch near present Broken Arrow; others of his family lined the Verdigris with ranchlands. Just a little east, Clement V. Rogers, a mixed-blood Cherokee, burned the CR brand into several thousand hides. To the north, Green Yeargin and A. W. Hoots, brothers-in-law through their marriages to Osage mixed-blood sisters, established ranches with their headquarters at present Sperry and Skiatook, respectively. Between them, their cattle grazed fifty thousand acres.

Outsiders swiftly joined them. William Halsell came up from Texas to take advantage of his wife's remote Cherokee ancestry and lay out a ranch that ran from the Verdigris to the Caney River and beyond, until it stretched nearly to the Kansas line. Employing fifty-five hands who required six hundred horses, Halsell soon needed an entire train to ship forty-five hundred head on the Frisco from Tulsa. All bore the Mashed O brand, one as famous across the Southwest as it was at his headquarters on Bird Creek, near the old site of Opothle Yahola's battle with the Confederates.

To the Osage lands lying within a stone's throw of the new city on the Arkansas came Texas cattle barons like Tom Waggoner, who built the great 3D ranch along the river's northern bank above Sand Springs. Kansas ranchmen crossed their state's southern border, taking out leases to as much as eighty-five thousand acres of Osage territory for an average of three-and-a-quarter cents per acre.

In 1883, the Cherokees leased a broad belt of grassland roughly 70 miles wide and nearly 110 miles long. It was the Cherokee Outlet, which ran west from the Arkansas River along the Kansas border. The lessee was the Cherokee Strip Live Stock Association, a consortium of cattle barons who divided the huge estate among themselves. The beneficiaries included the Bennett and Dunham Cattle Company, which took a large triangle, its southern and eastern sides defined by the Cimarron's confluence with the Arkansas. Another was the Saginaw Cattle Company, which covered thousands of acres with the Turkey Track ranch.

Under the circumstances, individual Creeks not only went into ranching but into the even more rewarding business of leasing. Josiah Perryman turned his acreage over to a white contractor. Thomas Perryman slapped the T brand on cattle ranging south of Broken Arrow. Legus Perryman ran about a thousand cattle and farmed 950 acres of bottomland. Alvin Hodge, a Perryman descendant, claimed a pasture that covered the intended site of the Tulsa depot and much else besides. Richest of all was George Perryman, who ran about three thousand head under the 5 brand. In addition, he got control of some sixty thousand acres that ran east from Tulsa to the Cherokee border. He then leased the eastern half to James Monroe Daugherty and the southwestern portion to Shanghai Pierce and Jay Forsythe. All three were Texans, and the money

LICENSE TO TRADE WITH INDIANS.

Be it known That James H. Hall of Tulsa, Ind. Ter. & Harry C. Hall of Springfield, Missouri,

trading under the name and firm of J.M. Hall & Co.,

having filed **their** application before me for a license to trade with the Creek

tribe of Indians

at the following-named place within the boundaries of the country occupied by the said Indians, viz:

Tulsa, Creek Nation Ind. Ter. (Union Agency)

and having filed with me a bond in the penal sum of

TEN THOUSAND DOLLARS, with Horace H. Crane, of Independence, Kans, and Owen H. Haworth of Tulsa, Ind. Ter.

as sureties, conditioned, as required by law, for the faithful observance of all the laws and regulations provided for the government of trade and intercourse with Indian tribes, and having satisfied me, as required by law, that they are citizens of the United States, and of good moral character, are hereby authorized to carry on the business of trading with the said tribe at the above-named place for the term of *ONE YEAR* from the 5th day of July, eighteen hundred and ninety-four

and to keep in there employ thereat the following-named person in the capac affixed to

name John Holland M H Mosher as clerks

I am satisfied, from the testimonials which have been placed in my hands, sustain a fair character and fit to be in the Indian country.

This license is granted upon the further express condition that the said J.M. Hall & Co.,

in accepting the same waives all right and privilege which they might otherwise have to any claim against the Government of the United States for losses or damages, or both, which may result from the depredations of Indians during the continuance of this license and pending the removal of their effects from the Indian country on the expiration or revocation of the same.

Given under my hand, at the Office of Indian Affairs, Washington, D. C.,

this 5th day of July, eighteen hundred and ninety-four.

D M Browning
Commissioner

14135 License had to be renewed every year

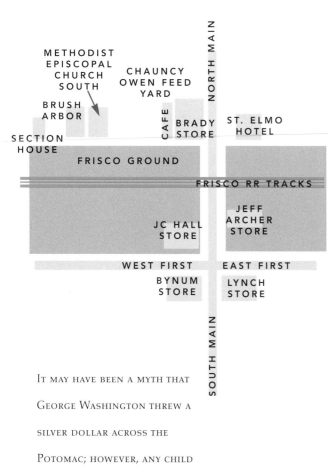

METHODIST
EPISCOPAL
CHURCH
SOUTH

BRUSH
ARBOR

SECTION
HOUSE

CHAUNCY
OWEN FEED
YARD

CAFE

BRADY
STORE

ST. ELMO
HOTEL

NORTH MAIN

FRISCO GROUND

FRISCO RR TRACKS

JC HALL
STORE

JEFF
ARCHER
STORE

WEST FIRST

EAST FIRST

BYNUM
STORE

LYNCH
STORE

SOUTH MAIN

It may have been a myth that George Washington threw a silver dollar across the Potomac; however, any child could have thrown a dollar across the Frisco tracks, and a strong one, aided by a stout wind, could have thrown one across all of Tulsa in the 1880s.

they paid comprised only part of the estimated twenty-five thousand dollars that the Perryman family soon was collecting annually through leases alone. When added to their other sources of income, it comfortably made the Perrymans the richest single family in the entire Creek nation.

George Perryman and his wife, soon to be known to all as Aunt Rachel, left their White House for a more imposing structure high on a hill that overlooked what there was of Tulsa to the southeast. Workmen had to drag the materials through waist-high weeds to build what neighbors regarded as the town's one real mansion.

If usually to less impressive quarters, others were coming too. Cowboys found the place a hospitable site for everything from home-cooked meals to church sing-alongs to less genteel recreation involving other forms of consumption and feminine fellowship. Their

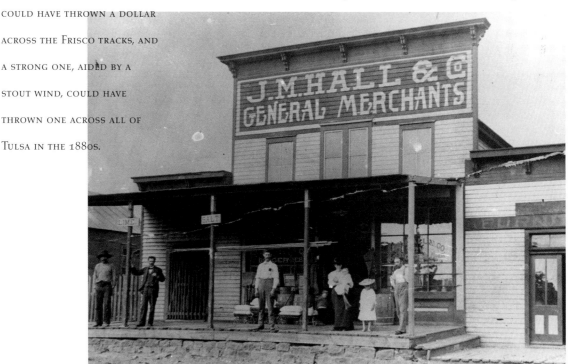

foremen and the ranch owners shared most of the same experiences and added to the fortunes of more stable and respectable businesses with orders for feed and supplies, barbed wire being an especially popular commodity.

Although the Frisco crossed the Arkansas in 1884 and later extended to Sapulpa's store, Tulsa remained a preferred shipping point despite the competition from the new west-bank facilities at Red Fork and those built subsequently at the town named for the Creek pioneer. With each fall, Tulsa saw the shipment of thousands of cattle grown heavy from lush prairie grasses and sleek from corn fed at huge pens like that operated by the Hall brothers. After every spring's roundup, chugging trains pulled out, the locomotives' sounds accompanied by the bawling of fatted and frightened calves.

The growing cattle industry provided local merchants a steady supply of customers, but hardly their only ones. In fact, their early trade with whites was much less important than that with either Indians or blacks. Storekeepers sometimes had trouble distinguishing between the two because there was considerable racial intermixture. Their economic interests and needs were virtually identical. Among the Native Americans, the more culturally and commercially advanced mixed-bloods usually bought and sold on a cash basis. Distrusting paper money as much as they did paper deeds, the numerous full-bloods were more likely to barter. They regularly brought wild game, fish, hides, and furs to the local stores, exchanging them for simple tools, home necessities, and food staples. The rate of exchange might vary from day to day, even from person to person, but some natives were legendary for driving hard bargains. The Osages were particularly known as shrewd customers who insisted upon an unusual measure of generosity.

The new community's environs turned out to have resources less obvious but no less lucrative than its grasslands and its game. Shallow coal beds lay about four or five miles east of the town, and residents were able to dig it cheaply from simple pits. The more enterprising took to selling it by the bushel. Under Creek law, nonresidents could neither mine nor sell coal or other minerals without buying permits and paying royalties to the nation, but few paid much attention to those rules. Even fewer honored the Creek prohibition of noncitizens' exploitation of the nation's timber resources. A lively, if thoroughly illegal, trade developed as newcomers picked up axes and felled the tallest hardwoods, including massive walnuts with trunks spanning as much as eight feet in diameter before they reached their first limbs, forty feet above. Because the walnuts and oaks were so rich and heavy that they would barely float, the lumbermen had to bind them with cheap cottonwood logs to build loose rafts that they could float down the Arkansas to awaiting sawmills. Lumber milled from them subsequently adorned eastern homes as expensive furniture, and the best walnuts became gunstocks prized around the world.

In all its various forms, business was so good that the original merchants all soon folded their tents in favor of more substantial structures. Jeff Archer put up the first, a tin-covered shack not much larger than a single room. Its original stock was several barrels of gingersnaps, but a more impressive frame building soon followed, and the contents verified that it was a general store. Competition came in the form of false-fronted buildings operated by the Perryman brothers, George and Josiah, and H. C. Hall and Company (the "Company" being his brother, J. M.). When Harry Hall moved on to open a new store at Red Fork, J. M. became sole proprietor of the original. Meanwhile, the Perryman place guaranteed itself regular traffic by doubling as the relocated post office.

Chauncey Owen already had put away his boarding tent and opened Tulsa's first real hotel, the St. Elmo, which boasted of having twenty-two rooms. In 1887, J. M. Gillette and Prier L. Price arrived to open a new grocery. The two subsequently parted. Gillette went into real estate, and Price stunned the community by erecting its first two-story structure to house his sand and lumber business. By then, Tulsa occupied three streets, the unimaginatively named First and Second Streets intersecting with the original Main. All were worn of grass, having replaced it alternately with dust and mud. Every street was littered with watermelon rinds in warm seasons and with horse apples year-round. Residents stepped over the refuse and were willing enough to put up with the dust, but they insisted that the streets be no more than eighty feet wide. Anything wider was too far to walk in the mud. No one had to walk to the bank; there was none for the first dozen years.

Maybe it was just as well, since there were people around who might have robbed it. One was a woman, the notorious Belle Starr, who passed through several times before her rendezvous with destiny and death in an 1889 ambush. Semipermanent residents included Bill Doolin, whom many locals fondly remembered for cowboying on the Turkey Track and other nearby ranches before he put together the gang that terrorized territorial banks, trains, and post offices. The Doolin gang got away with murder and robbery until 1893, when their luck ran out because they ran into marshals at Ingalls, about thirty miles west of Tulsa.

The four Dalton brothers were regular fixtures. Only a few Tulsans realized that they were cousins to the Younger family of Missouri, the boys that had ridden with Frank and Jesse James into crime, prison, death, and criminal renown. Most residents knew the Daltons as good boys who walked on the law's right side. The brothers occasionally sang in church choirs, and the oldest, Frank Dalton, served as a United States deputy marshal attached to the Fort Smith court of "Hanging Judge" Issac Parker. Frank died a hero's death when he was killed in service, and he was accorded a hero's burial. Grat Dalton then signed on with Judge Parker, and Bob and Emmett Dalton organized a police force for the Osages.

The surviving three soon straddled the line, however. All were fired for various infractions that amounted to their breaking the very laws they were supposed to

enforce. Afterwards, they crossed over far into the outlaw side and interspersed their assorted crimes with stops at Tulsa. If they spotted no lawmen's mounts from their lookout atop what came to be called Standpipe Hill north of the Frisco tracks, they boldly walked Tulsa's streets, ate at its cafes, and traded at its stores. Typical purchases included suspicious amounts of gunpowder and ammunition. Otherwise, they hardly bothered local businesses, since both

UNITED STATES
DEPUTY MARSHALS
ASSIGNED TO INDIAN
TERRITORY, CA. 1892.

THE ORIGINAL PRESBYTERIAN MISSON CHURCH STOOD AT FOURTH STREET AND BOSTON AVENUE, A LOCATION MANY TULSANS OF THE TIME THOUGHT TOO FAR SOUTHEAST TO BE CONVENIENT. THE BUILDING ALSO SERVED AS THE CITY'S FIRST SCHOOLHOUSE. AFTER INCORPORATION, THE SITE BECAME THE FIRST PROPERTY OWNED BY TULSA PUBLIC SCHOOLS.

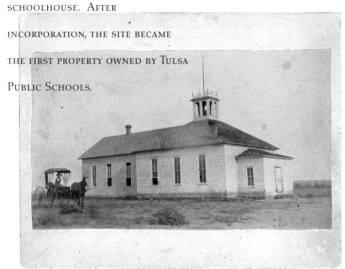

parties assumed a live-and-let-live attitude, the outlaws receiving shelter, the businessmen security.

The burghers of Coffeyville, Kansas, proved to be less tolerant. When the gang boldly attempted to rob two of their banks simultaneously, outraged townspeople shot them down in the streets. They killed Grat and Bob and two of their confederates outright, and they captured a badly shot-up Emmett. Coffeyville buried the bullet-riddled corpses, and Emmett Dalton served his time and later returned to Tulsa. He eventually ended up in Hollywood, where he made several shoot-'em-ups, none with live ammunition.

Happily for local residents, Tulsa also attracted its share of more decent types. Only a few weeks after the railroad building crew had reached the site, a Mrs. Slater—her husband was a carpenter with the Frisco—invited two adults and their children to her tent.

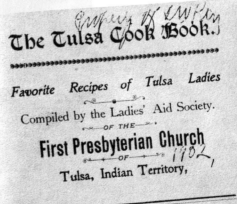

The Tulsa Cook Book.

Favorite Recipes of Tulsa Ladies

Compiled by the Ladies' Aid Society.

— OF THE —

First Presbyterian Church

— OF —

Tulsa, Indian Territory,

Eat as this Book tells you and deposit your money with the First National Bank. of Tulsa And your days will be many and filled with plenty This Book has 500 Recipes This Bank has $50,000.00 Capital And - - - - $10,000.00 Surplus Tulsa's First Bank Tulsa's Strongest Bank Main Street. Phone 130

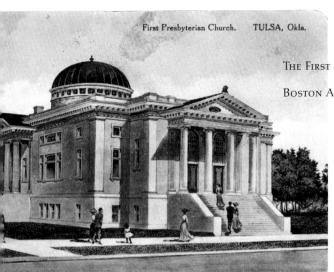

THE FIRST PRESBYTERIAN CHURCH, AT SEVENTH STREET AND
BOSTON AVENUE, AS IT LOOKED IN 1911.

There the grownups, Mrs. Slater (Congregationalist), Dr. Booker (Baptist), and J. M. Hall (Presbyterian) formed the community's first Sunday school. Because of denominational differences, it was a "union" Sunday school, but by the next spring the congregation had grown large enough to invite Tullahassee's venerable Robert Loughridge to preach the community's first recorded sermon. The Reverend Loughridge delivered it from the Hall store's front porch, the listeners arrayed before him on rough boards carried over from the new lumberyard.

The Presbyterians earned the honor of establishing the first formal church on October 5, 1885, when they organized themselves at the mission school maintained by that denomination. Among its charter members were fifteen Creek Indians, including the Tullahassee-educated Josiah Perryman. A few months later, communicants of the Methodist Episcopal Church organized at the same mission school, their twenty-one charter members including five Native Americans. Southern Methodists started meeting at the school in 1893 before moving to their own first site, a brush arbor.

Perhaps because they were less welcomed at the mission than were the Protestant denominations, Roman Catholics held their original services in a private home in 1890 before opening their first sanctuary on September 10, 1899. Seven years later, the parish got some land way out in the country. It was 1914 before the new church was completed, and by then the city had caught up with Holy Family Church, which would be dedicated as one of Oklahoma's two cathedrals (Oklahoma City's Saint Joseph was the other) in 1931.

That so many of the Protestant denominations began in the mission school was not surprising. Because most of them were not citizens of the Creek nation, the residents had nothing beyond their pooled resources to discharge even the most basic of civic responsibilities. Without authority to collect taxes and without anything much to tax in any event, the pioneers established their first school on a subscription basis, each family making monthly contributions toward the teacher's salary and expenses. Although they had been willing to do that, their will evaporated when the first teacher turned out to be a professional gambler.

Under J. M. Hall's leadership (Presbyterian Hall earlier had assumed the superintendency of the Sunday school), the community appealed to that denomination to establish a mission school. The Reverend W. P. Haworth, a Presbyterian missionary then assigned to Vinita, arrived in the summer of 1884 and began building Tulsa's first schoolhouse. Classes met in private homes until the white, barnlike structure was completed and crowned with a belfry. It remained the city's one school until 1899. For the last eleven of those years, it operated without the services of its founder. After Haworth had preached a strong Sunday sermon decrying the community's sins and lawlessness, a gang of toughs had beaten him into unconsciousness. He then had resigned and departed for the greener and presumably more peaceful pastures of California.

For the most traditional Creeks—including practically all of the Lochapoka people—the arrival of respectable men like the Reverend Haworth may have been even more troubling than the presence of renegades like the Doolins and the Daltons or the rowdies who finally ran the good minster out of town. Criminals and thugs were one thing. Town promoters, churchmen, and school builders were another, and they quite likely were more threatening. The first were transients. They probably would not have been there anyway except for the presence of the others. The latter were settlers, and they were there to stay. Every business that they opened, every sermon that they preached, every school that they established imperiled the physical isolation and the cultural autonomy of traditional folk.

The Creek government fitfully responded from time to time with statutes to restrict the flow of immigration, to regulate the granting of citizenship, and to preserve its people's patrimony. Subsequent councils repealed some of these. Others proved to be so poorly drawn as to be unenforceable. None had any more effect than a decree to sweep back the ocean by broom. The tides of change were too powerful for any merely statutory solution.

Under those circumstances, the Creeks' increasing unease began to take collective and violent form. When Tom Waggoner attempted to put his ranching empire south of the Arkansas on 250,000 acres of Creek lands, angry but well-disciplined citizens cut his fences, dispersed his stock, and drove off his cowhands. No one was hurt, but Waggoner gave up and temporarily had to content himself with the big spread in Osage country.

Less successful was the individual Creek—his name unrecorded—who threw a fence across early Main Street, a move that threatened to pen the city between the Frisco's iron rails and his wooden ones. No one but he was ready to strangle the infant Tulsa in its cradle; and even he temporarily changed his mind when Jeff Archer picked up a Winchester, stepped out of his store, and swore that he would kill the would-be infanticide. The fence came down, and the two went to court. Probably because both parties were Indians (Archer was a Cherokee citizen), a Creek court claimed jurisdiction and ruled that any such fencing would violate the old law that forbade blocking a public thoroughfare. As telling as was the episode and its judicial resolution was the fact that on this singular occasion, the court convened not in its traditional courthouse in the Coweta district but in J. M. Hall's Tulsa store. More than the judge's decision, the venue demonstrated where real power already lay.

The so-called Green Peach War satisfied any further need for evidence. Frustrated with their government's failure to control the incoming whites, a group that consisted primarily of the most conservative full-bloods picked up arms and rose in rebellion against the constitutional authorities under Creek Principal Chief Samuel Checote. The rebellion's leader was a determined and hidebound traditionalist named Isparhecher. Illiterate in all languages and able to comprehend only his native tongue, Isparhecher counted followers that included men like Tuckabatchee, Neha Harjo, Moosar Neharkey, and others—all from the Lochapoka group.

Fighting was sporadic but consumed nearly a year as it erupted in spots across most of the Creek nation. Tulsa was spared armed conflict, but some frightened newcomers retraced their footsteps homeward, and other, more established and more acculturated residents rallied to the government's cause. In March 1883, George Perryman assembled twenty-five men and set out to answer Checote's call for troops.

U. S. Army soldiers from Fort Gibson pushed Isparhecher's forces from the territory and finally apprehended them among Plains Indians near present Anadarko. Eight of the captured warriors were from the Lochapoka community. The warring factions made their peace that summer. Isparhecher entered and lost several Creek elections, but he usually received an all but unanimous vote from Lochapoka. The local voters, like others, accepted their man's defeat. They had no choice but to accept his cause's defeat as well.

TULSA'S FOUNDING BUSINESSMEN, AUGUST 27, 1885. THE PENCILED INSCRIPTION ON THE BACK OF THE PHOTOGRAPH IDENTIFIES THE GROUP AS "EARLY BUSINESS LEADERS AND TRAMP." PRESUMABLY, TRAMP IS THE DOG.

Rising Tulsa thereafter had no threat of Indian resistance and not much reason to think seriously about the older community that it was displacing. As the Indians still gathered beneath the ancient oak to reenact their ancient ceremonies, crowds of curious whites sometimes came out to watch. Pioneer merchants furnished supplies for the festivities, and a few of the gayer blades sometimes joined in the dances and games. Most probably regarded the spectacles as quaint and colorful relics from the past. Few had reason to doubt that the future was theirs.

They were right, and its shape was already emerging. Within not much more than a decade, the depot site had assumed the form of a real town. By the mid-1890s, Tulsa had its first bank (established by Jay Forsythe from his cattle earnings), two or more mills, and three newspapers: the *Tulsa Review*, the *Indian Republican* (predecessor to the *Tulsa World*), and the *Tulsa Democrat* (which became the *Tulsa Tribune*). Thirty-eight local persons bought annual permits to serve the Creek nation as traders, the number including nearly every occupation in addition to merchandising. Other businessmen were Creek citizens, who were legally exempt from fees, and unlawful intruders, who defiantly exempted themselves.

Far removed from this, Congress in 1889 had stretched federal judicial authority across all of the Indian Territory by establishing a United States district court at Muskogee, and the next year extended the laws of Arkansas over its American citizens. For the first time, the newcomers who were not Creek citizens had access to legal authority nearer than Judge Parker's Fort Smith bench. In 1895, Washington divided the territory into three judicial districts. Tulsa, along with all of the Creek, Cherokee, and Seminole nations, fell in the Northern District. In the fall of 1895, Judge William M. Springer ruled that the district's towns had the right to incorporate under the governing Arkansas statutes.

Tulsa's much larger neighbor, Wagoner, started the process required for incorporation almost immediately, but Indian protests, court delays, and internal strife consumed a full year before the community finally gave up in frustration. That experience probably accounts for Tulsa's delay until a rumor of indeterminable accuracy spurred immediate action. The rumor was that a faction of prominent men led by J. M. Hall was secretly negotiating with the Creek government to purchase Tulsa's entire townsite. They would then survey it, so the rumor went, and sell its lots to the very people who had made them valuable. At considerable cost to the occupants, the conspirators would reap enormous profit for themselves. However true or false, the rumor

THE FRISCO DEPOT IN 1905, WHEN TULSA STOOD AT THE THRESHOLD OF ITS MODERN ERA.

gained both credence and urgency when Hall and a presumed accomplice left town unexpectedly, bound for Saint Louis, where, it was said, they would get the money to execute the scheme.

Hall and his companion returned home on the very night that the aroused citizenry was holding a mass meeting of inquisition and protest. As the two entered the meeting, its chairman (whom Hall would sometime later recall as an honest enough old drunk) attempted to establish some semblance of parliamentary order by calling a question on a motion. "All of those in favor indicate it by saying 'yes,' and all of those opposed will go home," he bellowed. Just then someone pulled a gun, the lights went out, and the hall was filled with the disquieting sound of iron slapping leather. The meeting terminated in a roughhouse, but it featured no weapons deadlier than fists.

All escaped without serious injury (save to the chairman's reputation), but the need for official and immediate incorporation was certain. A quick census was taken to assure that the community had the requisite population of one thousand, and it barely did—although some suspected that a good number of transients and rural dwellers pushed the count to the target. A hastily drawn petition collected the signatures of

much of the town's stable and literate adult population. A delegation of leading men—Prier Price, Tate Brady, George W. Mowbray, L. M. Poe, R. E. Lynch, Dr. Samuel Kennedy, Edward Calkins, John Seaman, and the ever-present J. M. Hall—drew up the charter, proudly signed it, and sent it by horse-drawn buggy to Muskogee, where the federal court granted Tulsa its official charter of incorporation on January 18, 1898. The date thus marks the city's official birthday.

Within six months of incorporation, Congress passed the Curtis Act. The law provided for the termination of all tribal governments and the disposal of all tribal properties in the Indian Territory, including virtually all of the Creeks' national domain of just over three million acres. Most of that would be deeded individually to Creek citizens as allotments, which averaged 160 acres in size. Some 16,000 acres that held existing towns would be handled differently. The townsites would first be surveyed, platted, and appraised under the authority of separate townsite commissions. Lots then would be sold. Their occupants

could buy the land and any improvements at one-half to two-thirds the lots' declared values, the fraction determined by the extent of the claimants' holdings. Unused lots and those unpurchased by their occupants would sell at auction. All of the proceeds from townsite sales then would be deposited to the credit of the Creek nation. With slight amendments negotiated by the tribe in May 1901, this was the procedure by which Tulsa became private property.

Tulsa's townsite commission employed two brothers—Gus and Dan Patton—to perform the survey and create the plat. Experienced

in other territorial towns, the Pattons made the sensible decision to use the Frisco tracks as their base line. Main Street, long since shorn of grass, retained its original designation, and parallel to it they laid out avenues arranged alphabetically by the names of American cities. Those east of Main took names of places east of the Mississippi (Boston, Cincinnati, Detroit, et cetera); those west of Main honored cities west of the river (Boulder, Cheyenne, Denver, et cetera). Similar practicality dictated that the streets parallel to the Frisco track would be numbered (First, Second, Third, et cetera). This originally was true on both the track's north and south sides, although Tulsans soon would rename the north-side thoroughfares to honor pioneer settlers and the like, again in alphabetical order (Archer, Brady, et cetera).

Two circumstances interrupted the scheme's geometric logic. First, because the Frisco lay slightly askew from true east-west, the northbound avenues would later assume a perceptible jog at Tenth, where the original survey was corrected when later developers chose to continue the streets true to the compass. The second circumstance involved a handsome fruit orchard. Rather than destroy it, the Pattons narrowed and crooked East Third Street to preserve the orchard and threaten future generations of inattentive motorists.

The Pattons finished their work in December 1901, having surveyed a townsite of 654.58 acres. The townsite commission then set its value at $107,173.30, a figure that was exceedingly generous for the occupants who were anxious to buy but hardly fair to the Creek owners who were forced to sell. The sale of lots came in 1902. Nearly every occupant exercised the option of buying his or her lot at the one-half figure. In fact, the commission knowingly winked at several who avoided the higher price for multiple claims by purchasing them under the names of friends, relatives, employees, and other so-called dummies. Others used fake names to buy cheaply unused lots that contained no more improvements than hastily assembled shacks. So common were such practices that the total proceeds credited to the Creek nation for the sale of unoccupied lots was exactly $659. It was a pauper's price for what was

already princely property. Some land lying just outside the surveyed townsite was even more valuable than that contained within it. It lay in huge blocks of about 160 acres and was deeded separately to individual Creeks. To afford the Indians some measure of protection against the process that had been so destructive in Alabama, the agreement with the United States had "restricted" those allotments: most could not be sold within twenty years or more. One of the few exceptions to that rule governed land assigned to Creeks who thereafter had died. Their heirs were "unrestricted," meaning that they could sell the inherited land to anyone for any price once the Creek Agreement went into effect: March 11, 1905.

This was precisely the case for an allotment precious in economic worth and priceless in historic and symbolic value. Surveyors designated it a portion of the southwest quarter of sections eleven and twelve, township nineteen north, and range twelve east. It was the site of the Lochapokas' ceremonial square, still shaded by the branches of the Council Oak tree. It and the remaining 122.48 acres that surrounded it were allotted to full-blood Wehiley Neharkey. Because the old man died before receiving his formal deed, that particular piece of paper went to his son on July 5, 1904. He may have kept the paper, but he did not keep the land. In the early hours of March 11, 1905, developers Grant Stebbins and Samuel Davis bought the entire site for $6,400 from the heir, Moosar Neharkey.

The old Green Peach rebel thereby received a pretty pricey mess of pottage. Stebbins and Davis cut up his birthright into prime residential lots and began selling them off so fast and furiously that the transactions became barely decipherable in Tulsa's old land records. About all that one could figure out is that names such as James M. Hall and George Mowbray appear again and again, eventually to be joined by names like Sinclair (Harry and Earl) and Roberts (Oral).

Disturbed by the ethics of the process and the equity of the exchange, some judged the process harshly. Quite a few, then and later, condemned the entire affair as different in degree but not in kind from the frauds that Alabama had practiced on

the Indians two generations earlier. The Creek nation more soberly claimed itself the victim of many fraudulent lot sales and began a half-century of legal action and a half-century of futility.

Many individual Creeks pronounced the entire allotment process illegal and immoral. Many preferred to have nothing to do with it at all. The most stalwart, particularly among the full-bloods, vainly appealed to the promises made in their original treaty with Washington, promises that included that their new western homes would be theirs forever and governed by no authority greater than their own. In the end, however, those became merely the most recent in a long history of promises broken.

If there was moral blame, most of it had to go to the most powerful, and few of those lived in the Indian Territory, fewer still in Tulsa. One suspects that few Tulsans lost sleep to their troubled consciences. If they pondered at all the liquidation of the Creek nation, many might have agreed with the interpretation assigned one of the era's more notorious business deals: nothing was lost save honor. Most probably focused on what was gained: secure deeds, a dependable tax source, a formal framework of government and law, a path cleared toward statehood, an open field for investments—in short, the basis for better lives.

In the end, no contemporary judgment mattered. The future would judge, and Tulsa's long but uncertain future would have to justify this particular piece of its history. The next near century would issue history's pragmatic verdict upon the process by which Indian patrimony had become individual property and Tallasi had become Tulsa.

"Keep your eye

THREE

ON "Tulsa"

AS IF THE DUST WERE NOT
BAD ENOUGH, THE
NEWFANGLED AUTOMOBILES
KICKED UP WHAT EVEN THE
WIND LEFT UNDISTURBED.
EQUIPPED WITH HATS, VEILS,
AND GOGGLES, EARLY
TULSANS PREPARED FOR THE
NOVEL AND THRILLING
ADVENTURE OF AN
AUTOMOBILE OUTING.

MANY of the story's elements are apocryphal, but insiders have repeated them for so long and so often that even those parts have assumed the dimensions of truth. It has to do with oil, luck, and destiny.

Among its verifiable elements is the sad fact that in February 1906, a hard-pressed white farmer was forced to sell everything he owned. Frank Wheeler, his bone-tired wife, and their nine children (eight girls and a boy) probably stood silently as their rough furniture, their simple tools, and their hungry livestock passed under the auctioneer's gavel. Finally, the land itself was sold, and Wheeler took the bit of money earned (after all, the buyers were not much better off than the seller), using most of it to pay off his debts. What little was left went to buy the 160-acre allotment of Annie Jones, a Creek citizen deeded the place with the division of her nation's estate.

Frank Wheeler did not buy much because Annie Jones had not gotten much either. Most of the allottees in that corner of the old Indian country were irreconcilables, people who had refused to apply for land under the whites' system. The government had repaid their refusal by deeding them land available precisely because no one else wanted it. Frank Wheeler probably did not want it much either, but he had little choice, and he bought it because there was nothing better he could afford. Not even half of it could be farmed. Mostly it was hilly, rocky soil covered with blackjacks and other scrub timber. The place did have one creek running through its irregular hills, but even that asset ran dry most of the year. All in all, it was just about as sorry a piece of ground as anybody could find, a poor man's home on poor land.

The tale is that a stranger appeared at Wheeler's sagging door one evening about five years later. The visitor was looking for about the only things that the Wheeler family could offer: some warm grub, a dry place to sleep, and a little conversation. Life had treated the caller not much better than it had the farmer. He styled himself an oil-man (he liked to say that he could smell oil the way lesser men smelled perfume), and he had dirtied his hands in nearly every American oil field, all the way back to Pennsylvania and all the way westward too.

"You Said We Couldn't Do It, But We Did." In 1904, Tulsans built the bridge that built Tulsa.

Bridge at Tulsa J.T. 1/4 mile long

But not in any of those places, not even one time, had he ever found a drop of oil. It was an unrelieved record of failure that had earned him the nickname he despised: "Dry Hole." But, so the story goes, "Dry Hole" Tom Slick liked the Wheelers, and they liked him, and all agreed that he would lease the place.

With money borrowed from a banker over in Bristow, the county seat, Slick started a well a few miles over, then another, and another, and one more. All four fit his reputation: four wells, four "dusters." That was when he decided to try again, this time on Frank Wheeler's place, where he spudded a hole right by the farm's dry creek bed.

When the hole reached a thousand feet down, the original loan ran out, and Slick kept the cable tools working on promises alone while he headed over to Bristow. The banker refused to waste another penny and turned him down cold. He next appealed to the commercial club at the nearest little town, about ten miles away. Slick offered half interest for the $8,000 that it would take to finish the hole, but the Cushing Commercial Club had been burned quite a bit lately on bad investments, and this one looked even worse. With his last $100 (it borrowed), Tom Slick bought a train ticket and headed for Chicago, where he laid out the field's prospects for Charles B. Shaffer.

C. B. was an oilman, a real one, and he already had made several fortunes in Pennsylvania and other fields. Along the way, Shaffer had come to fancy himself something of an expert in what passed for geological science in that day. "Creekology," some called it, because it was based upon nothing more than the simple observation

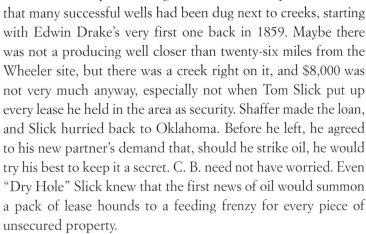

that many successful wells had been dug next to creeks, starting with Edwin Drake's very first one back in 1859. Maybe there was not a producing well closer than twenty-six miles from the Wheeler site, but there was a creek right on it, and $8,000 was not very much anyway, especially not when Tom Slick put up every lease he held in the area as security. Shaffer made the loan, and Slick hurried back to Oklahoma. Before he left, he agreed to his new partner's demand that, should he strike oil, he would try his best to keep it a secret. C. B. need not have worried. Even "Dry Hole" Slick knew that the first news of oil would summon a pack of lease hounds to a feeding frenzy for every piece of unsecured property.

Recapitalized, Slick pushed the drilling crew hard, and by February 1912, the tool pushers and roughnecks had reached nearly two thousand feet and an oil sand that appeared to be about fifty feet thick. Rather than accept his good—if limited—luck, Slick cased the oil off and insisted that the men push on. On March 12, their cutting tools reached 2,319 feet and cracked rock. Instantly, a huge deposit of natural gas roared into life, sending the first of that day's four hundred barrels rushing up

POSTCARDS PUBLICIZED
early Tulsa's firsts: The
ROBINSON HOTEL, ITS
FIRST LUXURY
ACCOMMODATIONS, CA.
1910, AND ITS FIRST FIRE
DEPARTMENT, FACING PAGE.
BELOW, MEMBERS OF THE
CITY'S FIRST TELEPHONE
CREW POSED FOR THEIR
PHOTOGRAPH IN 1904.

the hole into a towering geyser raining black gold onto what moments earlier had been rock-strewn, worthless soil.

As soon as he reached the scene, Slick inverted an old tub over the hole and used several hundred pounds of drilling equipment to hold it down. He ordered the drenched men to dig fresh dirt and rake it to conceal the oil-soaked earth around the rig. Every seventeen minutes, the workers had to stop as the accumulated gas pressure belched the old tub and heavy tools away and sent more oil cascading over the fresh soil. Meanwhile, Tom Slick wired Shaffer to come at once and bring along a small army of experienced "lease getters." He already had rented and hidden on the Wheeler place every horse, buggy, and carriage available at Cushing's three livery stables. Even should word leak, he figured, no one would be able to beat Shaffer's charging troops to the action.

Tom Slick was no longer "Dry Hole" Slick. He had hit the discovery well for the fabulous Cushing oil field, destined to be the world's largest and richest. Charles B. Shaffer's "creekology" had paid off. Soon real geologists could explain why: creeks like Wheeler's were surface indicators of anticlines and synclines, ancient folds that encased oceans of buried petroleum. Frank Wheeler was no longer poor. Within a month, his royalty interest was pulling in $145 a day, wells were sprouting all over his place, and he would not have to worry about spring plowing ever again.

But Slick, Shaffer, Wheeler, and everyone else would have to share their wealth. Word had leaked, and the very next train into Cushing carried men experienced at negotiating leases, drilling wells, and getting rich.

A few of them had found the only vehicle Tom Slick had overlooked—Cushing's one automobile—and reached the scene. Others had walked and run the ten miles. They probably ran most of it, for these were men used to running. After all, most of them had come into Cushing from a city where running was the norm and those who ran fastest ran richest. They had come from Tulsa, a city already well-off and just about to get a whole lot better-off.

It had been only ten years since the first Tulsan had bought the first deed to the city's first lot, but those ten years already had put Tulsa in first place in the nation's leading oil-producing state. It was a position much envied but little foreseen. Thoroughly documented, that story too was a tale of luck and of destiny—and of oil. Mostly, though, it was the work of leadership.

Like obscenity, leadership may be hard to define but is always recognizable on sight. One saw it often in Tulsa, even in its earliest years as a city. Take, for example, the matter of schools. Even before incorporation, key individuals had stepped forward from the village's small numbers to establish Tulsa's first school in the form of the Presbyterian mission. When the Presbyterians withdrew after the 1898-1899 school year, the community's children would have had no schooling at all had not leaders again acted boldly. J. M. Hall (the pioneer merchant who had lured his co-religionists in the first place), Jay Forsythe (the early cattleman), and a few other private citizens borrowed $1,050 on their own personal notes to take over the school and keep it running until the town could repay them. Because Tulsa could not possibly repay until secure deeds established a taxable base of real property, it was a loan of indefinite duration and uncertain status—interest free, at that.

Almost as soon as residents bought lots and received deeds, they levied school taxes, repaid the loan, and purchased the school and its site for the bargain-basement price of $426.23. Operations were charged to an elected board of education, and J. M. Hall was its unsalaried head. Within four years, school enrollment had grown so rapidly that the board persuaded residents to vote a $50,000 bond issue to build Tulsa's first high school on the site and a $25,000 bond issue for the first elementary school, on the city's north side. Neither would have been conceivable just a few years earlier, but leadership again made both possible. Sequoyah Elementary opened on North Boston with eleven classrooms and three hundred students in 1906. On South Main stood the city's pride: a new, three-story, domed high school with twenty-one classrooms, a full auditorium, and running water. Within two years, school leaders endorsed a second bond issue of $125,000, and Tulsa finished 1908 with seven schools—Sequoyah, Tulsa High School, Lindsay (renamed Riverview in 1917), Washington, Lincoln, Irving, and Celia Clinton. All in all, it was a remarkable record for any city, a dazzling one to realize in just six years, and a visible testament to the quality of leadership.

In other ways too, leadership asserted itself and made the difference. One famous to early Tulsans involved the building of the first nonrailroad bridge across the Arkansas. Because it was believed to be too costly for government and too chancy for outside investors, the project fell to three private citizens: M. L. Baird, J. D. Hagler, and George T. Williamson. With more faith than experience, the three formed a private toll company and set out to span the river known and feared for its unpredictable currents and shifting bed, which already had claimed one Frisco bridge. In 1904, they opened it. Across its first span ran a banner with these words: "You Said We Couldn't Do It, But We Did."

In many ways, the boast could have applied to others as well—to Robert Hall (Harry Hall's son and J. M. Hall's nephew), who organized the first telephone system in 1903; to William Halsell and Jay Forsythe, the cattlemen who left their herds to open Tulsa's First National Bank in 1905; to William Robinson, who built Tulsa's first luxury hotel (the Alcorn) in 1904 and followed it two years later with the Robinson, then regarded as the finest between the Mississippi River and the Rocky Mountains. There were men like Prier Price, Tate Brady, and J. M. Hall (of course) who worked with land developer Grant Stebbins to lure a little Presbyterian school away from Muskogee in 1907, place it on virgin prairie east of town, and eventually rename Henry Kendall College the University of Tulsa. In every case, any who said it could not be done were proved wrong. Tulsans did it. Before long, the merely difficult became the routine, and the impossible became the expected.

It sometimes was hard for one particular group to distinguish either the difficult from the routine or the impossible from the expected. Founded in 1901, the Tulsa Commercial Club never claimed to be the city's moral conscience but clearly embodied its business soul. Only after heated debate did the club vote to prohibit gambling in its facilities, but the gambling forbidden referred to that involving cards, dice, and other gaming paraphernalia. From its beginning, the commercial club took notable risks, most of which paid off handsomely, some incredibly so.

The very first one may have returned the highest dividends of all. The club's formation was hurried by the Katy Railroad's announcement of plans to complete a line from Muskogee to Pawhuska. The Katy intended for the rails to cross the Frisco tracks about seven miles east of Tulsa before proceeding through neighboring Turley to reach the Osage tribal headquarters. Tulsa businessmen quickly mobilized and approached Katy officials with a survey that seemed to save the company money by bending the line to run it right through their city. Likely more persuasive, however, was a pledge to secure free right-of-way (valued at $3,000) and an outright gift of $12,000, the latter in the form of promissory notes underwritten by virtually every merchant and business firm in Tulsa. Representing the Tulsans were men already well-off and well-known and about to become rich and famous: George Mowbray, Samuel G. Kennedy, J. M. Hall, L. M. Poe, and Jay Forsythe. All but the last had signed the city's charter of incorporation. All including the last were founders of the Tulsa Commercial Club.

Not least among the deal's immediate benefits was experience. When the

Midland Valley announced plans in 1904 to lay a line through Red Fork, Tulsa businessmen immediately changed the railway's tune (and route) with a $15,000 "bonus." Such assertiveness had equal—if cheaper—effect later in the same year. The Frisco agreed to build a line westward to Enid from Tulsa rather than from the planned departure point at Sapulpa, and the Atchison, Topeka, and Santa Fe (Santa Fe) altered its plans to extend its north-south line from Collinsville straight through the city rather than route it several miles to the east. Both came without price but not without reward. Consider just this: By 1905, Tulsa's future was set (not one railroad has come into the city since), and the fates of its immediate rivals, Turley, Red Fork, and Sapulpa, were sealed.

It was in 1905 that the commercial club came up with a stunning idea sure to put Tulsa on the nation's business map. A 1903 business excursion to observe "Indian Territory Day" in Saint Louis had drawn some favorable notice in that city, and the club decided that a lot more would be a lot better. With both ballyhoo and bravura, the club organized a band, installed a printing press in a railroad baggage car, and dispatched a special group said to include the infant city's top one hundred businessmen on a tour of twenty-five hundred miles to "boost" Tulsa in scores of midwestern cities and towns. A last-minute addition was the son of a nearby rancher. "Bill Rogers' fancy rope juggling," so the paper reported, was sure to attract much attention.

In other regards, the boosters may have been prone to exaggeration (the one hundred entrepreneurs amounted to no more than eighty-nine), but the sheer audacity of the project guaranteed it priceless front-page publicity as the loud train, the booming band, and the equally noisy boosters roared into successive cities. In fact, the head of Chicago's own commercial club was said to be so impressed by news of their imminent arrival that he decided he had to look up this "Tulsa" on the map—only to discover that there was no Tulsa on the map. One can be sure, however, that there was one indelibly on his and others' mental maps when the train departed. In the Windy City's case, the spectacle so moved the publishers of the *Chicago Inter-Ocean Appeal* that the paper exhorted its readers to "Keep your eye on Tulsa; we will."

So successful was the tour that the commercial club launched a second one—bigger, grander, and longer—in 1908. This excursion ran through Saint Louis to Chicago, thence eastward to New York City, ending in Washington, D. C. By then, Bill Rogers had moved on to bigger and better things under the name of Will, but

THE 1905 BOOSTER TRAIN DEPARTED FROM THE FRISCO DEPOT CARRYING THE CITY'S TOP HUNDRED BUSINESSMEN AND FANCY ROPE ARTIST "BILL" ROGERS. THEIR TWENTY-FIVE-HUNDRED-MILE TRIP WAS INTENDED TO "PUT TULSA ON THE MAP."

the Tulsans figured they had a perfect (well, not quite perfect) substitute: Emmett Dalton, sole survivor of the infamous outlaw band. Likely it was less Dalton's notoriety than it was Tulsa's new renown that accounted for this group's impressive reception. Chicago's Board of Trade suspended its wires for the first time in its history to greet the Tulsans. New York officials accorded them a parade down Fifth Avenue. President Theodore Roosevelt hosted a party in their honor at the capital.

The heavily promoted booster trips also bore fruit less visible but ultimately more rewarding. Some literally were so moved by the city's effort at self-promotion that they determined to move with and to it. Joplin, Missouri, mine owner George Bayne decided to cast his lot with the bold new city to the southeast, relocated in Tulsa, invested in utilities, and soon (with Eugene Lorton) transformed the old *Indian Republican* into the *Tulsa World*. H. O. McClure pulled up stakes in Chicago to move to Tulsa, where he opened a hardware firm and began to devote his boundless energies to nearly every civic project. Robert T. Daniel, already a millionaire developer, sensed that the grass was greener westward, relocated in Tulsa, and built two of the city's first skyscrapers, the Daniel Building and the Hotel Tulsa. He stayed in Tulsa even after the grass turned mighty green in his original home: Miami, Florida.

Newcomers like Bayne, McClure, and Daniel slid comfortably into what already constituted a Tulsa Establishment, the city's first true elite. Names like Hall, Poe, Price, Kennedy, Mowbray, Forsythe, and a few others appear so often on recent pages

for a reason: the same small group of names constantly reappears on older pages, these the frail and yellowed pages that document Tulsa's first years as a city. They adorn the newspaper columns that record civic activities. They show up in the financial pages as directors of the first banks. Their names (and their wives') emerge in the social columns reporting on the best clubs and the gayest parties. Their names are on the documents of incorporation, new plats and additions, and official records of public and private organizations. They reappear in every permutation in land records that record the buying and selling of prime locations as well as speculative property at the city's edges. As an elite, their hands shaped everything they touched. As an elite, their hands touched nearly everything of importance.

That was true even in mass politics. Like others of their generation, most were party men (if there were partisan women, they could not vote until 1920), and they divided fairly equally into Republicans and Democrats, the choice largely determined by the preferences of the places they had left to come to Tulsa. Thus, those of midwestern ancestry tended to be Republicans, those of southern stock Democrats. In election seasons, they might rail against the alleged perfidy of their partisan opponents, but one senses that they did so mostly out of habit and at least partly with tongue in cheek. Campaign passion

VANDEVER AND BEENE'S DRY GOODS STORE, 1904. FACING PAGE, YOUNG TULSA SWELLS SET ASIDE THEIR GLASSES TO POSE AT THE OASIS, A CHOC BEER JOINT ON BOSTON BETWEEN FIRST AND SECOND, 1909.

spent, they then closed their mouths, put their hands firmly on their wallets, and went about the business of government—which generally was business.

On most business matters, theirs was a remarkable harmony. Because they looked more to the future than to the present, they were deaf to the sirens of cheap government and confidently prepared and endorsed the bonds and taxes that were investments in Tulsa's destiny. Because they believed in ordered, rational growth, they set regular procedures to guide neighborhood development and city annexations. Because they trusted private enterprise, they entered creative public-private partnerships to provide utilities and other necessary services.

For the most part, Tulsa's more anonymous residents accepted the elite's values and habits. They almost always confirmed proposed bond issues with overwhelming majorities, and they paid the taxes with minimal grumbling. They applauded neighborhood development and appreciated the ordered and steady growth of an expanding city. They approved franchise arrangements in referenda, and a surprising number invested in the most imaginative public-private agreements. For example, well over two hundred purchased lottery chances for lots on the unbroken land surrounding the relocated Kendall College, individual acts of unnamed citizens that collectively generated most of the money to bring the school from Muskogee.

Thus, all of the sound and fury of early politics and campaigning usually signified nothing in the way of a divided Tulsa. There was, however, one public issue that did split Tulsans openly, bitterly, and repeatedly. It was the fight between the self-styled "open-town" and "closed-town" advocates. In its days as a cattle-shipping cen-

ter, Tulsa had been a "cow town," with all that implied. Frontier outlaws like the Daltons rubbed shoulders with rowdy cowboys, and both consorted with those whose daily work was considered downright criminal by some, pragmatically necessary by others, quietly tolerable by most. That work was running gambling halls (said to occupy nearly every second story of Tulsa's few two-story structures) and brothels (the cleanest and safest of which lined First Street). Tulsans also organized semiregular deliveries of booze across the Arkansas River. The joyful news that "the fleet is in" signaled a successful evasion of federal marshals and Indian police, and that news was welcomed by many a belly-warming toast.

While the cattle trade later succumbed to more lucrative industries, Tulsa retained its early reputation. In fact, it added to it. Illegal gambling parlors flourished openly, even on the ground floor. Bordellos spread to other locations, and First Street became known as "Bloody First" as the earlier establishments became wilder. Thirsty residents no longer worried about the fleet's status: bootleggers opened around-the-clock businesses to separate men from their senses and their money.

EARLY OIL'S NOVELTY EMBRACED BOTH THE ECONOMIC AND SOCIAL, AS DEMONSTRATED BY THIS GROUP, FACING PAGE, PHOTOGRAPHED ON A SUNDAY OUTING TO THE REFINERY. RIGHT, DR. FRED S. CLINTON, SHOWN HERE AT THE SUE BLAND NO. 1, FORSOOK PIONEER MEDICINE FOR PIONEER OIL.

Under the circumstances, the open-town, closed-town dispute simultaneously assumed the granitelike forms of a moral controversy, an economic clash, and a political row. None was easily amenable either to rational discussion or to reasonable compromise. Churchmen and churchwomen admitted to no doubt that their city was going to hell—probably somewhere on First Street. Others were unpersuaded because First Street afforded them a helluva good time. Sober business types held that Tulsa's reputation retarded investments. Their less sober counterparts answered that theirs was an investment, and a good one at that. Politicians found themselves in an impossible predicament. Here was an issue both unavoidable and controversial, one for which there was no safe side and almost no middle ground at all.

They widened what little ground they found with considerable hypocrisy. Both parties and nearly every political faction sought behind-the-scenes deals with powerful if less reputable elements, all the while promising the public to "clean up Tulsa" by throwing out the rascals and their allies, the "vice lords." In most cases, voters elected those who most fervently and credibly indicted sin, which, in the nature of things, generally meant the current nonincumbents. The winners usually proceeded to honor their private arrangements with Tulsa's demimonde, a process that led to their temporary enrichment. In the next election round, the once-virtuous "outs" became the newly soiled "rascals."

In the few instances in which newly elected officials honestly attempted to enforce antiliquor, antiprostitution, antigambling, and other moral laws, they discovered that quite a few citizens voted one way on election day but preferred to live another for the rest of the year. Moreover, the next election would find their opponents remarkably well financed and well organized. For these reasons, the voters would oust them in favor of more tolerant officials at the first opportunity. Whatever happened, the high-minded had their laws, the low-living had their outlets, and the politicians had a problem.

The one attempt to break the cycle through structural change came with a new city charter in 1908. Over strong opposition from working-class and minority precincts, a group of self-styled civic leaders (a group that included the great bulk of Tulsa's elite) promised to smash "machine" and "vice-corrupted" politics by replacing the old ward-based government with a city commission. Elected ward representation, so the argument went, fostered vice because it all but guaranteed that as many as three of the city's four council members would be agents of the criminal element operating in and occupying the two north-side wards and the working-class southwestern ward. Elect four men (and they had to be men) and a mayor citywide, place each of the four in charge of specified city departments, and Tulsa could guarantee itself honest, efficient government under proven administrators mindful only of the city's common good. Or so they believed at the time.

For more than seven decades, Tulsans would be governed by that charter, and the long-term consequences would be many and powerful. The short-term conse-

RESIDENCE OF BOB GALBREATH
OIL PRODUCER

quences, however, were few and revealing. The first mayor elected under the new charter was John Mitchell. Mitchell had been the nominee of a high-minded (and well-heeled) group of prominent businessmen who had assembled a nonpartisan ticket. He promised to clean up the city, and his victory seemed to signal the ultimate reform. Tulsa was now freed not only from the moral and social divisiveness reflected in its ward geography but from the bane of party politics as well.

The emancipation proved to be short-lived. At the first opportunity, voters repudiated the independents as "denizens of Tulsa's underworld" in favor of a Democrat, L. J. Martin. Mayor Martin promised to clean up the city. He actually tried to do it, but the effort failed to have any effect except to leave him exhausted and friendless. He declined to seek another term. Democrat Frank M. Wooden replaced him in 1912, promising to clean up the city. In no small part because a large number of black Republicans had been disfranchised, Wooden won a second term in 1914, again promising to clean up the city.

Within months, several shootings at gambling dens suggested that any cleanup remained incomplete. In July, Tulsans read the shocking report that W. J. Barber, a notorious bootlegger who had been their chief of police, had shot and killed two federal marshals in a liquor raid on his home. In February 1915, another shooting left five

BOULDER STREET SOUTH FROM 6TH STREET, TULSA, OKLA.

QUEEN CITY,
MAGIC CITY,
MAGIC EMPIRE,
OIL CAPITAL, CITY
BEAUTIFUL—TULSA
WAS TO NAME AND
RENAME HERSELF
OVER THE DECADES
AS HER
ASPIRATIONS AND
HER SENSE OF
IDENTITY EVOLVED.

Tulsa

OKLAHOMA'S
Queen City

Compliments of The Robinson

gamblers wounded and bleeding on South Boston. In August, a federal court sentenced William J. Creekmore, the so-called Bootlegger King and intimate of city officials, to the federal prison in Leavenworth, Kansas.

For once, concerns about public morality went beyond ministers' lamentations and politicians' promises. Judge Conn Linn impaneled a grand jury. State Attorney General Prince Freeling summoned Tulsa "madams" and other underworld figures before the panel. By December, the grand jury had heard enough and indicted (among others) Mayor Wooden, Police Chief Foster Burns, Police and Fire Commissioner Thomas J. Quinn, Tulsa County Sheriff James Woolley, and two Skiatook officials as well. The charges ranged from dereliction of duty to the solicitation and acceptance of bribes. Commissioner Quinn completed his term before judicial proceedings were complete, and others traded their offices for their liberty by resigning to have the charges dropped. Mayor Wooden lost both his office and his liberty after a jury found him guilty of a variety of crimes. Water Commissioner O. D. Hunt completed the deposed mayor's term. He promised to clean up the city.

By then, the task resembled cleaning the Augean stables, but the fault had little to do with public hypocrisy or official corruption. What really was involved was the phenomenon expressed in the frenzy that descended upon Tom Slick's discovery well on the Wheeler place. Before Mayor Wooden went to trial, before Attorney General Freeling subpoenaed the strumpets, before the city changed its charter, Tulsa's future already had been cast. In retrospect, the decisive moment may have come within a few minutes of midnight on June 24, 1901.

Dispute surrounds the details of the previous six weeks, but the important facts are clear. One is that on May 10, 1901, P. L. Crossman and a small crew began drilling near Red Fork on the allotment assigned a Creek citizen, Sue Bland. The work was slow, and the hole had reached no more than five hundred feet or so by late June, when Crossman left the site in charge of his son Luther and returned for a weekend visit to his home in Joplin, Missouri.

Late on the night of June 24, the drilling bit penetrated a gritty lime formation at 534 feet. Cracking the lime crust, the bit ruptured a gas pocket. Oil shot up the column and gushed over the wooden derrick, drenching it and the surrounding men from thirty feet above. An excited driller rushed to the nearest telegraph office, where he wired the thrilling news to the elder Crossman.

P. L. Crossman was not the last to know, but he assuredly was not the first. Before he could receive the printed news, every telegrapher between the site and Joplin already had heard it. Telegraph lines fairly buzzed as the word spread far and wide. Within hours, newspapers from Muskogee to Kansas City and at countless points in between were printing the news in bold headlines: The town had itself a real gusher. Red Fork instantly had become famous, and everyone agreed that a little community on the Arkansas was sure to be transformed.

They were half-right. Almost overnight, a mob of oilmen, land men, and con men descended on Red Fork, and quite a few loose women descended on them. By the time Crossman could get there, he barely recognized the modest hamlet that he had left; it had become (in his words) "one of the vilest spots in the area." But Red Fork's infamy lasted no longer than did its fame. When the gas pressure quickly dissipated, the gusher quit gushing. Hurriedly installed pumps daily managed to suck about six barrels from underground. At prevailing prices, that translated into about five dollars a day, enough to nourish hope but too little to feed hysteria. Later wells made modest showings, but Red Fork slowly slipped back into its sluggish ways.

Nonetheless, a town on the Arkansas was transformed, but that town was Tulsa. There was nothing inevitable about that. After all, Red Fork had been thoroughly independent of Tulsa since both were Creek towns. Red Fork lay right by the Bland place and other producing sites. Tulsa lay several miles away and on the wrong side of a treacherous river. Red Fork, not Tulsa, was then the Frisco's western terminus, and its 1900 population was not significantly less than Tulsa's.

In the end, not one of these advantages made much difference. The difference that made the difference had little to do with luck or location and a lot to do with leadership. Tulsans already had bridged the river, and the tools and lumber that went into Red Fork poured across that bridge. Tulsans had built hotels and eateries, and the men who worked in the Red Fork fields during the day slept and ate in Tulsa every night. Each morning, they boarded the "Coal Oil Johnny," a new train that Tulsa's early elite assembled, and went to work. Each evening, they took the "Coal Oil Johnny" back to Tulsa and home.

By the time the region had a real oil field and a real oil boom, it was Tulsans who opened it, and it was Tulsa that profited from it. The Tulsans were Robert Galbreath and Frank Chesley, the year was 1905, and the site was a farm about ten miles south of Tulsa. It belonged to Ida Glenn, and on November 22, 1905, it produced a true gusher. A second came the next March, when the partners hit another, larger one only three hundred feet away. One astounding success followed another, eventually defining a field more than eight miles long. By the end of 1907, more than ninety-five companies were operating in the field, having sunk more than a thousand wells. All but fifteen were producing—producing 19,926,995 barrels in the previous twelve months alone. People called it the Glenn Pool, and the industry was calling it "the Richest Little Oil Field in the World."

Glenn Pool's richness lay partly in the wealth that came up from the earth and partly in the money spent to extract it. As of January 1, 1908, the latter consisted of $4.5 million spent on drilling, $5 million on lease agreements, $3 million on wages, and $15.3 million on timber, iron, and steel for construction. A good portion of the income earned by the field ended up in Tulsa in the fortunes of a few lucky men like natives Galbreath and Chesley and newcomers like Harry and Earl Sinclair. Far more important, though, was Tulsa's share of the money spent, because a good part of that nearly $28 million was spent in Tulsa. It was spent as capital with drilling companies, freight companies, and supply companies. It was spent as wages in Tulsa's stores and for Tulsa homes. It was spent on necessities, on luxuries, on children—and on gambling, liquor, and women. It made Tulsa rich. It made Tulsa wild. And it made Tulsa big.

Against that, Tom Slick's efforts at concealment never had a chance. The first train to reach Cushing rolled in on the Frisco tracks, westbound from Tulsa because it was Tulsans who had won the line's extension from their city. It carried Tulsans because Tulsa had the experts who could identify the best leases and sign them fastest. Tulsa companies extended and developed the field because it was Tulsa that provided their headquarters and banks. The companies hired Tulsa drillers to penetrate Frank Wheeler's and others' lands because it was Tulsans who had the most experience and

the most equipment. Timber for derricks, iron for casings, steel
for holding tanks—all this and more they would ship through
Tulsa because it was Tulsa that had sought and won the railroads
that connected their city to the entire continent.

Unlike Glenn Pool, Cushing would never be able to claim
that it was "the Richest Little Oil Field in the World." No "little" would describe this field destined to produce nearly one-
fifth of all of the oil marketed in the United States. And Tulsa?
Tulsa already had earned its reputation as "the Magic City," but
there had been nothing magic about it. Nor would magic alone
account for the title it was next to assume.

1 9 3 1

Then and Now

Transportation technology
reshapes a city

CONTEMPORARY PHOTOS

BY SUSAN RAINEY, 1997

Boston Avenue
looking south
from Second
Street

ARCHER AND ROSEDALE

MAIN STREET LOOKING NORTH FROM SECOND STREET

8/18/09

LOOKING NORTH ON MAIN
FROM SECOND STREET
1909

1 9 0 9

Main Street looking south from the Frisco tracks

1 8 8 9

The people who put the magic in "the Magic City" thereby put Tulsa on the map, particularly on the maps that circulated in the offices of the oil industry. It made no difference if those offices were in New York, London, or Sumatra, in North America, Europe, or Asia. Anywhere people knew oil, people knew Tulsa. In fact, many knew it by its newest self-proclaimed title. Tulsa was "Oil Capital of the World."

Enough knew of its international status that the city received more than a few educated, urbane, and cultivated visitors. In every respect, they had nothing in common with its first visitors, the sweaty railroad workers of 1882. Nor did the place they visited physically resemble the Tulsa of 1882. Its skyscrapers and broad avenues having replaced tents and a single grassy street, this Tulsa really was a city.

One particularly inquisitive visitor was Herbert Feis, who came to Tulsa in 1923 as a representative of the eminently respectable Charity Organization Society of the City of New York. He was there for a purpose: to test a theory. Feis sensed that Tulsa would be an ideal place to apply William Allen White's advice to find a mid-American city of moderate size and "go down and see what a lot of Americans will do with a

Preceding pages: The Petroleum Industry War Service Board gathered for a victory banquet at the Mayflower Hotel in Washington, D.C., in 1919. Left, a view of the skyline Tulsa had acquired by the beginning of the First World War. According to local citizens, all roads led to their town. Below, *Tulsa Spirit* celebrated the city's churches and hospitals in the August 1927 Graphic Issue of the magazine.

1 First Christian Ch.
2 Sacred Heart Church
3 Christian Science Ch.
4 First M.E. Church
5 Boston Ave. M.E. Ch.
6 First Baptist Ch.
7 First Presbyterian Ch.
8 Trinity Episcopal Ch.
9 Holy Family Church
10 St. Johns Hospital
11 Morningside Hospital
12 Oklahoma Hospital

When Riot Stalked in

country if left pretty much to themselves." If White's formula was correct and if Feis's guess was good, Tulsa offered a model for all Americans—or at least for those "left pretty much to themselves."

What Feis found was a city that impressed even the well-traveled New Yorker. A quick tour of the swiftly growing downtown district was enough to convince Feis that "this small city reproduces some features of New York more exactly and truly than any other town in between." One new building, a fresh skyscraper built by Tulsa's Josh Cosden, "possesses in smaller scale the grace and purity of the Woolworth Building." Less than a block away, on Boston's corner with Third, stood the Exchange National Bank; next to it, at Second and Boston, was Central National Bank. In each,

thick carpeting, brass- and gold-adorned columns, polished marble floors, and long, shining counters looked for all the world like "a corner torn away from Wall Street." The price of a simple tea dress offered in a street-level shop (it was $110) persuaded Feis that Tulsa's Boston Avenue was in the same league as New York City's Fifth Avenue.

As Herbert Feis moved outside the shadows of the new downtown skyscrapers, he visited Tulsa's working-class areas, its largest industrial plant (Josh Cosden's refinery), and quite a few of its churches, pool halls, and street corners. Everywhere, he

found "friendliness, steadliness [sic], pride of achievement, a humorous self-independence, a great zest for ordinary things. Above all, a great striving for the perfection of accepted American standards, to be won, it is true, by wealth rather than by intellectual achievement."

Herbert Feis found such a life and he found it more abundantly at a function to which he had been expectantly invited and warmly received: the annual meeting of the Tulsa Chamber of Commerce.

One suspects that chamber officials and most ordinary Tulsans must have been pleased with Feis's final report and its tone. It is true that Feis had sprinkled a few negative observations along the way—maybe he had been a little too sensitive about anti-Semitism, a little too interested in this Ku Klux Klan business, and a little too naive about things in "the Negro quarter"—but he had been pretty fair. More important, he had been very optimistic, and that counted for a lot.

What really was portentous, however, was neither the report's fairness nor its writer's optimism. What was notable was White's formula and Feis's choice. Between the two world wars, Tulsans did reveal what people could do with a city "if left pretty much to themselves." Sure enough, it pretty much amounted to "what a lot of Americans" did under the same circumstances with the whole country. For Tulsans and for Americans, world war brought both national sacrifice and local strife. For Tulsans and for Americans, the 1920s brought both material abundance and social disorder. For Tulsans and for Americans, one decade's excesses and disorder predicated the next decade's depression and recovery. Any difference was chiefly in volume. Somehow, Tulsa managed at once to echo and to amplify the sounds of a changing America.

As those patterns unfolded between the wars, Tulsa's history acquired drama and pathos as well as significance and meaning. Any one of those qualities was as important, if not more important, than a simple declaration, even one as magnificent as its status as "Oil Capital of the World."

ONE OF THE PROBLEMS OF
CONTAINING OIL IN MASSIVE
STORAGE TANKS WAS THE
OCCASIONAL FIRE. NONETHELESS,
EVEN THIS STORAGE METHOD WAS
PREFERABLE TO THE LARGE LAKES OF
OIL THAT SURROUNDED TULSA
DURING THE EARLY DAYS OF THE
GLENN POOL FIELD. PIPELINES,
REFINING, AND OIL-EQUIPMENT
SUPPLY WERE AMONG THE
FOUNDATIONS OF AN INDUSTRY
THAT WOULD EMBRACE TULSA AS
ITS CAPITAL.

THE *Princes* of Petroleum

KE OF OIL, GLENN POOL OIL FIELD, NEAR T

VISION AND LEADERSHIP, not luck and location, placed Tulsa first among its immediate rivals for command of a rich area's early oil developments. Not Turley, not Sapulpa, not Red Fork, not even Cushing itself was to be the primary beneficiary of the oil that came from the earth surrounding each of them. Nonetheless, early Tulsa was hardly an oil capital. For a region no more than forty or fifty miles wide, it served as a shipping and supply center and a vice-ridden bedroom community.

In a remarkably brief period, however, that changed. Tulsa went quickly from a big boomtown to a proud and powerful city. Both its pride and its power shared a single source. Tulsa managed to rise above its rough origins by turning problems into opportunities, opportunities into successes, and successes into fortunes.

The first problem was obvious. Oil pumped from beneath the ground at Red Fork, Glenn Pool, or wherever was really no more valuable on the surface than it had been beneath it. Quite simply, it was smelly, messy, and abundant.

For its blackness to become golden, it would have to reach a buyer and then be refined into marketable commodities. Until then, someone had to find someplace just to put the stinking stuff.

The initial attempts consisted of crude earthen tanks, little more than large holes in the ground. Easy enough to build, they offered no realistic solution. Seepage from the tanks ruined the soil and wasted precious petroleum. Evaporation wasted more and fouled the air as well. Fire was a constant danger because the tanks, the grounds, nearby creeks, and the air itself became combustible. Most of all, the production was entirely too great to be confined to any pits dug by hand. The Ida Glenn No. 2, the second of Galbreath and Chesley's discovery wells, flowed seventeen hundred barrels during its first twenty-four hours. It overwhelmed every available pit, and no one was foolish enough to believe that men could move dirt faster than the earth could belch oil. Hastily constructed wooden tanks began to capture that particular well's overflow—just in time to become worthless when two new wells produced a steady fifteen hundred barrels per day.

The ultimate solution was to build huge tank farms with perfectly aligned steel-and-iron rows of massive, squat silos, each storing thousands of barrels. By January 1907, a good percentage of Tulsa's available labor force was hard at work building a tank farm in the then-independent community of West Tulsa, located south and west of the river. The first was built for the Texas Company, but other big companies followed right behind with their own. As had the little oil producers before, they paid Tulsa workers, Tulsa suppliers, and Tulsa shippers to get it done. What was new was

With the Arkansas River as a natural drain for waste products, the Mid-Continent was one of eighteen refineries eventually lining the west bank of the river. Drainoff of residue left the empire's capital peopled with "princes" living beside a sometimes malodorous moat. By century's end, new policies would do much to cleanse and renew the river.

A SERIES OF STELL TANKS GLENN OIL FIELD TULSA, OKLA.

35000 BBL TANK

Shooter loading shell
With Nitro-Glycerine

that all of these Tulsans cashed checks bearing the names of big and established companies.

The Texas Company's name (now Texaco) was one, but no name was bigger or more established at the time than that of the Prairie Oil and Gas Company. Despite its modest title, Prairie was a notable principality in John D. Rockefeller's global empire: Standard Oil. Prairie already had extended a two-inch pipeline connecting Glenn Pool via Bartlesville to Rockefeller's refinery six hundred miles away in Whiting, Indiana. In 1906, the company promised to replace it with an eight-inch line running right through Tulsa.

Pittsburgh's Mellon family immediately offered the Rockefellers a run for their money. The Mellons pledged to build a twenty-two-thousand-barrel loading station and a new pipeline to connect Tulsa with their interests in southeast Texas. The Mellons won the race by putting four crews to work simultaneously, one each at terminals in Tulsa and Port Arthur, Texas, and two working toward each end from the middle. The

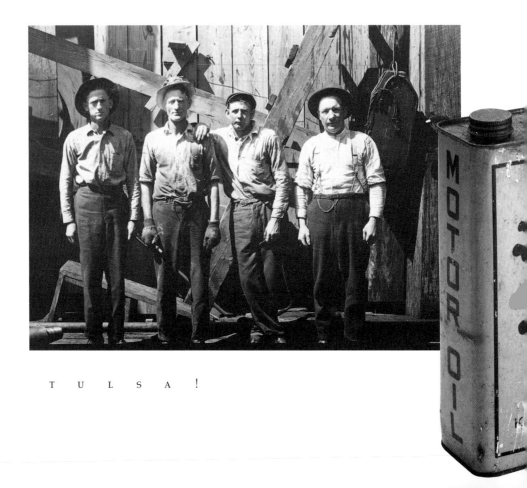

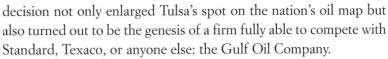

BRITISH PHILOSOPHER
THOMAS HOBBES LIVED
TOO EARLY TO SEE THE
PRINCIPALITIES OF OIL,
BUT HE UNKNOWINGLY
DESCRIBED THE LIVES OF
SOME OIL WORKERS
WHEN HE DECLARED
THAT EARLY LIFE WAS
"NASTY, BRUTISH, AND
SHORT." OIL-FIELD LIFE
COULD BE NASTY. FOR
MANY, IT WAS BRUTISH,
AND IN THE MOST
HAZARDOUS ROLES, IT
COULD ALSO BE SHORT.

decision not only enlarged Tulsa's spot on the nation's oil map but also turned out to be the genesis of a firm fully able to compete with Standard, Texaco, or anyone else: the Gulf Oil Company.

Rockefeller may not have welcomed the competition, but he did match it and more. In November 1906, Standard announced that it would build a new line connecting Tulsa directly to its big refinery at Baton Rouge, Louisiana. Working through a bone-chilling winter, Standard rushed the job to completion in record time. By April 1907, it was carrying twenty thousand barrels daily of Oklahoma crude—every drop passing through Tulsa. Still more important was the symbolic consequence. Oilmen sensed that the imperial Standard was anointing Tulsa its chosen capital for the province already called the midcontinent field, the vast region stretching from Illinois to the Texas Gulf coast.

That may have been why Patrick C. Doyle shipped an entire newspaper—printing press, type, newsprint, ink, and all—to Tulsa in 1908. Doyle had just bought the small weekly paper then called *Investor's Weekly*, and he insisted that Tulsa was its only proper home. Under its new name, the *Oil and Gas Journal*, oilmen everywhere came to study it, advertise in it, and refer to it as the industry's bible.

The relocation had powerful significance. Doyle resided in Oil City, Pennsylvania, center of America's first oil field. The paper that he relocated had been published in Beaumont, Texas, birthplace of the great gusher at Spindletop, the one that had ushered in the modern oil industry. There could have been no better evidence of Tulsa's rise.

Confirmation came in 1909, when Rockefeller ordered his Prairie Company to move its headquarters to offices in Tulsa's new Commercial National Bank Building. He also shut down Prairie's shops in Neodosha, Kansas; transferred $50,000 in equipment to Tulsa; and added one hundred Tulsans to his payroll. Within a month, a major oil-field outfitter, the Frick-Reid Supply Company, joined the exodus and relocated to Tulsa. The Texas Company followed next, taking over two complete floors of the new Mayo Building to oversee its own domain.

Other oilmen followed in short order. One was Mark Abrahams, who rushed all the way from Egypt to organize the Roxana Oil Company and locate it in Tulsa. The company's name might not have seemed weighty, but its presence had plain and potent international significance. Roxana was a branch of a huge international firm, the recently merged Royal Dutch/Shell Group. It represented the combine's first appearance in the United States, and it signaled Dutch and British intent to contest the mighty Standard on its own turf. It also measured Tulsa's stature. Tulsa was the chosen field for the battle, one sure to leave no scars upon the city.

The pipelines, suppliers, and producers would continue to come, particularly after 1912, when the Cushing field came on-line. Each one would bear the blessing and receive the boasting of the city's commercial club, but the club was anxious to move the city even higher up the oil industry's food chain, with refineries turning raw crude into finished wealth. So impatient was the club that it leaped at an earnest pro-motor's offer to build a massive refinery in Tulsa. H. H. Tucker promised that his Uncle Sam refinery would put Standard out of business and make Tulsa the capital of his own empire. The commercial club met his bonus demands in the spring of 1906 and eagerly awaited the results. It took a year for results to come—when Tulsans learned that H. H. Tucker had been hauled before a Kansas bankruptcy court.

Standard was safe for the moment, and the commercial club found a suitable (if less ambitious) replacement for Tucker. In June 1907, the club gave twenty acres of West Tulsa land to the Humboldt refinery to lure it away from Kansas. Local investors put enough money in the relocated plant to raise its capacity to two hundred barrels a day by 1909. Since the Glenn Pool alone was then producing seven thousand bar-rels every twenty-four hours, it was obvious that Tulsa still needed a strong dose of Tucker's ambition, cut with humility and practicality.

That is exactly what it got. The very next year, the Texas Company put in a West Tulsa refinery capable of handling five thousand to seven thousand barrels per day. Two years later, in 1912, Tom Slick's gusher on the Wheeler place prompted the Pierce Oil Corporation to announce plans for a big refinery north of Cushing at Yale. One day after newspaper headlines announced Yale's good fortune, the commercial club wired the company a counteroffer: a $10,000 bonus and a free 320-acre site to come to neighboring Sand Springs. Headlines had to be rewritten overnight, and the refinery turned out the first of its daily six thousand barrels of production on December 20, 1913. By then, smaller companies like the Constantin (in West Tulsa) and the Phoenix (in Sand Springs) were adding to Tulsa's refining capacity.

The greatest addition was built in the same year, 1913, and it was the work of one man: Joshua Seney Cosden. Born to a modest Maryland family, Josh Cosden had come west at twenty-seven to escape the East and modesty—the latter permanently. With borrowed money, he built a little fifteen-barrel-a-day refinery in Bigheart (pre-sent Barnsdall) in 1909. He did most of the labor himself, losing twenty pounds and adding ten years in the two months it took him to hammer, bolt, and weld the thing together. It lasted long enough to turn out exactly one run of gasoline before a torna-do blew it away. Josh Cosden borrowed a little more money, built another refinery, added more years, and lost more weight. He lost the refinery too when fire got this one within hours of its opening.

With the last money that he could possibly raise, Cosden rebuilt in Bigheart, and this time his plant survived and prospered. A millionaire at thirty-two, he took his earnings, organized Cosden and Company, and came to West Tulsa to open an eighty-acre refinery with a daily capacity of forty-five hundred barrels. Neither storm nor fire awaited him, but Cushing's immense flow did. Oil people said that Josh Cosden recaptured his entire $1.2 million investment in exactly two weeks.

Within two years, the plant had grown to cover six hundred acres, nearly a full square mile. Each day, it poured out a river of finished products from crude oil emptied the previous day through lines operated by the Cosden Pipeline Company. Much of it had come from wells owned by the Cosden Oil and Gas Company. Josh Cosden was suddenly a prince of petroleum, and Tulsa provided his throne.

For all these reasons, Tulsa was growing and, if its throne room never got exactly cavernous, it was becoming large enough to seat quite a few oil princes. A few were local people already in the city, some since frontier days of cowboys and Indians. One had been a pioneer physician: Dr. Samuel G. Kennedy. Arriving in 1891, Dr. Kennedy had received patients in his home and had driven his buggy across the trackless countryside to attend others. In 1898, he and his brother put up Tulsa's very first brick building to house his practice. He also began dabbling in real estate. Buying property just beyond the growing city's borders, he eventually controlled thousands of acres starting at Tulsa's northwest corner in the Osage. The Red Fork discovery shifted his interests toward oil. The Glenn Pool boom kept them there—and vastly enriched them. By 1907, Dr. Kennedy had abandoned his medical practice, and subsequent discoveries on his Osage lands topped his efforts with a prince's golden crown.

Dr. Kennedy was unusual, not because of his medical degree, but because he was already in Tulsa when oil was little more than a nuisance. In that regard, Josh Cosden was more typical of Tulsa's emerging royalty. Like him, most knew nothing of early Tulsa or Indian Territory. Like him, most came only after Glenn Pool alerted them to the city's opportunities. Like him, many desperately had needed those opportunities.

It happened that the development of Glenn Pool and the other fields that culminated with Cushing came at the very time several fields were playing out. The best days were over in Ohio, Pennsylvania, and West Virginia. Even the great Texas field at Spindletop had been milked dry by 1911, only a decade after its discovery. Thus, Tulsa's men of oil tended to be newcomers, chiefly from the Midwest or from Texas. They were newcomers ready to stay and anxious to develop their new hometown. They were newcomers who wanted to crown themselves princes.

Not all would achieve that lofty ambition. In a single month—March of 1913—twenty-two families moved to Tulsa from Marietta, Ohio, and another twenty-two also arrived from Pittsburgh, Pennsylvania. All were in Tulsa precisely because they expected to improve their lives, and surely most did. It is doubtful, however, that any of these unnamed families ever broke into the top layers of the city's newly emerging elite. Their significance lies in their numbers, not their success.

There were other kinds of newcomers as well. For these, the opposite was true: their small number was far less consequential than their enormous success.

One was Harry Sinclair. Born in West Virginia, raised in Independence, Kansas, and trained to take over his pop's little drugstore, Sinclair wanted to gamble for bigger stakes. He lost on a few (one bad deal cost the family drugstore), but he won on most. He started in oil by selling timber for derricks, got into swapping leases, and began putting together little oil companies. Some had no more assets than a single lease, but the sum of them was a stack of chips that he pushed into Glenn Pool's pot. Sinclair drew a flush hand: swapping, drilling, buying, storing, and selling oil. He made a fortune producing oil and a bigger one on what others produced. During peak production, independents were lucky to get ten cents a barrel for their oil. Harry Sinclair was even luckier to buy it for a dime and luckiest of all when he held it off the market until the price reached $1.20. He made so much money that he had to send for his brother Earl to help him manage it all. Tulsa thereby got two princes named Sinclair.

Hotel Tulsa. TULSA, Okla.

Two others were cousins, Robert McFarlin and James Chapman. They were Texans bitten by the oil bug during the big Spindletop boom of 1901. News of Galbreath and Chesley's Ida Glenn No. 1 summoned them to Tulsa and into the Glenn Pool field. Once there, they combined their little capital, their enormous energies, and their family names to found the McMan Oil Company. They made so much money in Glenn Pool and elsewhere that it took less than ten years for McMan to become the world's largest independent oil company. Still the money came pouring in. In 1916, they sold their holdings to Magnolia (later Mobil Oil) for the princely sum of $55 million—the equal of more than a half-billion of today's dollars.

HOTEL TULSA OPENED IN 1912. TULSA HAD MUCH TO SELL AND MUCH TO BUY AND THE NEW HOTEL OFFERED A PALACE FOR THE EXCHANGE.

And there was William Grove Skelly. His father had been a teamster in the Pennsylvania oil fields. At sixteen, Bill Skelly hopped a freight and began five years' hard work as a $2.50-a-day tool dresser in Oil City, the town's name saying it all. After serving in the Spanish-American War, Skelly took just enough classes at a business college to get bored and lit out for Gas City, Indiana, that town's name also saying it all. He made a little money there and more in Ohio and Illinois. Around 1910, he made a lot of money in West Texas during the heyday of the Electra, Desdemona, Burkburnett, and Ranger oil fields. Soon, there was a Skelly-Sankey Oil Company, and Skelly moved it all in 1912 to the only logical site, the Oil Capital of the World: Tulsa, Oklahoma. Tulsa's title said it all—loudly.

Tulsa Home Makers
MAGAZINE

17th Anniversary Number --- Summer 1925

(Above) A "Modern" home in Tulsa, 17 years ago, as shown in a booklet published by the Commercial Club at that time. (Below) The palatial residence built by Blair Bros., especially for Mr. and Mrs. W. G. Skelly at 2101 South Madison.

PUBLISHED BY

The Genet Furniture Company

TULSA · OKLAHOMA

Tulsa oil made Tulsa fortunes, Tulsa banks, and Tulsa oilmen. It also made the American automobile industry and some Native Americans (most notably the Osages) extremely wealthy. Facing page, Osages ride in a Pierce-Arrow for the 1918 Confederate Veterans' Reunion parade.

If Tulsa was a capital by 1912, the Hotel Tulsa (opened on May 12 of that year) was its Buckingham Palace. Located at Third and Cincinnati and managed by veteran innkeeper William Robinson, it was only ten stories high, but by the only measure that mattered—money—it was the tallest thing around. In the next fifteen years, a billion dollars in oil deals would be transacted there, a cool $100 million per floor. Harry Sinclair ran a suite of offices on the fifth floor, where he also played poker, drank whiskey, and (according to legend) put together the Sinclair-White Oil Company one night in its hallway. Another legend—this one confirmed by dozens of witnesses—was that Josh Cosden once nonchalantly wrote a personal check for $12 million over a table in the Hotel Tulsa's lobby.

At one time or another, everybody who was anybody in oil passed through that lobby, making deals, swapping information, hustling business, and hustling each other. On a typical evening, one might see Tom Slick, Skelly, and one or both of the Sinclairs trading jokes beside one of its marble-clad pillars. Cosden, McFarlin, and Chapman might be huddled around another, whispering quietly while some newcomer lounged purposefully nearby, hoping to pick up some information he could use. If that newcomer happened to be (as it was around 1914) a young man named J. Paul Getty, one could be sure that he was picking up information. He used it to found Getty Oil Company. The company's original headquarters were next door in rooms 810, 811, and 812 of the Daniel Building.

Such tales are the stuff of legend. More than that, they are expressions of power. Whether over drinks in the lobby of the Hotel Tulsa or over balance sheets on the desks at their corporate offices, men like Cosden, the Sinclairs, McFarlin, Chapman, and Skelly were making decisions that affected the lives of millions worldwide. Nowhere, however, did oilmen's decisions have more immediate or greater impact than in Tulsa. As early as 1920, the city's telephone book listed 431 oil and gas companies. It was a staggering figure, triple the number of grocers and nearly double the number of doctors and lawyers combined. Even

the 431, however, did not include the refining companies
(12), petroleum companies (17), or gasoline companies
(42). In that year, the largest 16 oil-related companies
alone employed 13,961 workers—over half of Tulsa's
wage earners and just under a fifth of its entire population.

By and large, it was the same small group that affected even more Tulsans with other decisions made in other
capacities. These were not merely presidents of corporations. They were princes of a principality, and they exercised powers over all they surveyed. For Tulsa, that meant
control not just of oil companies and their employees but
also of the major banks and those dependent upon their
services and credit. The most famous of them was Exchange National Bank. It grew out of the old (by Tulsa
standards) Farmers National Bank, a respected institution founded in 1903 and holding just under a million dollars in deposits as
late as September 1, 1909. Those deposits started falling as rumors
of weakness spread. By February 1910, they were down to
$400,000, when the collapse of its subsidiary, the Kiefer State
Bank, ignited smoldering rumors into flames of panic. On the very

Compared with life on the many small farms that dotted Sooner thin soil, oil fields and oil camps promised change and improvement, particularly for the young and ambitious. The lodging might be crude and poor (as in this board-and-batten house), but it was home. Men pushed sophisticated tools and worked hard. Women used simpler tools and worked just as hard. Together, men and women maintained homes and families and built better lives.

night that the Kiefer bank went down, C. J. Wrightsman, a prominent attorney and oilman, summoned Tulsa's oil elite to his office. They emerged to announce that they were taking over the institution, renaming it Exchange National Bank, and personally guaranteeing every dollar of every deposit. "They" included Harry Sinclair and P. J. White (of the oil firm) and Robert McFarlin, representing McMan.

Eleven years and several consolidations later, Exchange National was operating out of a beautiful new building at Third and Boston, held deposits of nearly $28 million, and was known internationally as the bank most closely identified with America's oil industry. That was little wonder. Exchange's board of directors was a veritable *Who's Who* of midcontinent petroleum.

That may have been remarkable, but it was hardly unique. The Central National Bank, located just a block away at Second and Boston, had eight oil executives on its twelve-member board. Although founded by cattlemen in 1896 as Tulsa's original bank, the First National Bank similarly listed nine oilmen among its seventeen directors in 1924. Most of the remainder had substantial investments in oil, but (as far as is known) not one owned a cow. Even the city's largest life insurance company, Atlas Life (established in 1918 as Tulsa's first and only the third in Oklahoma) was an oilman's company. Its directors included nearly every major producer and refiner in the city.

For the community as a whole, the fullest institutional expression of oil's power and authority lay neither in hotel lobbies nor in corporate boardrooms. Nor could it be found in city politics, which generally lay lower among oilmen's interests than the deepest deposits of crude. For common citizens, though, elections remained hotly contested. Active voters still showed intense loyalty to their parties and their leaders. Both Democratic and Republican politicos continued to tar the other with every conceivable charge, both fair and foul. The unchanged political issue—the need to "clean up" the city—managed to fit into both categories. It was fair because Tulsa still needed a thorough moral cleansing that no administration managed to effect. It was foul because those who used the charge to replace incumbents had no more success and (one suspects) no more intent either.

That may have been one reason that so few Tulsans bothered to vote at all. Sometimes barely a tenth of the potential electorate managed to make its way to the polls for city elections. Such evidence of political disaffection had to have causes. Cynicism bred of "open-town" and "closed-town" fights, fights with neither end nor consequence, was one of them. There were others. The 1908 charter "reformed" government with citywide mayoral and commission elections. The consequence was to reduce the effect that any one class or area had. In that circumstance, thousands of potential voters may have made an entirely rational decision: not to vote at all. Economically better-situated people might have reckoned the same. If they neglected their civic duty, though, it may have been because they sensed that the really important decisions were not always made at the ballot box or in city hall.

Some decisions were made in the mayor's office. Others were made in the commission's chambers. Quite a few, however, were made in another part of city hall. That part consisted of the rooms that the city had turned over to a private corporation, one insulated from popular elections. Chartered by the state of Oklahoma on October 20, 1915, its official name was the Chamber of Commerce and Federation of Allied Interests of Tulsa, Oklahoma, Incorporated.

The chamber represented the combination of the old commercial club with three other business groups: the Tulsa Traffic Association, the Tulsa Retail Merchants Association, and the Merchants Credit Association. It also represented something else. Clarence B. Douglas, who liked to call himself colonel and served the chamber as its managing director, put it this way in his three-volume *The History of Tulsa, Oklahoma: A City with a Personality*: "The evolution of the Commercial Club into the Chamber of Commerce brought new men on the scene."

That it did. Although most, if not all, of the men who had founded the old commercial club fourteen years earlier were still active, not a single one of them was an officer or director of the new chamber of commerce. They may have been members—after all, 1,073 Tulsans were by 1916—but they did not control it. Old-time haberdashers, grocers, undertakers, real estate peddlers, and assorted small-

business owners paid their dues. They just did not make the decisions. Decisions were the province of the chamber's officers, directors, and major committees.

The early presidents were, in order, J. H. McEwen (whom Douglas recalled as "one of Tulsa's most successful business men and manufacturers"), Robert M. McFarlin (oilman, banker, and three-term president described by Douglas as "Oklahoma's wealthiest citizen"), and Harry H. Rogers (whom Douglas identified as "a business associate of Mr. McFarlin"). Successive boards of directors were filled with men like these, particularly after about 1918, when McFarlin finally replaced those he had inherited from the original mergers.

A similarly small group also controlled the chamber's chief committees. None was more significant than the finance committee. That committee wrote checks to promote the city and to finance campaigns encouraging the citizenry to think and vote right on public questions. Describing its composition, the chamber's official organ, the *Tulsa Spirit*, once disarmingly noticed:

> Recently when President McFarlin was making up a list of committees for the year for the Chamber of Commerce, as is usual on such occasions a finance committee was named, and in going over the list of members, Mr.

McFarlin selected, largely at random, 44 prominent Tulsa citizens who constitute this committee. An analysis of the committee shows it consists of 44 men each of whom is worth more than $1,000,000, the wealth of some of them being estimated at $10,000,000 to $15,000,000.

If the author was right to be impressed, his "largely at random" claim was too cute by half—or by several million. Either way, it was not surprising, since the forty-four included the city's leading manufacturers, major bankers, and oilmen: Josh Cosden, Earl and Harry Sinclair, Dr. Samuel Kennedy, Charles Page, John O. Mitchell, F. Constantin, Earl Harwell, H. G. Barnard, L. E. Z. Aaronson, Harry Rogers, James Chapman, J. E. Crosbie, and (of course) President McFarlin.

Many were princes of petroleum, and Tulsa was their home. Tulsa also was their city, and they constituted almost a shadow government. More than adopting a nuisance ordinance, hiring a few cops, or shifting a hundred dollars here and there in the city budget, these men focused on the decisions that really shaped the city. They brought it wealth. They brought it growth. They even brought it water. And therein lies a tale.

For all of its genius at extracting oil from the ground, Tulsa never had much luck getting water out of it. The Arkansas River was the city's original water supply, and a private firm operated the pumps and pipes that carried it to Tulsans. It did so to unceasing public criticism, one year receiving almost as many formal complaints as did the post office.

BELOW, THE "PRINCESSES OF PETROLEUM" ASSEMBLE FOR A PHOTOGRAPH
ON THE FRONT LAWN OF THE RESIDENCE OF MRS. GRANT R. McCULLOUGH
IN 1928.

RIGHT, NORMA SMALLWOOD, TULSA'S QUEEN. NORMA CARRIED THE
BANNER OF MISS TULSA TO THE 1926 MISS AMERICA PAGEANT AND WON
THE NATIONAL TITLE. UPON HER RETURN, SHE MARRIED THOMAS GILCREASE,
IN A UNION THAT ENDED IN DIVORCE IN 1936. HER BEAUTY, MATCHED BY
HER CHARMING DISPOSITION, CAPTURED THE HEARTS OF A CITY.

Photo by J.L. Rinslia
—26.

Not everything was the company's fault.
The river was an undependable source, usually
muddy except when it was dry. It was a pollut-
ed one as well, since it served both as a source
of water and as an open sewer for untreated
wastes. In 1908, the city bought out the company for $172,000. The purchase did little to
improve the quantity or quality of the water but
added to discontent with a municipal government that could provide neither a clean city nor
clean water.

By 1915, the situation was intolerable.
Tulsa's population had multiplied by a factor of
five since the buyout, and eight refineries had
begun dumping into the Arkansas above Tulsa.

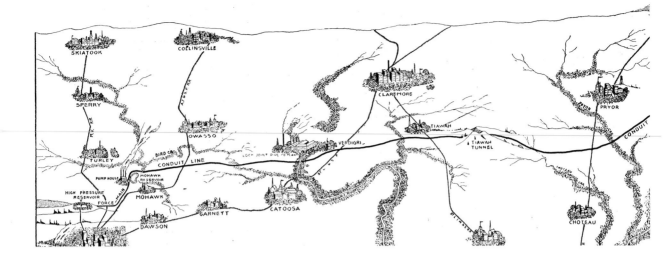

The water was less dependable and more loathsome than ever. For common drinking and bathing purposes, Tulsa was still on the bottle. Its residents spent $750,000 a year to buy as many as fifty thousand bottles per week of Crazy Water and other brands.

An opportunity presented itself in 1915, when private investors offered to solve the problem once and for all with a dam on Shell Creek in Osage County, about eight miles upstream from Tulsa. Trapping every drop from the creek's twenty-eight-square-mile watershed, the dam would impound billions of gallons of nearly pure water and do it at a cost of $600,000. In a rare display of initiative, the elected government realized that the city itself could build the same dam with the same benefits at the same cost. Demonstrating even rarer resolve, the city commissioners voted unanimously to submit a $600,000 bond issue, ordered the city attorney to prepare the ballot, and set the election for November 9, 1915. All of that was in place by October 8.

Twelve days later, the chamber of commerce received its charter and dissolved the older, separate business groups. Each of those now-defunct organizations had expressed support for the Shell Creek project. Joining them had been the Tulsa County Medical Association, which had endorsed it unanimously. Not so, however, the new chamber of commerce. Within days of its organization, the chamber dispatched a special committee down the hallway to visit the commissioners. The records contain no hint of why or how, but they do show a remarkable result. A few private citizens had persuaded the elected government to postpone the scheduled bond election. The postponement proved to be permanent. Tulsans would never vote on the Shell Creek option.

In time, they did vote. They had to because there was no other legal way for the city to obligate itself. A public election in 1922 authorized the sale of nearly $7 million in bonds for a water system based upon damming distant Spavinaw Creek and sending its waters through fifty-three miles of pipes and tunnels to a giant reservoir in far northeastern Tulsa. The intervening years had been consumed with engineering studies, court challenges, newspaper broadsides—and the use of ever more filthy water.

COMING DOWN FROM SPAVINAW

Words and music by Tulsa Water Commission

1. Coming down, coming down, Coming down from Spavi-naw; Water
2. Let it flow, let it flow, Let it flow from Spavi-naw; Clear and

flows. Tulsa grows. Finest town you ev-er saw. We have
cold. Pure as gold, Nothing like the Arkan. In the

dreamed. Planned and schemed
tub. — No more mud!

down, Coming down— Co... ...aw!
flow. Let it flow. Le... ...aw!

Publis... ...Commerce

W. R. HOLWAY IS SILHOUETTED AGAINST A PAGE OF SHEET MUSIC CELEBRATING THE COMPLETION OF HIS SPAVINAW WATER SYSTEM. ALTHOUGH THE ARTISTRY OF THE SONG MAY BE CONTESTED, THE ART OF HOLWAY'S MAGNIFICENT ENGINEERING PROJECT IS UNDISPUTED. SPAVINAW ALSO REVERSED THE DAYS WHEN TULSANS PAID MORE FOR A GALLON OF WATER THAN THEY RECEIVED FOR A BARREL OF OIL.

THE MAYO
TULSA
"OKLAHOMA'S FINEST HOTEL"

600 ROOMS, EACH WITH BATH   SERVIDOR SERVICE
LARGE SAMPLE ROOMS   CIRCULATING ICE WATER
"RATES WITHIN THE REACH OF ALL"

JOHN D. MAYO, Managing Director

The one constant presence throughout was the chamber of commerce. Having derailed the Shell Creek option, it was the chamber of commerce that picked engineer Henry A. Pressey to evaluate every alternative source of supply. It was the chamber of commerce that guaranteed Pressey his $12,000 fee. It was the chamber of commerce that consistently killed any attempt to bring Shell Creek's waters to Tulsa, even after private sources had gone ahead with the project and offered clean water at bargain-basement prices. It was the chamber of commerce that whipped up support for Spavinaw through "mass meetings." It was four of its directors—Grant McCullough (First National Bank), Arthur Farmer (Sunbeam Petroleum), Earl Sinclair (Exchange National Bank), and Charles Hopkins (Lawrence Petroleum)—who comprised the water commission that directed the process and oversaw the project. Nonpartisan, it also was nonelected.

And that is the point. Time would totally vindicate the chamber's choice of Spavinaw. Completed in 1924 as the then third most expensive municipal project in American history, Spavinaw and its waters carried Tulsa through the remainder of the century.

The choice would not have been made but for the chamber. Thus, an Aesop telling this particular tale might draw as its moral that the contest belonged neither to Tulsa's elected government nor to Tulsa's electors but to Tulsa's Establishment.

Different from Tulsa's original Establishment in composition, it was even more different in power and achievement. Tulsa's first elite had brought railroads to town. Its successor built the city's first airport, shipped the nation's first airborne freight across state lines, and financed a plant to build airplanes. Tulsa's early business leaders built hotels to attract travelers from nearby places. These leaders founded and funded the International Petroleum Exposition, an industrial world's fair that brought to Tulsa oilmen from around the world.

Tulsa's original elite had built bridges. Its successor built highways. U. S. 64 connected Tulsa to Little Rock, Arkansas, on the east and Raton, New Mexico, on the west. U. S. 75 put Tulsa on the highway stretching from Canada to the Gulf of Mexico. U. S. 66 (originally running along Boston Avenue and Third Street) put the city near the exact center of America's Main Street. Because he sat on the executive committee of the American Association of State Highway Councils, the chamber of commerce's Cyrus S. Avery almost single-handedly managed to route every one of them through Tulsa. In fact, it was Avery who assigned their numbered designations and designed the uniform markers used on all federal highways.

Early Tulsa leaders had organized subscription schools and had built the city's first wood-framed high school. This generation's leaders replaced it with a new Central High School, which occupied an entire city block. The largest school west of the Mississippi (and third largest in the United States), it also may have been the best. Having availed themselves of three gymnasia, two swimming pools, a cafeteria, and a full complement of courses (including one on banking), 60 percent of the school's graduates went on to college.

Tulsa's first elite had platted subdivisions to house oil-field workers. This elite built some of the finest residential areas in the nation to house the workers' employers (and sponsored one of America's first comprehensive zoning plans to keep them separate). Maple Ridge, extending south from Fifteenth Street, provided homes for most corporate executives and nearly every chamber official after the early 1920s. Later in the decade, Claude Terwilleger planned a subdivision of nearly equal stature, named its main thoroughfare after himself, and opened it just to the east. Meanwhile, the most established of the Establishment built custom mansions in any style they wanted anywhere they wanted. Three of them (Josh Cosden and the two Sinclair brothers) erected lavish homes on the site of the old Lochapoka ceremonial square.

If they stepped outside on a warm summer's night, Cosden, the Sinclairs, or their guests would have seen little recognizable to old Achee Yahola and his suffering people. The stately old oak was still there (in Harry Sinclair's yard, in fact), and the river still made its way slowly through sandy banks. Its waters may not have been quite so clean, but one would not have seen that at night. If the wind blew from the west, one might have noticed that the air was not as pure as it once had been. But to these noses, the refineries gave off the smell of money.

The Tulsa that such men built bore little resemblance to the Tallasi that the Lochapoka people had known. No longer was it a village dependent upon a few garden crops and game from nearby hills and valleys. Their principality had earned its title of Oil Capital of the World. By 1927, Tulsa provided the headquarters for fifteen hundred oil-related companies, and the city was at once the nerve center, the heart, and the guts of the midcontinent fields, which produced two-thirds of the nation's oil. Its refineries furnished more gasoline than any other city in America. Its pipelines ran to each coast. Its producers were directly responsible for 90 percent of the crude oil flowing from Oklahoma fields, which, in turn, accounted for a third of all the oil originating in the United States.

Such success deserved celebration, even ceremonies. Unlike an ancient Creek boosketah, however, these ceremonies tended to take place not publicly on foot-worn squares but privately in thick-carpeted corporate offices, bank boardrooms, and executive suites. Fasting accompanied none of them.

Over $8,000,000 Invested in Tulsa's Public School System

SCHOOLS
1 Monte Casino
2 Typical Ward
3 Central High
4 Cascia Hall
5 Woodrow Wilson Jr. Hi.
6 Lee Stadium
7 Theo. Roosevelt Jr. Hi.
8 Administration
Bldg.~Tulsa U.

Honoring Our Friends The N.E.A.

COSDEN & COMPANY
WEST TULSA REFINERY

From his palatial residence in Stonebreaker Heights near the Creek Council Oak, Josh Cosden reigned over an empire of iron, steel, and brick. The city was prospering as well. Bottom, Eighteenth Street looking east from Madison, principal thoroughfare of the new Maple Ridge, in 1919.

Refinery office

TULSANS IN THE 1920S HAD MUCH TO ADVERTISE WITH PRIDE. THEY ALSO HAD MUCH TO GIVE THEM

SHAME—BUT THEY CHOSE NOT TO ADVERTISE THAT. MOST UNADVERTISED OF ALL (IN FACT, IT WAS

LONG SUBJECT TO A CONSPIRACY OF SILENCE) WAS THE DISGRACEFUL AND DISASTROUS RACE RIOT OF

1921. SHOWN HERE, GREENWOOD AVENUE ON THE MORNING OF JUNE 1, 1921.

Sheets OF Terror

DESPITE THE RAIN, Tulsans lined their downtown streets to witness the great Memorial Day parade of May 30, 1921. Hundreds of young but veteran doughboys, most still able to fit into their uniforms, marched past as the crowd's cheers echoed off nearby walls. The Great War had ended not three years earlier, and Tulsans were proud to salute the ex-soldiers. They were prouder still to remember and honor the many local boys who had not returned.

When the morning parade ended, the marchers returned home to pack away their uniforms, and the spectators set aside their red silk poppies. Everyone resumed normal lives. The rain stopped, but a steamy humidity cloaked the city. The ninety-degree weather only made it stickier. Some stayed downtown, and some came back, perhaps to catch the William S. Hart matinée at the Lyric. Others preferred Norma Talmadge's new feature, *The Passion Flower*, which was showing at the Strand. Mostly, though, it was office workers and shoppers who filled downtown sidewalks that afternoon. Many of the latter headed for Renberg's, an elegant clothing store located in the Drexel Building at 319 South Main.

As they passed through the Drexel's lobby, few had reason to notice a young man patiently waiting for an elevator. Like some of the shoppers, nineteen-year-old Dick Rowland was taking a break from work. Unlike many of them, however, he worked for none of the oil firms, banks, or the shops that catered to their employees. Dick Rowland had dropped out of school to shine shoes. It was a rational choice for a young African-American male like Rowland. The stand's white owner paid him only five dollars a week, but the trade was brisk in downtown Tulsa, and the tips were generous. There were inconveniences, though, and Dick Rowland was in that lobby because of one of them. Since neither Renberg's nor any other store in downtown Tulsa allowed blacks to use its public restrooms, he had to take the elevator upstairs to the dirty little cubicle marked "Colored Only."

At last, the elevator arrived, and the door jerked open. It was empty except for its operator, a seventeen-year-old white woman named Sarah Page. Dick Rowland stepped into the elevator—and into history.

The history into which Dick Rowland was so casually stepping was part of the history that had sent that morning's marching veterans to war. Few realized it on that hot summer day. No one could have anticipated it when the war had begun seven years earlier. Reports of the event that triggered the Great War—the 1914 assassination of Austrian-Hungarian Archduke Francis Ferdinand in Sarajevo—had merited only a one-column story in the *Tulsa Democrat*. If few Tulsans until then had heard either of Francis or of Sarajevo, probably none foresaw that the effects eventually would extend beyond Austria-Hungary and beyond all of Europe to reach into their own city.

The war came to America partly because Americans went to it. Those who went to France in 1917 answered the call of country. Tulsans also answered the call of the chamber of commerce. In the summer of 1916, chamber officials had solicited recruits to form a Tulsa-based infantry company. Expecting to be sent to Mexico to chase Pancho Villa, the unit got no closer to the bandit than Fort Sam Houston in Texas. The men returned to Tulsa on March 21, 1917. Twelve days later, the United States declared war on Germany, and the unit remobilized as an ambulance company in the famed Rainbow (Forty-second) Division. By the following February, the young Tulsans were in battle. They transported the wounded from Champagne, Château-Thierry, and Verdun. They were in the thick of things in the Meuse-Argonne on November 11, 1918, when the Armistice silenced the last gun.

Near them was a second Tulsa volunteer unit, Company D, Second Battalion of the 111th Engineers. Ending only with the Armistice, these volunteers had fought sixty-two consecutive days, starting on the night of their arrival at Saint-Mihiel. Until then, many had known no danger greater than a final examination. Most had been students at Kendall College (the name did not become the University of Tulsa until 1920). They had left school and signed up because chamber executives decided that Tulsa needed a second volunteer unit only five days after the war's declaration. They

Just before "Mess."

Lined up for Roll Call + Mess.

ended up working on roads and bridges leading to the barren hell called No Man's Land. They left behind a campus with hardly a single male enrolled.

Back home, citizens were ready to do their part, and they did. Money was never a problem.

When the war began, European generals had expected that this one would be like all of them, powered by horses at the familiar ratio of one horse for every three fighting men. For all the dead horses and all the dead men, the war ended that equation. "The Allies," Lord George Nathaniel Curzon observed afterwards, "floated to victory on a sea of oil." He might have added that they flew to victory, transported their troops to victory, and drove their tanks to victory the same way.

Much of that oil was from America's midcontinent, and the Allied governments paid top dollar for it. From a low of 40 cents a barrel, nominal prices shot up to $2.25 by the war's end, and premiums brought it considerably above that. Production climbed as well. Midcontinent fields increased their flow by nearly half between 1915 and 1918 to reach nearly 180 million barrels per year.

Awash with money, Tulsa's oilmen invested money to make even more money. Harry Sinclair dissolved the old Sinclair-White company and replaced it with a bigger one under his name alone. Josh Cosden spent $1 million to double his refinery's capacity. Other refiners followed suit, and the Frisco had to add another fourteen switch tracks to handle the resulting traffic.

Tulsa's overall business had never been so good; never had so many clamored into the city. Furniture shipments crammed every available warehouse, and several hundred carloads piled up on sidings. In the spring of 1918, railroads announced that they no longer could ship household furnishings to the city. Quickly, though, a permit system broke the logjam. Newcomers had only to present a permit certifying that they had a place to put their goods. The permits were issued by the secretary of the Tulsa Chamber of Commerce.

It was just one way that the chamber was doing its part. There were others. The U. S. Treasury Department proposed to raise $17.5 billion through the sale of

AMID THE FEVERISH
BUILDING BOOM FUELED BY
THE GREAT WAR, TULSANS
COULD NOT ESCAPE THE
PRESENCE OF THE WAR'S
DEMANDS. MANY GAVE THEIR
MONEY, OTHERS THEIR TIME,
AND SOME THEIR LIVES. IN
EACH CASE, SOME
WERE BLACK;
SOME WERE WHITE.

"Liberty Bonds" and assigned every American county its quota. Chamber president Robert McFarlin and board members Newton R. Graham (of McFarlin's Exchange National Bank) and J. M. Berry (president of Central National) were determined that Tulsa would meet its quota. Under their direction, five Liberty Loan campaigns raised $32,499,150 from Tulsa County. More than 90 percent of that came from the city, and the total exceeded the Treasury Department's assignment by nearly $9 million. Apparently, the giving hurt neither Tulsans nor those who led them. Tulsa ended the war with record bank deposits of over $60 million. Exchange National held nearly half of the total ($24.9 million), and Central National occupied second place with $10.6 million.

If there was a problem, it was only that the giving was sometimes less than voluntary. The first Liberty Loan subscriptions exceeded the county's quota by 127 percent. Although Tulsa also passed its quota in the second bond drive, it did not generate the enthusiasm measured for the first one. By the third campaign, which opened on April 6, 1918, McFarlin, Graham, and Berry needed help and added (among others) the chamber's Cyrus Avery and Colonel Clarence Douglas to the committee organizing the drive. With or without their direction, they also profited by the timely reappearance of a group calling itself the "Knights of Liberty." Masked and cloaked in black robes, bands of Knights swept through the county in search of "disloyalists" who were not buying bonds. They had little trouble finding them and even less trouble convincing them of their errors. Beatings and whippings made fearfully persuasive sales pitches. In later campaigns, the Knights generally had only to warn "slackers" of what awaited those who did not give—generously, if not freely.

This was a problem. As in much of Oklahoma—and the rest of America, for that matter—Tulsa's support for its doughboys became more than that. Somehow, love of one's country aroused suspicion of one's neighbors. Nationalism became confused with submission, and patriotism gave way to paranoia. If Tulsa's elites did not cause that, neither did they stop it. In fact, some of them celebrated it.

The so-called Knights of Liberty provided one example. No documents survive to record who organized it, financed it, led it, or served in it. The record does reveal, however, what some prominent Tulsans thought of it. In his postwar history, the chamber's Clarence Douglas almost gloated when he included it among the civic organizations that had made Tulsa so proud during the war:

> Unique in its organization, with nothing like it in the entire United States, with its membership unknown, the Knights of Liberty early in the war attracted national attention by the quick and effective means which they used in stamping out disloyalty in this city and in this vicinity.

One as well informed as Douglas had to have known how the Knights interpreted "disloyalty" and just what their "quick and effective means" involved. "Disloyalty" amounted to the slightest resistance to war, whatever its source and whatever its form. Along with those unwilling (or unable) to buy Liberty Bonds, the definition embraced pacifists. Religious convictions kept them out of the war but not out of trouble. Such was the experience of a lonely Collinsville Mennonite whom the Knights nearly hanged.

Douglas's history did not include that particular episode. Neither did it include the torture of a young man accused of keeping company with a woman whose husband was serving in France. Neither did it include the rounding up of more than two thousand men who had no draft cards on their persons when the Knights accosted them. All, however, had registered and were released—with frightful warnings—when they produced their cards.

In fact, only one specific act made its way into Douglas's postwar history, and he recounted it with downright glee. With all the cuteness he could muster, Douglas wrote about "Tulsa's famous coming out party." By his telling, it was a regular wingding, a "social function." The ceremonies included a "receiving line, with probably fifty patriotic citizens officiating." The honored guests—"honored" with brutal beatings—were what Douglas called "Reds."

The men whom Douglas wrote off as "Reds" were oil-field workers. Like their bosses, they were gamblers. The difference was the bosses gambled with their money in high-risk ventures; workers gambled with their lives in a deadly occupation. When oilmen lost, they came back to gamble again. When workers lost, Oklahoma's law denied compensation to their widows and children. When the employers won, they won fortunes. Workers who won earned four dollars for a ten-hour "tour" (pronounced "tower") on the drilling rigs. Semiskilled workers, called roustabouts, were lucky to get twenty-five cents an hour.

Successful oilmen counted their flow of earnings by every hour on the clock. Workers moved from job to job, with idle weeks and no income in between. Tulsa's oilmen lived in luxurious additions just east of the river. West of the river, where many of

their workers rented homes, few had running water or electric lights. The aristocrats among the oilmen were worth millions. The aristocrats among the workers were those in the refineries. They earned an average of $726.78 per year. Subsistence wages at best, the sum equaled dire poverty at worst—when a breadwinner was laid off, when a child took sick, or when food prices doubled, as they did during World War I.

Such circumstances cried out for organization, but the same circumstances made it a formidable challenge. Field personnel worked in small groups, sometimes singly. They worked in widely diffused places, all across sprawling fields. They were migrants who rarely stayed anywhere long enough to put down roots. Most came from agrarian backgrounds and distrusted authority from any source not their blood relatives. For all of these reasons, oil-field workers were about as easy to organize as fleas on a bluetick hound. It would take an unusual type of union to get it done.

The Industrial Workers of the World was unusual, and it made an impressive start. Born in Chicago in 1905, the IWW had diverse parentage and a troubled childhood. Its organizers included radical Socialists, hard-rock (and hard-living) miners, and individualists as rugged as Tom Hagerty, a defrocked Catholic priest from Hobo Hollow, Arkansas, a little community about sixty miles from Tulsa. Its annual

conventions tended to attract both working stiffs and ideologues, the latter tossing around big words of French derivation, words like *syndicalism* and *sabotage*. But the working stiffs made its history, and they wrote it in plain American words. They wrote it on the floors of textile mills, in the huts of lumber camps, in the shafts of copper mines, and on windblown port docks. "Wobblies" wrote it with hope that the lowest-paid, hardest-working, and least-appreciated workers could form the One Big Union. As Joe Hill, their songster, was supposed to have said, "Where working men fight for their rights/It's there you'll find Joe Hill."

One would not have found Joe Hill in Tulsa in 1917 (Joe Hill had been executed by a Utah firing squad in 1916), but one could have found Arthur Boose. A veteran IWW organizer known as the Old War Horse, Boose set up the Oil Workers Industrial Union No. 450 in a little office in the New Fox Hotel at Main and Brady. At least that is where the office was until November 5, 1917, when the Tulsa police raided the place. Without a search warrant and without uncovering a single piece of evidence linking a single person to a single crime, they arrested each of the eleven men present. Police added a twelfth the next day when they nabbed him "loitering" near the deserted site.

Municipal Judge T. D. Evans opened their trial on November 8 and concluded it at 10:30 P.M. on the ninth. While the prosecution failed to tie any defendant to any criminal act or even to show that any had a criminal record,

GREENWOOD'S SONS WHO PUT ON THEIR UNIFORMS AND TOOK UP THE BURDEN OF WAR RETURNED HOME TO CIVILIAN CLOTHES AND THE SECURITY OF FAMILY. IN LITTLE TIME, THOUGH, THEY WOULD FIGHT ANOTHER WAR—THIS ONE WITHOUT UNIFORMS, THIS ONE AT HOME, AND THIS ONE NUMBERING AMONG ITS CASUALTIES THEIR OWN FAMILIES.

BELOW, A. L. WILLIAMS, OWNER OF THE DREAMLAND THEATER, MOTOR WITH HIS FAMILY, CA. 1920.

five men stepped forward to testify for the defense. Nonetheless, Judge Evans fined each $100 for the "crime" of not owning a Liberty Bond. For good measure, he summarily arrested, tried, convicted, and fined the five defense witnesses too. "These are no ordinary times," Judge Evans reasoned. At least he had that right, as did too many judges in these hysterical times.

The extraordinary times then led to an extraordinary aftermath. Police took the prisoners from the city jail and turned them over to forty or fifty black-clad Knights of Liberty. The Knights carried weapons provided them by the Home Guard, an official group organized a month earlier in the rooms of the Tulsa Chamber of Commerce. The chief of police and another officer then robed themselves in black and joined the vigilantes. Also with them, undisguised but obviously invited, was the managing editor of the *Tulsa World*, Glenn Condon, who brought along his wife.

The entire group then proceeded to a secluded ravine on Tulsa's west side. By the light of torches and circled automobiles, the Knights took the captives' shoes, stripped them to the waist, and beat each one with heavy, doubled hemp rope. They then poured hot tar over their raw wounds and added layers of feathers. The torture completed, they sent their victims hurrying northward accompanied by hoots and gunshots. Before returning home, a committee of Knights posted a printed warning—"Don't let the sun set on you in Tulsa"—on Charles Richardson's front door. Charles Richardson was the attorney who had represented the defendants at trial.

Clarence Douglas was terribly wrong to find honor here. But he was right in finding significance. The significance was that Tulsa's history during the war included vigilantism, mob violence, masked marauders, and brutal suppression.

As Tulsa's blacks could have testified, that history did not arise from a vacuum. They were part of Tulsa before it was Tulsa. When it was still called Tallasi, blacks had lived among its Creek inhabitants, some as freedmen, many as the offspring of interracial unions. Creeks since their Alabama days had intermarried freely with

blacks, and many Creek families had high percentages of African blood. Such was the mixture that federal census takers, including those who compiled the tribal rolls necessary for the final allotments of the Creek nation, arbitrarily identified some close kin as Indians, others as Negroes.

With Tulsa's development, these became the nucleus of the city's black community. Its numbers swelled with the arrival of black immigrants from surrounding states, as well as those from Oklahoma's rural areas. Although originally no law required it, most settled north of the Frisco tracks, many along a single street. In making the city's original survey, the Patton brothers had named it for their hometown: Greenwood, Arkansas.

After the city annexed the area in 1909, the so-called Greenwood district ran northward from the Frisco tracks to Independence Avenue, bounded by the Midland Valley tracks on the east and Cheyenne Avenue on the west. Almost entirely confined to that area, Tulsa's black population rose from 1,429 in 1907 to 2,754 in 1910 and 8,803 in 1919. Although numerically impressive, the growth was only slightly faster than the white increase. The black percentage of Tulsa's total population increased from just under 7 percent to slightly over 9 percent during those years.

Nonetheless, Greenwood was larger than all but a few of Oklahoma's towns. By 1921, the black population had grown to nearly eleven thousand. Serving them were

two black schools (Dunbar and Booker T. Washington), two black newspapers (the *Tulsa Star* and the *Oklahoma Sun*), three black lodges (the Masons, Knights of Pythias, and Odd Fellows), thirteen black churches, two black theaters, one black hospital, and one black library.

In each instance, the adjective *black* underscores that Tulsa was not one city but two. Some of that was by Greenwood's choice; most of it was not. Schools were separate because the state constitution of 1907 mandated racial segregation for all state schools. White private associations excluded blacks either by policy or by attitude. North-side developers papered housing tracts with restrictive covenants forbidding blacks to own, buy, sell, or occupy property in that part of town—with the telling exception of overnight occupancy as domestic servants. After 1916, Tulsa's municipal ordinances merely codified what was already true. A new ordinance forbade persons of either race from living in or maintaining a public facility in any city block in which three-quarters or more of the population was of the other race. Although the United States Supreme Court invalidated all such laws the very next year, Tulsa defiantly kept its ordinances on the statute books.

By legal fiction, the two Tulsas were "separate but equal." Half of that was true; the other half was a lie. Schools were separate, but a black teacher earned barely 70 percent of a white teacher's pay. A sizable police force patrolled south Tulsa, but a single officer, African-American Barney Cleaver, served all of Greenwood—and the department emphasized that Barney Cleaver could not arrest a white person. State constitutional amendments of 1910 and 1916 introduced patently unfair literacy requirements for voting, which Tulsa election officials applied by forcing would-be black voters (but no one else) to copy page after page of the state constitution.

When Dick Rowland stepped into the Drexel's elevator on that fateful day in 1921, he was crossing the line between the two Tulsas. No one knows just what happened between him and Sarah Page over the next few moments. Sarah Page later said that she had been assaulted. Dick Rowland said that he accidentally had bumped into her as he stumbled. Either way, Sarah Page ran screaming from the elevator, and the police arrested Dick Rowland the next day, Tuesday, May 31. By that evening, local newspapers were printing sensational front-page stories about their encounter and openly speculating that Rowland would be lynched. Unconscionable exaggeration characterized the news but not the prediction: fifty-nine blacks had been or would be lynched in America that year, most after accusations like those of Sarah Page.

Dick Rowland would not be one of the fifty-nine. To protect him, seventy-five to a hundred black men gathered that evening outside the county jail. Many were veterans, some carrying their government-issued Colt .45s. More than fifteen hundred whites gathered too. Some were there out of curiosity, some out of malice. Many were armed. Lawmen, including Barney Cleaver, tried to separate and disperse both assemblies, but they failed. By then there were two mobs, separate but unequal. Within each, there was frightened talk. Between the two, frightened talk became heated exchanges. Heated exchanges became angry words, including words like *nigger* and *cracker*. Someone fired a shot, several guns answered, and a dozen bodies dropped. In a flash, one Tulsa was at war with the other Tulsa.

The war was just about as one-sided as had been everything that led to it. In the first few hours, whites broke into sixteen pawnshops and hardware stores. They carried off $42,923 in merchandise—mostly guns and ammunition. Armed gangs then invaded the Greenwood district. Overcoming black resistance, they proceeded to shoot, rob, and burn their way across black Tulsa.

The city wired Oklahoma Governor James B. A. Robertson to rush the National Guard to Tulsa. Waiting for their arrival, Mayor T. D. Evans—the same T. D. Evans who had presided so injudiciously over the IWW trial—devoted his night to commissioning scores of "special deputies." Most of them spent the next several hours apprehending some six thousand blacks (mostly the males, who might have defended their neighborhood) and sending them to one of the three internment camps that authorities had designated. In doing so, they left the Greenwood community to the mercy of other "deputies" who had hurried down to join the pillaging mob.

URNING OF CHURCH WHERE AMUNITION
WAS STORED — DURING TULSA RACE RIOT

CHARED NEGRO
KILLED IN TULSA RIOT 6-1-1921

INCREDIBLY, BOTH
OF THESE
PHOTOGRAPHS
WERE USED
COMMERCIALLY AS
POSTCARDS.

The train carrying the guardsmen reached Tulsa at 9:15 A.M., and Adjutant General Charles Barrett declared martial law about two hours later. By then, most of the damage had been done. The damage embraced thirty-five city blocks that had been looted systematically before being burned to the ground. The homes of 1,115 black families lay in smoldering ruins, and those of another 563 had been robbed of everything of value. In the first twenty-fours of restored order, 184 blacks and 48 whites required surgery. Most suffered from gunshot wounds. Another 531 people of both races received medical care from the Red Cross during the first three days. There were no official death totals (presumably because officials had no earthly idea), but informed estimates ran anywhere from fifty-five to three hundred. Even now, nobody knows.

What is known is that numerous outside agencies offered Tulsa aid in rebuilding its black district. Pridefully, Tulsa officials turned them down; Tulsans would solve their own problem. The report of the grand jury impaneled to investigate the riot left no doubt as to how official Tulsa understood that problem:

> The presence of the armed negroes was the direct cause of the riot, . . . [but] there existed indirect causes more vital to the public interest than the direct cause. Among them [was] agitation among the negroes of [for?] social equality.

The grand jury proceeded to indict sixty-four blacks on a series of charges (mostly for the capital offense of inciting a riot), and one white man. That was Police Chief John Gustafson, whom it indicted on several unrelated charges and a single count of dereliction of duty for allowing the riot. In July, a criminal jury convicted Gustafson of the lesser offenses but absolved him of responsibility for the disaster. In the end, Tulsa's criminal justice system punished exactly one person for the most disgraceful mass disaster in the city's entire history. Garfield Thompson served thirty days in the county jail for carrying a concealed weapon. Thompson, not surprisingly, was black. Preferring to put the matter quietly and quickly behind them, prosecutors pursued none of the other indictments.

THE LAW OFFICE OF B. C. FRANKLIN AND P. A. CHAPPELLE IN TEMPORARY QUARTERS IMMEDIATELY AFTER THE RACE RIOT.

Sarah Page never filed charges against Dick Rowland. Sarah Page and Dick Rowland disappeared. Both apparently left Tulsa permanently. They remain, however, central in its story: two people from two Tulsas that made one history.

Within weeks of the riot, hundreds of Tulsans assembled to extend that history. The site was Convention Hall, most recently used as an internment center. The occasion was the appearance of Caleb Ridley, a Baptist preacher on a mission from Alabama. After a warm introduction by Wash Hudson, a celebrated local attorney and powerful state senator, the cleric took as his text accounts of the recent riot, which his message described as "the best thing [that] ever happened to Tulsa." He then issued his call on behalf of the community of believers who had sent him: the Imperial Knights of the Ku Klux Klan.

Within days of Ridley's visit, fifteen hundred Tulsans formed the city's first (and Oklahoma's second) "Klavern," the basic local unit of the national Klan's swiftly expanding Invisible Empire. In January 1922, the Klavern incorporated as the Tulsa Benevolent Association. Under that name, Klansmen paid $60,000 to buy the Centenary Methodist Church, razed the building, and spent another $200,000 to erect what they called Beno Hall. With a seating capacity of three thousand, it was the largest assembly hall in the state and one of the largest in the Southwest. Occupying the corner of Main and Easton, its three stories nearly dominated the whole of downtown Tulsa. It towered over nearby Greenwood, just to its east. To the Greenwood community, *Beno* represented not benevolence but the certainty that there "Be No" blacks, Catholics, Jews, or foreigners welcomed there.

None was. But Tulsa's white, Protestant, male population supplied more than its share of the estimated 150,000 Oklahomans (one-tenth of the eligible population) who joined the hooded order. Thousands of Tulsa women also enlisted in the Klan's female wing, the Kamelia, which had its national headquarters thirty miles away in Claremore. Quite a few also joined the Junior Ku Klux Klan, an order for boys twelve to eighteen. All bought their proper regalia through Atlanta: cheap sheets sold as expensive robes and hoods. State and national Klan executives split the enormous profits as well as the flood of income arriving monthly as membership dues (ten-dollar "Klectokens") from each of the faithful. The leaders' zeal needs no further explanation.

The members' devotion does. With an estimated two thousand black Tulsans still living in tents during the winter of 1922-1923, Klansmen had only to look around Beno Hall to know that white supremacy was secure in Tulsa. While national Klan spokesmen railed against Jews, Catholics, and immigrants, Tulsa hardly had enough of any of these to merit notice, much less terror.

A properly supplied Klansman needed one further item to complete the Klan outfit. That was the official KKK whipping strap, a piece of top-grain leather four inches wide and three feet long, its last six inches sliced into ten slits better to cut a victim's back. Tulsa's Knights bought them by the hundreds, and they did not have to look far to find backs on which to use them. Immediately south of Beno Hall stood the district that held fourteen bordellos. Some of the city's fifty gambling spots were there too. Others were in roadhouses that lined the highways leading into the oil fields and nearby towns. At any hour of day or night, their parking lots held fifteen to twenty cars. Drivers and passengers sat inside drinking "Choc" beer, playing the slot machines, or paying women to go back to the cars with them. Scattered among the Choc joints were another thirty or so narcotics dens, which sold cocaine, morphine, and heroin by the pound.

None of the politicians' biennial promises to clean up Tulsa had done much good. If anything, the war-induced boom had left it dirtier, sleazier, and nastier than ever. Tulsa's elite had profited generously from that boom, and they lived in safe neighborhoods far away from the Choc joints and dope dens. Arguably, it was in their immediate economic interest to cast a blind eye on the downtown vice district and the outlying roadhouses. They attracted and temporarily pacified the young and rootless men needed for the refineries and oil fields. That may have been why Tulsa's Establishment turned a deaf ear to the raucous noise of the wicked and to the outraged cries of the righteous.

BELOW, ROOM SERVICE DELIVERS ILLEGAL REFRESHMENTS, CA. 1923. FACING PAGE, AUTHORITIES CONFISCATED 40,800 BOTTLES OF BEER FLOATED BY BOOTLEGGERS INTO TULSA VIA ITS STORM SEWERS, CA. 1923.

The sum of it was that neither Tulsa's official government nor its unelected powers could or would clean up the city. Action fell to those who saw the consequences most closely (law-enforcement people, chiefly) and those whose status and places of business rendered them most morally incensed and economically threatened (generally skilled workers and small-business owners). Neither princes nor peasants, Tulsa's Klansmen were the squeezed middle class, squeezed on one side by an economic aristocracy they never could enter, squeezed on the other by a caste whose morals they never could accept. Enlisting in the Klan's Invisible Empire, they struck at both by concealing themselves in Klan attire, picking up their Klan whips, and meting out rough justice to those who lived beyond the elite's self-interest and the law's bounds. In doing so, they asserted their independence of the powerful. But in doing so, they consciously placed themselves beyond the bounds of law too.

In the early 1920s, residents of Tulsa County did that on the average of once a week. The most notorious instance involved a white veteran, Nathan Hantaman. Hantaman (like many others) had acquired a drug addiction while recovering from wounds in a government hospital during World War I. After the war, he supported himself and his habit by smuggling dope from Mexico and selling it from his wife's Tulsa boardinghouse, the Colorado Rooms.

On the evening of August 10, 1923, Tulsa Police Captain Ned Gritts arrested Hantaman on a vagrancy charge. After routine processing, the police released him. As he left the station, a car pulled beside him, and a man jumped out and hit him over the head. Others pulled him into the automobile. His abductors beat him continuously until the car reached a farmer's field. Stopping the car, the men bound Hantaman to a tree and proceeded to lash him fifty times with a bullwhip.

Hantaman passed out, but the men revived him and began a second series, this time with an official Klan whipping strap. Its specially designed ends served their intended purpose and more. Already bleeding profusely, Hantaman again passed out and nearly died when the strap split his penis open. Their blood lust satisfied, Hantaman's abductors dumped him in front of a Tulsa hospital.

After a minimum of emergency treatment, Hantaman prevailed upon some friends to drive him directly to the state capitol, where he demanded to see the governor, John Walton. The governor happened to be in Sulphur, Oklahoma, so Hantaman told aides the grisly story and displayed his bleeding wounds. Upon his return, Governor Walton responded with a declaration of martial law on the city and county of Tulsa.

For a second time in two years, military forces occupied Tulsa. They set up headquarters in the Hotel Tulsa and immediately suspended the elected city and county governments. When the *Tulsa Tribune* editorialized against this violation of popular rule, guardsmen shut down the newspaper too. With armed soldiers patrolling the streets, a military tribunal began taking testimony regarding the Klan and its activities.

By the time the military left the city a few weeks later, the authorities had collected information on 220 separate incidents, the bulk of them originating in Tulsa, Collinsville, and Broken Arrow. Only four appeared to be race related; the remainder amounted to general acts of moral terrorism. The state indicted thirty-one admitted Klansmen. Yet all but four escaped punishment, several regaining their freedom because of the legal talent of their fellow Knight Wash Hudson. Upon their release, the freed men were counseled by the local Klavern's Kludd (chaplain), who reminded them that Saint Paul too had been jailed for floggings before going on to spread the Christian faith.

There is no evidence that any of these men followed in Paul's footsteps. Their deeds remain a living witness to something much less than the truth expressed in Paul's most beautiful doctrine: "Faith, hope, love abide, these three; but the greatest of these is love" (I Corinthians 13:13, RSV).

Brother, Can You Spare a Dime

FOR A Barrel of Oil?

HARRY SINCLAIR should have stayed in Tulsa. Instead, he announced that he had to "shake off provincialism," left for New York City, and encountered no trouble raising the $50 million that it took to build his next company. Like his old Tulsa firm, this one produced oil. The difference was that the new Sinclair Consolidated Oil Company did everything else too. It found oil, pumped oil, transported oil, and refined oil. It sold oil products beneath signs bearing huge green dinosaurs. With Texaco, Gulf, and a few others, it was a "major," one of America's ten largest. On the day that Harry Sinclair moved into his new president's office in New York City and took over an impressive mansion on Long Island, he was three months shy of his fortieth birthday.

The trouble was that when Harry Sinclair left Tulsa, he moved into the world of big-time industries, big-time deals, and big-time politics. In fellow oilman Edward Doheny, he found all three. A onetime prospector, Doheny was reputed to have used a knife and bare hands to fight off a hungry mountain lion. After that, he moved into oil, became a millionaire several times over, and fought off hungry competitors with his hands full of cash. He thought to distribute much of it to pliant politicians.

One of those politicians was New Mexico's Republican United States senator, Albert Fall. Habitually clad in a black Stetson, Fall looked exactly like what he was: a lawyer, rancher, and mine owner just a few years (and several million dollars) away from his days as a two-fisted, gun-toting frontiersman. He never outgrew the belief that the publicly owned resources of the West should be privately developed—developed by men like himself. Senator Fall became Secretary Fall in 1921, when President Warren Harding named him to head the Interior Department. "It would have been possible to pick a worse man for secretary of the interior," one outraged conservationist bemoaned, "but not altogether easy."

For Harry Sinclair and Edward Doheny, there could have been no better choice. On very generous terms, Fall assigned Doheny a lease to the government's oil reserves at Elk Hill, California, also guaranteeing a market for every drop Doheny could squeeze from the rich field. The market was the United States government. As it turned out, Fall's generosity was awakened after

"TWO MANY STRAWS IN A TUB"— THE OKLAHOMA CITY FIELD BEFORE PRORATION.

Edward Doheny's son had handed the cabinet officer $100,000 cash in "a little black bag." Doheny the younger thus became known as the "bagman," and a phrase thereby entered the American vocabulary. Another joined the lexicon of American scandals when investigators discovered that Doheny's sidekick, Harry Sinclair, had given Fall several hundreds of thousands of dollars in exchange for an even sweeter lease to the government's Wyoming reserve: Teapot Dome.

For his role in the Teapot Dome affair, Interior Secretary Albert Fall went to jail, the first cabinet officer convicted of a felony committed while holding public office. Edward Doheny escaped imprisonment when a jury acquitted him following a lengthy trial. It proved, one cynic said, that "you can't convict a million dollars in the United States." Harry Sinclair's two trials (one for contempt of Congress, the other for contempt of court) proved that occasionally you can convict a millionaire, though. Harry Sinclair left his Manhattan office and Long Island estate to spend six-and-a-half months in one of America's most provincial quarters: a federal penitentiary.

If Harry Sinclair's Tulsa buddies were ashamed, they did not show it. If anything, his disgrace only affirmed that he should have stayed in Tulsa longer and should have stayed away from politics altogether. The latter judgment was so self-evident to Tulsa's oilmen that they had no need to proclaim it, but that scarcely prevented their doing so.

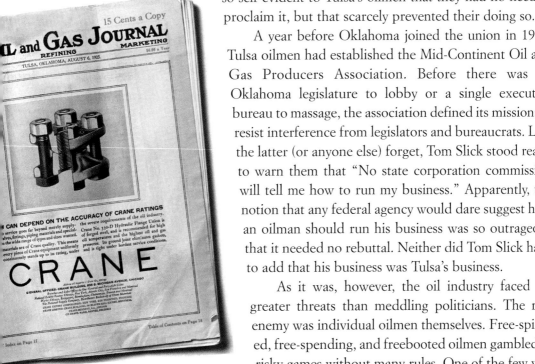

A year before Oklahoma joined the union in 1907, Tulsa oilmen had established the Mid-Continent Oil and Gas Producers Association. Before there was an Oklahoma legislature to lobby or a single executive bureau to massage, the association defined its mission: to resist interference from legislators and bureaucrats. Lest the latter (or anyone else) forget, Tom Slick stood ready to warn them that "No state corporation commission will tell me how to run my business." Apparently, the notion that any federal agency would dare suggest how an oilman should run his business was so outrageous that it needed no rebuttal. Neither did Tom Slick have to add that his business was Tulsa's business.

As it was, however, the oil industry faced far greater threats than meddling politicians. The real enemy was individual oilmen themselves. Free-spirited, free-spending, and freebooted oilmen gambled in risky games without many rules. One of the few was the so-called rule of capture. Like much in Anglo-American jurisprudence, it was a legal doctrine originating in medieval circumstances. Specifically, the rule denied a landowner claim to damages when a neighbor captured (or killed) wild game that had entered his own estate from the other's.

Whatever the doctrine's consequence for the English grouse population, its effect upon early American oil was decisive. Once a drilling bit pierced an underground reservoir, it freed the oil beneath to flow horizontally as well as vertically, and the rule of capture came into play. Any producer who failed to exploit his holdings immediately risked ruin if his nearest competitors' wells captured the riches beneath his lease. To the prevailing Darwinian faith in the survival of the fittest, the rule of capture thereby added the doctrine of survival of the quickest. Each seeking individual survival, as many oilmen as possible produced as much oil as possible from as many wells as possible as fast as possible.

The weight of these individual acts smashed any rational equation between supply and demand and set in motion a monotonous history that followed every discovery of every new pool. Scores of companies rushed every available man and drilling rig to the new area. Rivers of oil flowed forth, and prices began a downward tumble. In little time—only months, in some cases—fields played out. Supplies shortened, and prices nudged back upward until a new discovery began the process all over. The lesson—too often unrecognized—was that individuals' struggles for their separate survival threatened the extinction of their collective species.

Even the most self-reliant and independent-minded oilmen had to sense that the result was economic waste. In the 1920s, a few oilmen began to understand that the process involved incalculable physical waste as well. Fields played out quickly because the bedlam of drilling and producing dissipated the reservoir pressure necessary to reduce the buried oil's viscosity and allow its extraction. When the boom chasers moved on, they left behind as much as two-thirds of entire reservoirs lost forever. "Too many straws in a tub" was the colloquial explanation. Reckless ruin was the inevitable result.

The industry delayed, if it did not escape, the worst immediate consequences through the Great War and the first years afterward. While oil was fueling the war's planes and ships, the automobile became for Tulsans and other Americans not a plaything of the rich but a commodity for the masses. Detroit's Henry Ford got rich making cars. Tulsa's Fred Jones got rich selling them. The city's oilmen stayed rich and their employees stayed working, producing the oil and refining the gasoline filling those cars' tanks.

That is why Oklahoma's crude prices actually rose from their wartime peak of $2.25 a barrel to reach $3.36 in 1920. They did not stay there long, however. The discovery of vast reserves in neighboring Osage County, in Oklahoma City, and in the Greater Seminole field flooded the market in the late twenties. The industry thereupon returned to its familiar ways, and prices resumed their familiar patterns.

The event that destroyed those patterns forever occurred on October 3, 1930. The place was Daisy Bradford's little farm in Rusk County, Texas. Then and there, Columbus "Dad" Joiner, a wildcatter heretofore more successful at bedding widows than finding oil, hit the discovery well of the fabulous East Texas field. Within six months, 340,000 barrels flowed daily from the thousand wells hastily sprigged among the region's pine barrens and scrub timber, and someone was spudding in a new one every hour. Even at that rate, it took another year to delineate the field's full extent—and maybe longer for anyone to believe it. Forty-five miles long and five to ten miles wide, the East Texas field covered 140,000 acres. Oilmen referred to it as the "Black Giant," the adjective denoting not merely oil's physical color but this particular oil's sinister consequences. Sixteen months after Dad Joiner had made Daisy Bradford rich, this monster doubled total American oil production and threatened to impoverish an entire industry. All by itself, East Texas yielded more than enough to satiate fully the nation's thirst for oil.

Prices did not fall; they evaporated. By mid-1933, crude stood at a dime a barrel, and much Texas and Oklahoma oil sold at six cents. Desperate oilmen even sold some for as little as two cents a barrel. No one was safe at such prices. For the first half of 1933, the giant Sun Oil Company earned a net income of exactly fifty-three cents. Tulsa companies probably envied Sun its good fortune. Many went into holes metaphorically rivaling their deepest wells. Going down with them was a sizable percentage of the city's labor force. The industry fired half its production hands, two-fifths of its pipeline workers, and nearly a third of its refining employees. Those who kept their jobs did so at greatly shortened hours and greatly reduced pay scales.

There is no way to measure accurately the human cost these cold fractions represented, but one contemporary effort was revealing. In 1933, Tulsa Methodists conducted a door-to-door inquiry into living conditions in the working-class district along the west bank of the Arkansas. By the church workers' count, 684 families containing 2,781 people lived there. Fewer than a quarter of those families (164) owned their own homes, and some of those homes were tents. The investigators considered just 78 of the rented homes to be in good condition. They placed 217 of the remaining 457 into the category of "bad." Among all housing categories, outside privies served the majority of homes. In some cases, the outhouses were the only facilities available for twenty or more people.

Just over a fifth (146) of the families had no breadwinner present. Only half of those with a resident breadwinner were blessed to have one who was earning a paycheck. The area contained 405 children of preschool age. On the day that the investigators called, 305 of those children (75 percent) were suffering from contagious diseases. Thirty-two residents had died during the previous year, which meant the area's morbidity and mortality rates exceeded those of Calcutta, India.

More moving is the investigators' house-by-house description of west Tulsa's once-proud working class. At 209 South Maybelle, a man, his wife, and four children were "living on a dirt floor." At 1107 West Twentieth Street, "25 people [use] one outside toilet, [and the] users complain there is no top on it." At 1110 West Twenty-first Street, there were "seven in [the] family. All sleep on the floor." Two blocks away, at 1354½ West Twenty-first, home for a family of four consisted of a "tent and improvised toilet." Three families shared the rental house at 1350 West Twenty-first. Each paid "$8.00 a month, and 27 [share] one toilet." At 714 West Twenty-second Place, none of the four children, ranging in age from seven to twelve, attended school—because none had clothes.

During the oil industry's feast days, black Tulsans had missed even the crumbs. "Tulsa may be the Oil Capital of the World," one observed at the time, "but the Negro in Tulsa has neither the oil nor capital." In the entire state, not one African-American owned an oil company and only 104 worked for one in 1930. Just seven of those lived in Tulsa. The industry's implosion had little direct impact upon Tulsa's black oil workers for the simple reason that there was almost none to be affected.

A chain is no stronger than its weakest link—

If the oven of your range you buy, rusts out in a year or two, you may have reason to recall this old adage—for without an oven, a range is little better than a $5 hot-plate.

Roper, along with other manufacturers, had long experimented with numerous so-called rust-proof oven linings. Some materials stood up very well for a while. But Roper guarantees his oven linings and sooner or later all but one kind had to be replaced.

Even though the merchant and the manufacturer do their best to prevent it, there must be some annoyance about having your oven linings give way—and about having to replace them.

"Better Cooking In the Home," is a valuable booklet that is yours, free for the asking. It contains a wealth of time and temperature recipes, as well as menus for full meal oven cooking, together with full instructions and charts for Cold Pack Canning in Roper Regulated Ovens.

So Roper adopted this one material universally admitted to be rust proof —PORCELAIN—and beginning this year every Roper is porcelain lined. This improvement—added to the Roper Fresh Air Oven—and Complete Heat control, made Roper look so good to us that we—at Genets— secured Roper Ranges for you.

Complete   Oven Control

Roper Porcelain-lined Ranges with porcelain outer door panels, splashers and pans—begin at $65.00. ($58.50 for cash.)

These are beautiful models at $85, $88, $108, $125, $150, $180 and $320.

The all porcelain $375 Roper pictured here has six burners, two baking ovens, a boiling oven, a broiler, a warming closet and shelf and a canopy top.

17 years ago the Dodge Electric Co. occupied a 12-foot frontage at 108 S. Boston

That dubious blessing was a part of a larger pattern. Most southern and southwestern cities routinely assigned a few public-service jobs to African-Americans, but Tulsa did not do even that. Eight black policemen patrolled Greenwood (after the 1921 riot, the police department had beefed up its presence), but the city of Tulsa otherwise did not have a single black employee. The city and its private utility companies were almost unique in hiring only whites as meter readers in the all-black neighborhoods. Tulsa also was one of the few American cities in which only white carriers delivered mail to the black community. In the downtown federal building, 425 people worked on the U. S. government payroll—417 whites and 8 blacks. Four black men swept the floors during the day. When the men went home, four black women came in to scrub them.

In that climate, the black population of predepression Tulsa had found regular employment chiefly in the few niches unoccupied (and often undesired) by whites. The most respected provided African-Americans with goods and services not easily available—if available to them at all—outside the community. There was a sizable professional class, including 55 clergymen, 16 physicians, 13 attorneys, and 128 schoolteachers. The last group received salaries from the school board. The others relied upon offerings and fees, almost all coming from black patrons. More numerous were the community's businesspeople, who owned and operated every type of business. To mention one: Tulsa's Greenwood of 1926 had more hotels for blacks than did New York City's Harlem.

The reason for that remarkable fact was that Greenwood, even more than Harlem, lived beneath the long shadow of racism. Its visitors needed hotels because none in the rest of Tulsa accepted black guests. Greenwood, unlike Harlem, also had been rebuilt hastily and incompletely after a devastating race riot left it in ruins. Many of its residents had to have access to multifamily lodging simply because there was not enough single-unit housing available.

The segregated housing market made what little there was abnormally expensive. Blacks buying homes struggled under mortgages bearing 10 to 20 percent interest rates—this at a time when Oklahoma's maximum lawful rates were 4 to 6 percent. Most of Greenwood's families rented, annually paying rents that averaged 10.2 percent of their houses' values. That rate made Tulsa the most expensive city for African-Americans of any of the nation's eighty cities with a black population greater than ten thousand. For their money, Greenwood's people got entire blocks without street paving, without running water, without city sewers, and without regular trash pickup.

Black Tulsans paid relatively much but received relatively little because they had no choice. If they could afford to, it was only because of decent predepression incomes. Most of Tulsa's African-American wage earners received ten to twenty dollars a week, and quite a few earned twenty-five to thirty. They earned it not as oil workers, not as professionals, and not as business owners, but in the one capacity that many Tulsans presumed was their race's special calling: domestic service.

In 1930, 39 percent of black Tulsa's male workers and 93 percent of its female workers served white Tulsa families. They were butlers, chauffeurs, porters, yardmen, maids, nannies, cooks, laundresses, and the like. So prevalent was the practice that the Tulsa public school system maintained a special yearlong vocational-training curriculum for Greenwood's girls. Boys at all-white Central High School already trained to be bankers. Under this plan, girls at all-black Booker T. Washington got to train to become white folks' "help." Incredibly, the school system publicized its curricular innovation—until the National Child Labor Committee discovered that the "training" consisted of forcing black children to spend their school hours doing the laundry of well-placed white families. Even before then, however, all but a very few of Tulsa's white families had been reduced to washing their own laundry, cooking their own meals, mowing their own grass, and scrubbing their own floors. In time, the national economic collapse of 1929 made its presence felt even in the Oil Capital of the World. It did so just as the city was reeling from the disintegration of oil prices. Black servants become expensive luxuries that few could afford. Unable to make their mortgage payments, many discharged African-Americans lost their homes and their equities. (By 1936, at least 30 percent of Greenwood's real property belonged to white-owned loan companies.) Other black families, unable to pay their rents, began moving, sometimes at each month's end, in the hope of staying one step ahead of their landlords. Before long, the landlords were having to move too. Dependent upon an unemployed black clientele, African-American professionals and businesspeople reduced their expenses by cutting their own payrolls. With ever fewer solvent customers, they soon became not much better off than those they had dismissed.

The cycle was a metaphor for what was happening to many other Tulsans—to all Americans, for that matter. In the city and in the nation, the process demonstrated the choices a lot of Tulsans and a lot of Americans had made when left pretty much to themselves. In the good times, both produced too much. They greeted the first hint of bad times with economic contraction. Once contraction set in, layoffs and wage reductions followed. With more and more people able to buy less and less, the contraction tightened. More layoffs and more wage cuts followed. Even tighter contraction was the result.

One had no need to see the soup lines in Chicago or the apple salesmen in New York to understand the consequences. Tulsa would do. In working-class west Tulsa, in African-American north Tulsa, in the shopping district of downtown Tulsa, in middle-class residences in south and east Tulsa, even in the upscale homes of Maple Ridge, all Tulsans suffered, even if some suffered more than others. They suffered from an economic machine that turned out to be not self-governing but self-destroying. It had pretty much locked up by 1931 or 1932. And all the oil in East Texas was not going to unbind it.

In desperation and bewilderment, many of the city's needy turned to Tulsa's municipal and county governments for relief. Mayor George L. Watkins could come up with nothing better than a job-placement service. It was a piece of well-intended foolishness, since its only service was to place the unemployed in jobs that had disappeared with their own dismissals.

Those who turned to county officials believed they had the law on their side. Oklahoma's statutes clearly obligated its county commissioners to "relieve and support all poor and indigent persons lawfully settled therein, whenever they shall actually

need assistance." In practice, most counties had discharged that duty (if at all) by assigning to charity what little money was left (if any) after funding every other project.

Tulsa County usually had done somewhat better, but in this crisis the county commissioners responded to the pleas of the poor by pleading poverty themselves.

The official response was that the county had available no more than a few thousand dollars. A report by independent auditors, however, calculated that the commissioners could make available well over $100,000 a year. All they had to do was sacrifice just a few of their most wasteful and self-indulgent practices, many of them detailed in the report. The embarrassed commissioners made a sacrifice all right; they sacrificed the needy. Commissioners angrily washed their hands of relief and turned the whole problem over to private parties.

As in the best of times, in these, the worst, many roads ended up leading to the same place: the Tulsa Chamber of Commerce. In the fall of 1931, the chamber undertook to study Tulsa's potential to address the economic disaster. No one involved even imagined that there might be a publicly funded relief program. Instead, they trusted completely the curing capacity of private charity—if it was properly limited and managed. Given such predilections, the inquiry came up with two chief policies. First was the insistence that any charity be strictly limited to the "deserving," defined as the elderly, the disabled, and the families lacking a male breadwinner. Second was the resolve that all private relief efforts (those available from the Red Cross, the Salvation Army, and others) should be coordinated for maximum efficiency and impact.

Demonstrating the unreality of this approach, the study maintained that the entire effort could be managed by just a few private citizens. A "Committee of Five" would be sufficient to supervise every single relief and charity program in Tulsa. In due order, the chamber adopted the report and swiftly appointed four men to the Committee of Five. Each was a chamber member; two were directors. Then the chamber bowed to public pressure and filled the fifth position with a municipal judge who had a strong prolabor record.

Through the remainder of 1931 and beyond, the Committee of Five assumed control over the only relief available to most Tulsans. Seeking oversight of every single private charity, the committee got it, if only because it persuaded the city to close noncooperating charities. To avoid the prospect of any person's receiving aid from more than one source, it directed that every Tulsan seeking relief register with its Social Service Bureau. It required that applicants of apparent Hispanic descent present naturalization papers before being registered. The Committee of Five would not register those without papers, even if the absence was because of the applicants' birth in the United States. What it did instead was to direct the sheriff's office to remove them from the county.

The Committee of Five also ordered the police department to round up unsightly "panhandlers." It similarly commanded the city government to tax sidewalk vendors out of business. Among the casualties were local versions of the depression's famous apple salesmen.

Like Christ's followers, Tulsans still had the poor with them. But the Committee of Five just made it harder to see them. It was a remarkable, if all too typical, record for five private citizens.

The poor Tulsans most impacted were the several thousand families who cleared the committee's hurdles to draw upon private charity. None received much. Better-off Tulsans bragged that they could assist the needy at a unit cost of six cents a day. Of course, those judged less than deserving did not get even that.

Inevitably, the working definition of deserving came to reflect not just economic circumstances but social prejudices as well. On one side, the Committee of Five urged needy middle-class white people to schedule personal appointments to register for aid. It was an offer extended to spare them the humiliation of standing in long lines filled with poor people. On the other side, black Tulsans had to stand in lines—often with no effect. Despite African-Americans' disproportionate needs, only ninety-six black families were approved for charity aid out of the total seventeen hundred Tulsans who were receiving it in April of 1935. One reason was that many white Tulsans still believed (and openly said) that black poverty was necessary if African-Americans were not to be permanently ruined for their proper place as servants.

Whether getting aid or not, black Tulsans received almost no other social services at all, not even access to youth programs. Tulsans were particularly proud, for instance, of the city's Girl Scout program. Probably most neither noticed nor particularly cared that there was no such program for black girls. When a nonresident social worker did notice and asked about it, one of the local organization's directors answered with guileless and revealing candor:

> Of course the Negroes need Girl Scouts, but if the Negro girls wore the
> Scout uniforms down the street, the white girls would take theirs off.

It was just one way that too many Tulsans—and too many Americans—understood "deserving."

In time, nearly everyone recognized that the depression had broadened the definition of deserving in at least one sense. The able-bodied unemployed had to have work, even if that meant that work would have to be created for them. Again, the Committee of Five set the parameters: all work must benefit the city materially, as much as possible must be performed without costly equipment and machinery, and as few local tax dollars as possible must fund it. A single episode shows what that meant.

It snowed heavily all day on December 14, 1932. In that evening's *Tribune*, relief directors published the names of four hundred unemployed men picked from the several thousand Tulsans registered for work relief. If they wanted to work and if they provided their own tools, they could cut some timber along Bird Creek for firewood that relief workers would distribute to unemployables. If interested, they were to report by eight o'clock the next morning.

Every single one of the four hundred was there, waiting patiently in the cold, at the dawn's first light. Each brought his own tools. Unfortunately, only one person had responded to the directors' call for the more fortunate to loan trucks to carry the men from their North Main gathering point to the work site on Bird Creek. The truck was an undependable old flatbed. It could carry only a few men at a time, and it exposed them full time to the elements. Under the circumstances, relief officers suggested that most of the men go back home.

Rather than lose a day's pay, every man begged to be allowed to walk. Several hundred men walked eight miles to Bird Creek, eight miles back, and then walked home. They walked through muck and mud and cold and dark. They walked so they could spend eight hours swinging axes, pushing saws, and pounding sledgehammers. They walked so they could earn thirty cents an hour, a quarter of the $9.60 that the Committee of Five permitted each family for a maximum of four days' work a month. If they managed to get in the other three days, their families received enough to cover their month's food costs, but not much else.

Those who know that story can appreciate the enthusiasm with which most Tulsans greeted Franklin Roosevelt's election in 1932, his inauguration in 1933, and his launching of the New Deal in his first one hundred days. Tulsans finally had a government ready to fight the depression and to aid its most immediate victims. That government was in Washington, D. C., thirteen hundred miles away. Changes neither the municipal nor the county government of Tulsa could conceive, changes the chamber of commerce could not envision, changes the Committee of Five would not permit became national policy. And Tulsa was part of that nation.

Within months, many of Tulsa's neediest began earning paychecks issued by the new Federal Emergency Relief Administration. Young people earned money working on projects for the Civilian Conservation Corps. High school and college students stayed in school with the help of the National Youth Administration. Many of the high schoolers went to new high schools—Will Rogers and Daniel Webster—built with moneys from the Public Works Administration. Thousands of Tulsans, many unemployed for years, went to work on projects sponsored by the Works Progress Administration. They laid sidewalks in front of Lee School. They put in a football stadium at Carver Junior High School. They constructed benches, tables, and shelters for Mohawk Park. They built armories in Tulsa, Sperry, and elsewhere. They dug foundations, poured concrete, raised joists, and laid bricks to erect rural schools all over the county. Some even compiled the first good history of the city—*Tulsa: A Guide to the Oil Capital.*

On everything they built, they left imprinted a shield bearing the initials WPA. Those letters represented not a bureaucracy in Washington but people in Tulsa, white people and black people and Indian people and Hispanic people. All were treated equally because all were needy. Because all were equal, all were paid equally.

Some of the Oil Capital's oil capitalists grumbled about the "dole," mouthed shibboleths about "free enterprise," whispered fearfully about "creeping socialism," and scoffed at the "worthless" projects of the WPA. "We Piddle Around," they called it, and they called FDR a whole lot worse. No such talk swayed the great mass of

Tulsa's citizens. All it did was obscure what may have been the New Deal's largest single contribution to Tulsa's economic recovery. The federal government saved the oil industry from the oilmen.

No one, least of all the oilmen, disputed that the industry needed salvation, if not resurrection. The trouble was that almost no one, including the oilmen, knew where to find it. They savagely abused one of the few of their own who had any notion at all. That one was Henry Doherty, who spent the 1920s as a prophet without honor in his own industry.

Doherty was an entrepreneur of humble background and magnificent achievement. He left school when he was twelve, and (like one of Horatio Alger's characters) rose by pluck and luck to become a captain of industry, of many industries, for he eventually served as a director of no fewer than 150 corporations. Many of them were utility companies servicing cities with gas and electricity. It was perfectly natural for Doherty to add oil to his interests, and he eventually acquired Oklahoma's most poetically named company, Indian Territory Illuminating Oil. I.T.I.O., as the old-timers called it, became the basis of Henry Doherty's more prosaically titled Cities Service.

Less natural was Henry Doherty's preaching that the industry had to exchange its rugged-individualist predilections in favor of outright government regulation. Given the prevailing ethos, the message was so unnatural that it was a perversion. Three times Doherty pleaded for the American Petroleum Institute (API) to consider his proposals; three times it turned him away. Barred from one API meeting, he resorted to hiring his own hall to address whoever would listen. Few would, and still fewer believed.

Doherty believed, though. He believed that independent oilmen had to think of each oil field not as an arena for their own cutthroat competition but as an entity, a single unit to be managed rationally. "Unitization," he called it. He also understood that for it to work, the government would have to enforce it. Only government could assign and rigorously enforce "allowables" among the field's owners, the oilmen who held its separate leases.

Henry Doherty never changed his mind—but neither did he change many other people's. Finally tired of rejection, Doherty left the cause to others. "The oil industry is in for a long period of trouble," he predicted, "but I will stake the last shred of my reputation that the day will come when every oil man will wish we had sought federal regulation." Henry Doherty said that in 1929.

The day of Doherty's prophecy broke on October 3, 1930, the day that Dad Joiner, Daisy Bradford, and the "Black Giant" broke oil prices and broke the back of an unregulated industry. Under the circumstances, only the most stubborn ideologue dared assert his individual sovereignty in an unfettered marketplace. Regardless of any other principles oilmen might have had, the right to unassisted suicide was not one of them.

Some tried to restrain themselves with agreements to limit production voluntarily and separately. Because compliance was voluntary, however, each producer ended up acting separately. Production actually increased; prices dropped further. Some then turned to Oklahoma Governor William Henry David Murray.

For Tulsa's oil princes, this was an act of unspeakable desperation. Governor Murray, known to all and detested by many as "Alfalfa Bill," was something of a professional rustic. Generally displaying the dirty cuffs of his longhandles, even during the hottest summer months, Murray also was noted for a chin that frequently dripped tobacco juice and a mouth that more frequently drizzled profanity. Although dead broke and just returned from a long self-exile in Bolivian jungles, Murray had won the governorship in 1930 after a campaign of ruthless vituperation and creative demagoguery.

They undoubtedly swallowed hard, but the city and state's oilmen had no choice. They could not save themselves; perhaps the state's chief executive could save them. Murray tried in the manner befitting one who proudly bore the title "Alfalfa." In August 1931, he issued a declaration of martial law upon 3,106 specified sites: every producing oil well in Oklahoma. He thereupon sent armed state militiamen to each of the 3,106 sites and ordered them to withhold production until prices reached "a dollar a barrel."

To the relief of many and to the surprise of most, Murray's bold move paid off. Prices moved toward the magic one-dollar figure. They never did and probably never could have gotten there, since even the strongest enforcement was weakened by the seepage of "hot oil." With almost the calculable certainty of a mathematical equation, each penny's increase in crude prices encouraged more independent oilmen to undermine the system by illegally producing, transporting, and refining oil—the so-called hot oil. For a price, guardsmen could get awfully sleepy or find some emergency to call them away. Acting individually, quite a few oilmen paid that price, surreptitiously restored production, and drained off thousands of barrels in violation both of the governor's decree and of their industry's collective interest. The lesson was that state authority exercised in a global marketplace never would break the industry from the habits of its youth.

Franklin Roosevelt and his so-called New Dealers came to power at high noon of the long day that Henry Doherty had foreseen. To Albert Fall's old job, the president appointed Harold Ickes, a new interior secretary who was everything that Secretary Fall was not. Self-righteous, morally incorruptible, and politically liberal, Ickes had built a career opposing business in general and big business in particular. If politics makes strange bedfellows, depression politics made downright weird ones. Harold Ickes and leading American oilmen sat down, made their peace, and effected the industry's salvation.

The details would shift, dependent upon changing statutes and evolving court and administrative decisions, but the basic arrangement was and remained this: The federal Bureau of Mines would periodically calculate future market demands and "recommend" to the governors of oil-producing states each state's "suggested" share of the total. State agencies (in Oklahoma's case, the corporation commission) would then "prorate" state production among individual producers. Federal and/or state authorities would punish any violators.

Under these arrangements, Tulsa's oilmen finally realized the profitability and stability they never could have achieved alone. In 1934, oil prices reached and passed the dollar-a-barrel mark. Between 1934 and 1940, they stabilized, never less than $1.00, never more than $1.18. The result was a dependable flow amounting to hundreds of millions of dollars to float a grounded industry off the shoals of rugged individualism.

Thus it came to pass that the Great Depression's chief consequence for Tulsa was not the few mites disbursed to widows and others on "welfare." The Great Depression's real legacy was that Tulsa's oil princes finally had to limit their own sovereignty.

Many of them still talked like Tom Slick ("No state corporation commission will tell me how to run my business"), but they had learned the cost of acting like buccaneers. They might have learned it a little quicker and a lot cheaper had they listened to one of their old neighbors, one of Henry Doherty's few early converts, Harry Sinclair.

Harry Sinclair made it a point to call on Secretary Harold Ickes just after Inauguration Day. It was his first visit to the interior secretary's office since he and Ed Doheny had carried cash to Albert Fall. Whatever their differences, Harold Ickes and Harry Sinclair demonstrated that they both knew what oilmen did to an industry when left pretty much to themselves. The first had learned it; the second had lived it. That is why Harry Sinclair and Harold Ickes agreed on one thing: The federal government would have to save oilmen from themselves. Sinclair emerged from the meeting and publicly said as much. After all, he confessed, ruinous competition, voluntary self-restraint, even state martial law—all had proved to be "about as effective as prohibition."

Harry Sinclair knew of what he spoke. After all, he said it from conviction.

COMMEMORATIVE ASHTRAY BY FRANKOMA POTTERY.

GILLETTE HOME, 2130 EAST FIFTEENTH

The Homes That Oil Built

A legacy of graceful domestic architecture

BRADSTREET HOME, 1635 SOUTH CARSON

MAYO HOME, 1401 SOUTH CHEYENNE

Stebbins home, 1030 East Nineteenth

SPRINGER HOME, 700 NORTH OSAGE DRIVE

KISTLER HOME, 1016 EAST NINETEENTH

CROSBIE HOME,
1437 SOUTH BOULDER

TRAVIS HOME
2415 SOUTH PEORIA

WINKLER HOME, 605 NORTH DENVER

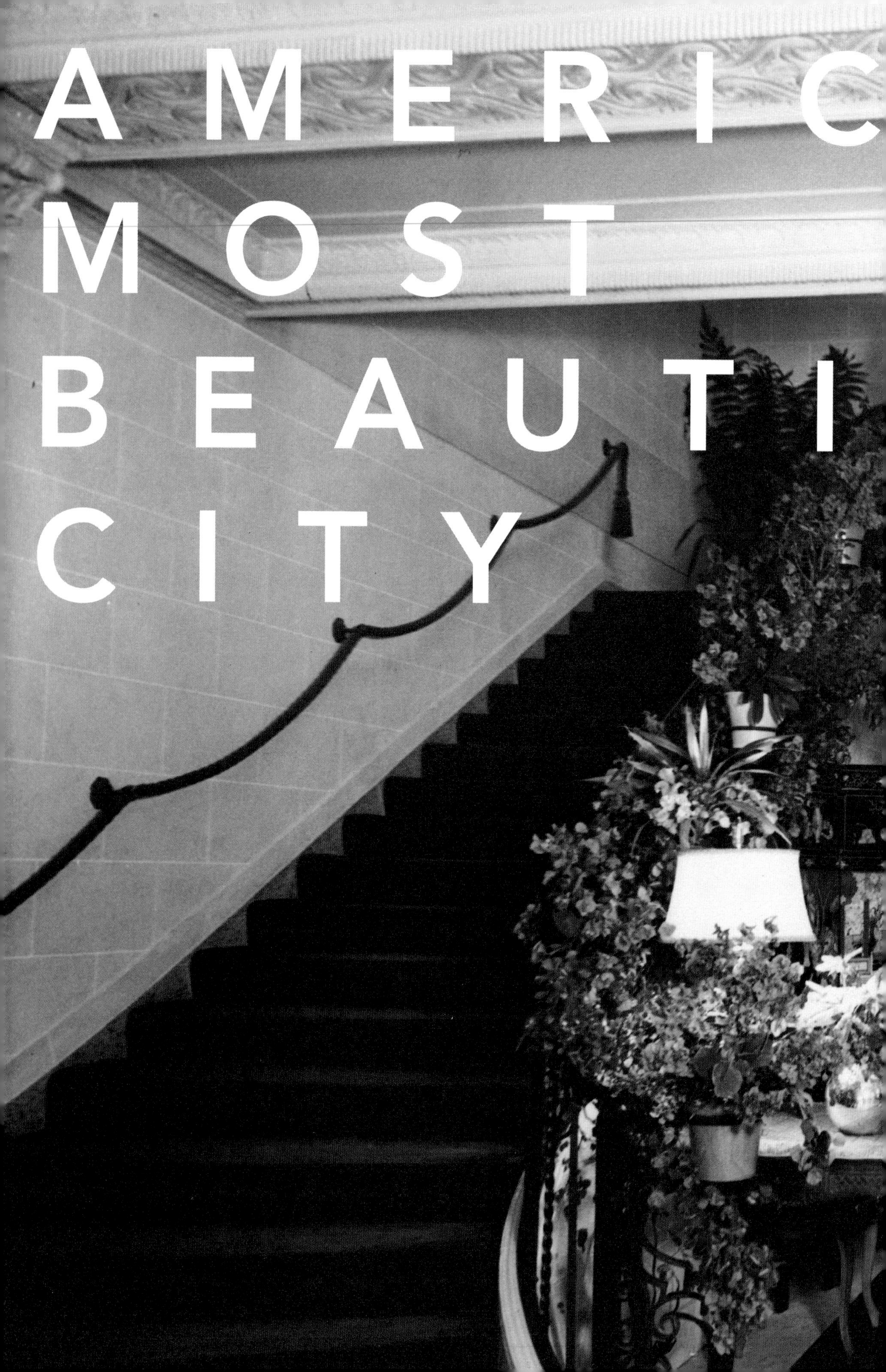
AMERIC
MOST
BEAUTI
CITY

Later, there would be cynics who said that the author obviously never had visited San Francisco. The really cruel ones said he never must have gone to Wichita or Amarillo either. No one was mean enough to claim that the writer never had seen Oklahoma City.

Those were the scoffers and the wiseacres, though. Most Tulsans were absolutely thrilled that Daniel Longwell had come to Tulsa, had loved what he had seen, and had written it up for what they considered the perfect publication. It appeared in the June 1957 issue of the *Reader's Digest*, and its title said of Tulsa that it was one American city "Where Beauty is Everybody's Business." The reader had to read no farther than the fourth paragraph (and the *Reader's Digest* specialized in very short paragraphs) to find Tulsa's newest claim to an identity. Tulsa, Daniel Longwell declared, was "America's Most Beautiful City."

Those who had not seen it recently might have marveled at the appellation, which in the thirties would have seemed no more accurate than the first builders' claim that Tulsa was "the Magic City." The fact was, however, that Tulsa recovered completely from the economic collapse of the 1930s. As had been true before, credit belonged less to magic than to leadership. An earlier generation of Tulsans had used the blessed discovery of oil to turn a town into a metropolis by the time of the First World War. This generation used the occasion of the Second World War to turn depression into prosperity.

Several things were striking and fresh about this renewed prosperity. One was that it was not oil based. Oil still accounted for a significant portion of the city's economic well-being, and the enormous demands of global war made themselves felt

THE GRAND THEATER ON SECOND STREET WAS "GRAND" FOR 1906. HOWEVER, FAR GRANDER THEATERS TOOK ITS PLACE IN LATER DECADES, CULMINATING IN THE RITZ IN 1926. THE RITZ LOBBY (FACING PAGE) WAS A PRELUDE TO AN EXTRAVAGANT ARCHITECTURAL SHOW THAT OFTEN SURPASSED WHAT WAS SEEN ON ITS SCREEN.

in everything from refinery workers' paychecks to oil executives' country-club dues. The fact was, though, that neither oil's contribution to Tulsa's wartime recovery nor the city's contribution to the Allies' war effort justified its claim to being a seat of global economic power. Tulsans and others might still think of the city as the Oil Capital of the World, but it was, at best, a provincial seat for part of America.

If anything, World War II underscored oil's declining significance, and nothing in the postwar era reversed that. What the war and the next years did see was an economy revitalized as it broadened. New plants employing new workers for new industries were signs of Tulsa's liberation from depression as well as its liberation from an overdependence upon a single industry.

Like the oil-fueled boom of the 1920s, the economic upswing of the war and postwar period brought more things to more Tulsans. The difference was that the latter generation of Tulsans seemed unsatisfied with mere things. They contemplated not the quantity of their belongings but the quality of their lives. To their parents' devotion to accumulating the goods of life, they added a dedication to achieving the good life.

Daniel Longwell was right to capture one particular expression of that desire. Whatever the skeptics might say then or later, Tulsa was a beautiful city, at least a contender for the title of America's most beautiful. Longwell surely was not the only visitor who noticed its landscaped airport, its gaily decorated public buildings, its award-winning new shopping center on Utica, or its publicly owned Tulsa Garden Center and adjacent Municipal Rose Garden. It may have taken an expert to know that the last was regarded by "rosarians [as] one of the best in the United States," but even the casual visitor and the resident nonrosarians realized that Tulsans had made their city something special.

Tulsa's people and its visitors who stayed any length of time learned how very special the city was. From faint and oily beginnings, the city became a regional center of national reputation for refinement as well as for refining in post–World War II America. The cultural cognoscenti knew of its sym-

phony, opera, and dance companies. Wherever paintings and sculpture were known, discussed, appraised, sold, or displayed, its museums were famed as special American treasures.

Others could argue, though, that Tulsa was not quite as special as Longwell and the *Reader's Digest*'s faithful wanted to believe. There were Tulsans who rarely, if ever, flew in or out of the landscaped airport, shopped at south Tulsa's tony shopping centers, attended its operas, or joined the rosarians at the rose garden built with tax dollars. Those particular Tulsans might have stopped reading at Longwell's fifth paragraph, the one in which he declared that Tulsa was so new that it had "few run-down sections."

Tulsa did have run-down sections, and there was nothing in the least special about that. Neither was it novel that the most run-down of those sections were concentrated in a single area of the city, one that was literally on the other side of the tracks from everything that so impressed Daniel Longwell. Finally, there was nothing at all singular in the fact that the residents of those sections lived there because they had little if any choice. They were black, and they knew intimately of several ways in which Tulsa was and was not special.

Their neighborhoods might have been run-down, but they were not run-down people. Moreover, during the war and early postwar years, they proved that they would not be run-over people. In that—no less than in its landscaping, its culture, or its art—Tulsa demonstrated real beauty and its opposite too.

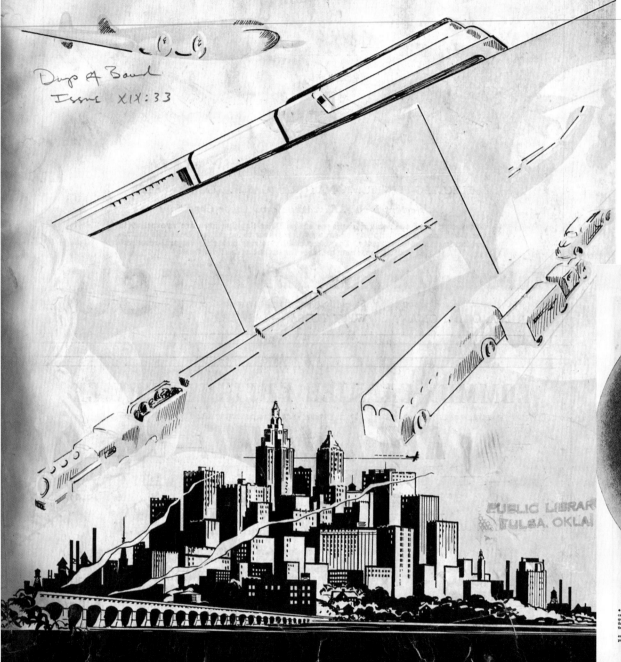

transportation ● 1945

Days & Bound
Issue XIX:33

THE TULSA SPIRIT

War AND *Deliverance*

J. PAUL GETTY CAME BACK to Tulsa. In the two years of his first stay, Getty had made the first of many subsequent millions in the Stonebluff field, near Muskogee. When he had left in 1916, he was just twenty-three and already a multimillionaire. He also had gained an education, one considerably more profitable to him than that he already had acquired in the classrooms of the University of Southern California or in earning degrees from the University of California and Oxford. "After my experiences in Tulsa," Getty would recall nearly six decades later, "I knew all the nuts and bolts of the oil industry. And I suppose the greatest lesson I learned, which I was to apply to other phases of my life, were those qualities that I have defined as determination, persistence, and mulish stubbornness."

In men like Skelly, McFarlin, Chapman, and Sinclair, early Tulsa had the perfect faculty to teach those lessons. After all, each had earned advanced degrees from schools of the prestigious hard-knocks league. If he learned from them, J. Paul Getty learned well, and what he learned he applied thoroughly. After leaving Tulsa, he started a lifelong habit of approaching his own physical well-being as he would a tough business deal, becoming something of a fitness fanatic. He later challenged and held his own against heavyweight boxing champion Jack Dempsey. Even the Manassas Mauler was impressed. After the fight, Dempsey observed that Getty was "well-built, pugnacious by nature, and quick. . . . I've never met anybody with such concentration and willpower—perhaps more than is good for him. That's the secret."

Getty's concentration and willpower were no secret to his business competitors, and they served him well against those he met outside the squared circle. In the 1920s, Getty Oil became a sizable firm exploring for oil—and finding it, mostly in California. In the 1930s, the collapse of oil prices only made the company bigger and Getty richer. When oil-company stocks plummeted, Getty took to prospecting for oil on the floor of the New York Stock Exchange. One of his best deals involved the acquisition of 557,557 shares (the controlling interest) of a major independent. It was the Skelly Oil Company, and the shares were those that had belonged to its founder, William G. Skelly. The student who once had hung on every word uttered by his mentor Skelly was now the master.

Although he otherwise was not one to trust and empower subordinates, Getty made an exception in Bill Skelly's case. The Skelly Company kept its name and identity, Skelly retained its president's office and salary, and Getty pretty much left the older man alone. At least, he did when it came to oil. Getty respected Skelly's credentials in oil, and Getty trusted him implicitly.

What brought him back was not Skelly Oil but one of its minor assets, a small firm established by Bill Skelly back in the twenties. Wholly owned by Skelly Oil, it went with the company and became a piece in the growing Getty fortune. Unlike other Getty interests, it neither located, produced, transported, nor refined oil. It only used oil to fuel what it did produce: airplanes manufactured by the Spartan Aircraft Company at 1900 North Sheridan Road, Tulsa, Oklahoma.

That is why J. Paul Getty was back. William G. Skelly could run the oil company. Getty was back to run something even more important to him than oil. The date was February 22, 1942, and there was a war on.

The decision might have seemed purely eccentric if only because Getty was pretty eccentric himself. As he had grown richer, J. Paul Getty had grown odder. Not even bothering to conceal his sexual preference for teenage girls, Getty had recently undergone his second face-lift and had taken to dyeing his hair a funny reddish-brown. The combination made him look more like a young cadaver than anything else. Having tried (and failed) to buy himself a diplomatic post, he had sought an officer's commission in the United States Navy when the war began. The government had rejected his noble and patriotic offer, largely because of his notorious friendships with leading Nazis and other Fascist elements. Officially, J. Paul Getty was a security risk.

Altogether, then, Tulsa seemed like a good place to spend the war. Getty ordered a concrete bunker built at Sixty-ninth and Virgin. Because it was near the plant, he would run Spartan Aircraft from the bunker—and live in it too. Some speculated that it was to save money, others said to protect himself against the German Luftwaffe. Each explanation was as absurd as the other, but both were less ridiculous than Getty's idea of home and home life. At home in the bunker, J. Paul Getty maintained his habits of chewing each bite of food exactly thirty-three times and hand-washing his underwear every night.

However eccentric, Getty had grown rich not for his peculiarities but for his vision. In that regard, his foresight was a perfect twenty-twenty. Oil would be a major factor in the war, and Tulsa would have a share in it. That share, however, was to be remarkably small, particularly coming from the city that had styled itself the Oil Capital of the World.

The First World War had broken permanently the equation of fighting men to horses. Not the number of cavalry mounts but the horsepower of gasoline and diesel engines became the measure of military might and an accurate predictor of battlefield success. The Second World War demonstrated just how important oil had become. At the peak of fighting, American forces in Europe consumed one hundred times as much fuel in World War II as they had in World War I. The average American division of the First World War required 4,000 horsepower just to move. In the Second World War, the need was a phenomenal 187,000 horsepower. Nearly all of the fuel to feed those mechanical horses came from American oil fields, and the same fields also had to supply the war machines of the Soviet Union, Britain, and other allies. Under the circumstances, it was appropriate that Marshal Joseph Stalin would offer a toast during the war's darkest days: "This is a war of engines and octanes. I drink to the American auto industry and the American oil industry."

If few Tulsans heard of Stalin's toast, even fewer might have felt comfortable returning it. The fact was, however, that little of the dictator's sentiments properly fell upon Tulsa. During the First World War, Oklahoma supplied roughly 35 percent of the nation's oil, of which Tulsa firms accounted for 90 percent. Oklahoma's oil production peaked in 1927, before the midpoint of the interwar years. After 1930, Texas and California both caught and passed the Sooner State in oil production. The only significant pool developed in the following decade was at Oklahoma City, and that city's new oilmen were jealously independent of their Tulsa cousins.

Nearer to Tulsa, many of the once-grand fields were played out or barely staggering along. Oilmen still reminisced about and dreamed of gushers, but the fact was that 87 percent of the state's wells of 1940 were "stripper wells," producing as little as two or three barrels a day. The sum of Oklahoma's entire production did not amount to even 9 percent of the nation's oil output in the 1940s. There was so little slack in Tulsa's oil economy that the war took up all of it in its first year. After that, there was nothing left to give—or to get.

J. Paul Getty was right: Tulsa was to be his wartime home, but oil was not to be his business. Fortunately for Tulsa, other, less idiosyncratic leaders made the same calculation. Tulsa was their home too, and they already knew that the city had to free itself from its dependence on oil. The long agony of the Great Depression proved the hazards of Tulsa's being a one-industry town. When oil profits and wages ran down, the Oil Capital's fortunes slid down the greased slope with them. A decade after it had begun, the Great Depression remained the most immediate problem in Oklahoma and in Tulsa. The state's per capita income had peaked in 1929 at $464 per person. Despite all the efforts of the New Deal, the figure steadily declined until a slight rise brought it to $314 at the end of 1937—just about two-thirds of the precollapse figure. Conditions only worsened immediately thereafter. Tulsa's retail sales declined a whopping 25 percent in 1938 and fell further in 1939.

The long depression had another consequence. A few of Tulsa's early oil princes went under, others went away, and more went into retirement. For all these reasons, the depression left gaping holes in the city's established leadership. This was most visibly so in its clearest institutional embodiment: the Tulsa Chamber of Commerce.

By the war years, men like Josh Cosden, Charles Page, and Robert McFarlin were gone, dead, or inactive. Others took their places, but those others were not princes of petroleum. Tulsa's new elite sprang from far different (and generally lesser) orders. By the early forties, not even one of the chamber's officers was an oilman. Just six of its forty directors were with oil or oil-related companies, and only one headed a Tulsa bank. The overwhelming majority of the chamber's directors ran local retail or manufacturing shops or were managers sent to Tulsa by large corporations such as Southwestern Bell Telephone or Sears, Roebuck and Company.

If from lesser ranks, this new elite had no less vision. France's fall to Nazi armies in the spring of 1940 and the ferocious Battle of Britain that followed created a national crisis. Powerful congressmen debated neutrality legislation in Washington before finally passing huge military spending bills. Prominent intellectuals organized isolationist America First committees in most eastern cities. Plain people everywhere worried about their sons' fates in a second global conflict. In Tulsa, the city's elites did not debate; they only organized and worried. With unhesitating resolve, they organized to enlist the city in what President Franklin Roosevelt called the "Arsenal of Democracy." They worried only that Tulsa would not get its share of military dollars being spent to save Britain and arm America.

There was reason to worry. Nearly all of the increased military spending of early 1940 passed by the state and city. Oklahoma's total share of that spending was a barely calculable 5/100ths of 1 percent, and Tulsa's portion was exactly zero. Most contracts went to industries on the east and west coasts. Their recruiters lured away some of Tulsa's most skilled workers. As their numbers fell, Tulsa's chance to attract future military spending fell too.

What really soured Tulsa's chances, though, was the city's abysmal housing situation, and the souring was the rotted fruit of earlier decisions. During Tulsa's fevered growth of the oil-boom days, the city's leadership had not recognized housing as a communal issue. Private developers had opened additions as the marketplace dictated. In the nature of things, that led to handsome tracts in Maple Ridge, Terwilleger Heights, Forest Park, and similar additions. All were well planned, well built, and well serviced precisely because all paid the developers well, extraordinarily well.

Developers did handsomely too in more middle-class areas like Florence Park, where the market for distinctive bungalows was strong. Affordable but solid working-class housing offered less obvious returns. As a result, private developers built relatively little, most of what they did build they threw up cheaply, and working-class housing deteriorated more quickly because it was substandard.

At least, it would have been substandard had there been standards to apply. In the days before the New Deal, before "Big Government," and before the Federal Housing Administration (FHA), there were no national standards at all. The city did have building codes, but many of their provisions were trivial, and most of them went unenforced. Those with power saw no great cause to enforce them, and those without had no great chance to enforce them. Finally, the roar of gushing oil wells and the hosannas offered to free enterprise completely drowned out earlier voices calling for rational city planning, most notably in the case of an urban-development plan proposed as far back as 1924.

To those sins of thoughtless omission, Tulsa's early leadership had added another of calculated commission. Just after the 1921 race riot, when the black-owned property immediately north of the railroad tracks lay in charred ruins, the directors of the Tulsa Chamber of Commerce decided (as recorded in their official minutes) that "we must forget the causes of the riot and find a solution that is right." The next sentence defined what was "right": "We must determine whether this area is physically suited for a [railroad] terminal point." Apparently, it was. The chamber swiftly adopted the following resolutions:

> Whereas, the recent fire [!] in the northeast section of the city has made available a thoroughly feasible and practicable site for the Union Station and Joint Terminal,
>
> Now, therefore be it resolved, that it is the unanimous sentiment of the Chamber of Commerce and Federation of Allied Interests of Tulsa, Oklahoma, that the railroads and interurbans of the city of Tulsa immediately take steps looking toward the erection of a Union Station and railroad and interurban terminal, . . .
>
> Be it further resolved, that the Chamber of Commerce and Federation of Allied Interests of Tulsa, Oklahoma, by unanimous vote, pledges its unqualified support and backing to this proposed project, which it believes will inure to the benefit of the city of Tulsa, and to the various railroads and interurban systems.

With the same support and backing, the city adopted its first comprehensive zoning plan in 1923. It zoned the entire Greenwood area for industrial purposes. Should any future industry offer to locate there, the chamber's plan was to fill Greenwood with "cheap shacks . . . because when the proper time comes to condemn it, it will be possible to finance the proceedings." For the same reason, the city thereafter ignored its own housing and sanitary codes in Greenwood. In addition, when Tulsa's Union Depot opened in 1931, it took up much of what had been Greenwood's better residential and commercial sites. Add to that mix private restrictive covenants used in virtually every American city, and this is the result: an unspeakable housing crisis that, nonetheless, spoke volumes about what was supposed to "benefit the city of Tulsa."

In the emergency of global war, this problem threatened to be especially costly for Tulsa. Securely situated midway between coasts, blessed with inexhaustible sources of cheap fuel, famed for its network of roads and highways, endowed with a vast pool of trained workers, Tulsa had only one drawback as a site for military contracts, and it was largely self-inflicted. The city had nowhere to put the thousands of new workers necessary to make Tulsa a center of war production.

Civic leaders found an answer where the oil industry had found its salvation in

the thirties: the federal government. When America entered the war in December 1941, Washington's war orders multiplied geometrically, and no problem became too big to solve. Tulsa moved with lightning dispatch to get as much as possible as fast as possible. Working directly with the National Housing Board and the War Production Board (WPB), the chamber got the government to agree to hurriedly construct hundreds of new dwellings. Most were small (two- and three-room units), some were barracks, and many were substandard, so that the city and the FHA both had to waive their codes. Nevertheless, they solved one immediate problem and offered a future potential solution to another. The chamber reasoned that when the war ended and the war workers moved on, the cheap, shoddy properties would provide perfect homes to relocate some of Tulsa's overcrowded black population. Of course, they also would preserve the segregation that had caused the overcrowding in the first place.

The promotion of wartime housing was only one of the chamber's efforts to place the city in the hunt for military spending, and the hunting ground was Washington. Russell Rhodes, the chamber's general manager, logged thousands of air miles flying to the capital, where he met with procurement officers and enlisted the state's entire congressional delegation in the crusade to send defense dollars to Tulsa. William G. Skelly, one of the few old-timers who still served as a chamber director, used his influence within industry and as Oklahoma's national Republican committeeman on the city's behalf. Fred Jones proved to be a valuable ally on the War Production Board as one of the famed "dollar-a-year" businessmen donating their services to advise the government. Fred Jones offered his advice with a strong Oklahoma accent. At home, the government agreed to clear defense contracts, war-related regulations, and other business through the chamber. The chamber assisted by securing personnel and office space for local branches of the Office of Price Administration, Army Finance, Army Ordnance, and the WPB's Office of Priorities and Contract Distribution.

By the time of the Second World War, Tulsa's Greenwood district had recovered from the ashes, if not from the memories, of the race riot two decades earlier.

All of that work paid off handsomely, perhaps more handsomely than anything local businessmen had done since they had bridged the Arkansas back in 1904. If there was no banner proclaiming "You Said We Couldn't Do It, But We Did," it was because there was no need. This time, no one dared say that Tulsa couldn't do it any more than anyone doubted that America could answer President Roosevelt's call to produce warplanes at the unheard of rate of fifty thousand per year. No one in Tulsa, at least, was surprised to learn that many of those planes would come from Tulsa, Oklahoma.

Eleven months before Pearl Harbor, the War Department announced that it had chosen Tulsa as a potential site for a $15 million plant to be operated by the Douglas

ASSEMBLING B-24 LIBERATORS IN 1943

Aircraft Company. City and chamber officials nailed the deal down by moving quickly to prepare a $750,000 bond issue, which voters approved by an eleven-to-one margin.

Fly ahead with Tulsa in 1941

Vote **YES** on the Bomber Plant
Bond Issue ❖ March 25

(Speakers' Handbook, Issued by the Mayor's Advisory
Committee March 19, 1941)

Dexter Publishing Co.

The money bought one thousand acres of land and built runways just east of the existing municipal airport. Tulsa won the Douglas plant, a victory that the chamber savored as the greatest since the discovery of oil. Chamber, city, military, and industry officials turned out for the ceremonial groundbreaking on May 2, 1941. The Japanese bombing of Pearl Harbor accelerated the project enough that contractors finished the steel framework for the plant on December 18—thirty-five days ahead of schedule. By the summer of 1942, the plant was in full operation. It occupied a building nearly a mile long, with one-and-one-half million square feet of floor space.

APPLICATION FOR ENROLLMENT

SPARTAN SCHOOL OF AERONAUTICS,
P. O. Box 2649,
Municipal Airport,
Tulsa, Oklahoma.

Gentlemen:

Please enter my application for enrollment in the following course checked below:

TUITION FEES

☐ REGULAR MECHANIC'S COURSE $ 135.00
Twelve weeks or 360 hours instruction on
motors, etc. 30 minutes Dual flying instruction.

☐ MASTER MECHANIC'S COURSE 225.00
Twenty weeks or 600 hours instruction on
motors, etc. One hour Dual flying instruction.

☐ MASTER MECHANIC'S FLYING COURSE 275.00
20 weeks or 600 hours instruction
on motors, etc. 10 hours flying.

☐ PRIVATE PILOT'S COURSE 260.00
10 hours Dual instruction — 10 hours
solo flying—180 hours Ground School

☐ LIMITED COMMERCIAL COURSE 650.00
15 hours Dual instruction — 35 hours
solo flying—500 hours Ground School

☐ TRANSPORT PILOT'S COURSE 1,975.00
35 hours Dual instruction—165 hours
solo flying—500 hours Ground School

☐ SPORTSMAN PILOT'S COURSE
10 hours flying time

I will enter School about ....

Signed..

Street..

City..

Age..................years.

TULSA **Airview News** DOUGLAS

Vol. III—No. 19   Friday, August 17, 1945   Tulsa, Oklahoma

Peace Halts A-26 Production

Douglas Photo by F. M. McCormack

More than ten thousand Tulsans provided the initial labor force. Many had been oilfield hands, barbers, clerks, or common laborers. Others had been housewives, waitresses, or beauticians. Still others were newcomers who had been farmers. Quite a few had not worked in so long that they had forgotten just what their occupations had been.

They immediately set to work rearming 226 Boeing B-17s, the Flying Fortresses that were preparing to carry the war to Hitler. That finished, they built 615 Dauntless dive-bombers to take the war to Tojo's forces in the Pacific. They then assembled 954 B-24 Liberators and 1,343 A-26 Invaders that flew the skies in both theaters. Along the way, they also modified nearly 4,000 other aircraft, including many of the C-47 Skytrains that left British airfields for Normandy on June 6, 1944. Between major contracts, Douglas workers produced, crated, and shipped more than forty million pounds of spare parts for military aircraft.

The cost of their work to America's enemies was fearful. To America's taxpayers, the cost included another $5 million required to expand the plant almost as soon as it opened, in the fall of 1942. As many as fifteen thousand workers on its payroll earned an average of over $185 per month.

That kind of money was enough to interest even J. Paul Getty. From his Virgin Street bunker, he placed the Spartan Aircraft Company in position to get a share of it. The company already had some experience in building military-type aircraft. Under Skelly's leadership, Spartan had introduced its Executive Model 7-W in 1935. A low-wing monoplane, it cruised at 190 miles per hour and had a range of 950 miles. With proper training and fifteen minutes' time, a crew could convert the aircraft into a fighter-bomber armed with two fixed machine guns in the wings, a swivel-mounted machine gun atop the cabin, and bomb racks for ten bombs. Neither the U. S. Navy nor the Army Air Corps showed interest in such a fancy, if versatile, plane. In fact, one of its few owners was Iraq's King Faisal, whose custom-built model included inlaid tiles, Persian carpeting, and solid-gold fixtures.

Early in the war, the navy did contract with Spartan to build more modest aircraft. These were primary trainers known as the Spartan PN-1. The company produced two hundred planes for a fee of $1.8 million. Spartan completed the contract after Getty arrived and instituted around-the-clock shifts to turn out a plane a day. Getty thereafter kept the plant humming at full capacity under a steady flow of subcontracts with major aircraft firms. Through the remainder of the war, Spartan workers turned out wings, bomb-bay doors, fuselages, and other parts for companies like Grumman, Curtis-Wright, Lockheed, Boeing, and Martin. Several hundred other employees overhauled airframes and engines for the Army Air Corps.

In all these ways, Getty achieved his purpose of keeping Spartan Aircraft running at maximum capacity virtually every hour of every day after his arrival. The result was not a massive company but one just the perfect size to be terribly lucrative, especially since the increased production required almost no investment for physical expansion. Even Getty's decision to expand one of Spartan's programs required little capital expenditure. The beefed-up program—the Spartan School of Aeronautics—was destined to play a major role in Tulsa's economic development.

The school had opened in 1928. Using the facilities of the municipal airport, it originally offered ground and flight training for a modest number of students seeking federal pilots' licences. All of that changed with the fall of France and the launching of the Nazi blitz on England. Under contract with the Canadian government, Spartan trained three hundred men—Canadians and Americans, mostly—to fly the Spitfires of the Royal Air Force (RAF).

With America's entry in the war, Britain contracted directly with the school. Using British military aircraft, Spartan turned out five thousand pilots for the RAF. Scores of classes received their wings at Spartan's auxiliary field in Miami, Oklahoma. Fourteen cadets were killed during the training; their bodies lie in a Miami cemetery. Of those who returned to face the German Luftwaffe in the ongoing Battle of Britain, entire classes perished in the skies. Among those who died over Britain or the Continent were some of the twelve thousand American pilots that Spartan also trained as one of only nine private companies approved by the Army Air Corps to prepare military aviators.

The school turned out another six hundred civilian pilots as well as more than five thousand certified aircraft mechanics. Nearly all of the mechanics left Spartan with their diplomas, walked a few hundred yards, and signed on at the Douglas plant. They discovered that almost all of their foremen, supervisors, and managers were earlier graduates of Spartan themselves.

SPARTAN C4-240

It was a remarkable record for the little company out on North Sheridan. Having compiled it, the odd man in the concrete bunker left Tulsa again and returned to oil. In a few years, he used some of the profits from Spartan to lease a site that bore some promise. It was an undivided interest in a region of Saudi Arabia. Within ten years, it would earn J. Paul Getty the title of the "World's Richest Man."

Well before then, however, Getty proved that the government had misjudged him as a security risk. With his employees at Spartan and the workers at the Douglas plant, J. Paul Getty had helped America defeat the dictators of Germany, Italy, and Japan. At the same time, Getty proved that he had judged Tulsa correctly. Oil would remain important to the city's future, but oil never again would dictate what that future would be.

The evidence was everywhere and abundant. After nearly doubling in the booming 1920s, Tulsa's population barely held its own through the depressed 1930s. Between 1940 and 1945, however, it grew by nearly a third to reach 185,000. The long decline in per capita income reversed course and raced toward a record of $1,470 in 1946, five times the prewar figure. After the slump of 1938 and 1939, retail sales soared by 187 percent between 1940 and 1945. Bank deposits increased by 236 percent during the same years.

Feeding that growth were millions of investment dollars, many dispatched through Washington. Despite labor and materials shortages, Tulsa's factories spent $7,242,000 to expand their plants during the war, not including the aircraft industry, which spent another $20 million or more. Manufacturers had employed eleven thousand Tulsans in 1939, almost all of them in the refineries and other oil-related fields. By 1945, forty-two thousand Tulsans worked in manufacturing, and only a small minority depended upon oil for their jobs. Overall, the United States Department of Labor calculated in 1945 that only two American cities (Long Beach, California, and Wichita, Kansas) changed more with the wartime's industrial expansion.

While he was presenting some of those figures at the chamber's first postwar Public Affairs Forum, Russell Rhodes paused to note that the war had presented Tulsa with another powerful legacy. This one was not measurable by percentages or numbers of dollars. Perhaps for that very reason, this was the war's most important bequest of all:

> The victory era into which we are entering can never be the same as the pre-war period. We have undergone too many changes, both psychological and actual, ever to return to the attitudes and methods of the 1930s.

Russell Rhodes was right. World War II had delivered Europe and East Asia from tyranny and established the foundations of the modern world. The Second World War also had delivered Tulsa from its own past and pointed it toward its uncertain future.

TERRIFIC AS ALL CREATION
THE TALKIES REBORN
MIGHTIEST DRAMA OF THE AGES
EDNA FERBER'S COLOSSAL
CIMARRON
RICHARD DIX
IRENE DUNNE ESTELLE TAYLOR
WM. COLLIER, JR. AND A GRAND ASSEMBLAGE OF SUPERLATIVE ARTISTS
WESLEY RUGGLES PRODUCTION
Radio PICTURES

"A Cultural Sahara"

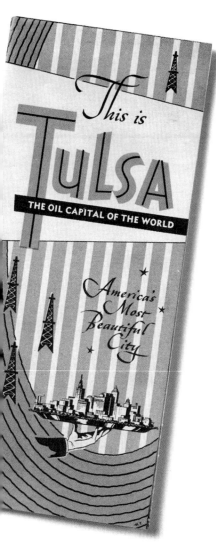

SOME PEOPLE SAID that Edna Ferber only needed to have stayed in Tulsa longer. More said that she never should have come at all. The truth was that she did not stay long when she came to the city in the late 1920s, near the peak of its fabulous oil-boom era. The Tulsa stop accounted for just one of her research visits during the entire thirteen days that she had set aside to research completely her planned next novel.

As in her other best-selling books, *So Big* and *Saratoga Trunk*, the central figure for this novel-to-be would be female, and this one would be based upon a living woman, Elva Shartel Ferguson. She and her husband, Thompson B. Ferguson, had founded the *Watonga Republican* back in Oklahoma's territorial days. Thompson Ferguson served Oklahoma Territory as its governor while she ran the newspaper. After his death in 1921, Elva Ferguson continued to edit and publish the paper under her own name. Politically active even before Oklahoma permitted woman suffrage in 1920, she headed the state's delegation to the 1924 Republican National Convention. Along the way, she had helped her son, Walter Ferguson, launch his own career as a journalist in Tulsa.

So Edna Ferber came to Tulsa to interview Walter Ferguson and see for herself the difference that oil had made to the state that her fictional family had pioneered. She saw it, all right. Chauffeured limousines delivered oilmen and their jewel-encrusted ladies to the home honored

to host the celebrated guest. It was the new, palatial residence of one of their own, Waite Phillips. The cream of the city's high society was absolutely giddy to meet the best-selling novelist, playwright, and resident wit of New York City's famed Algonquin Roundtable.

Cimarron was the book that resulted. Its Sabra Cravat bore some resemblance to Elva Ferguson—not much, Mrs. Ferguson allowed, but some. It was not likely that many Tulsans would have known that, though. It was even less likely that the oil princes or princesses ever bothered to read it. As it turned out, they already had all they wanted of Miss Ferber. Before *Cimarron* hit the bookstores, she had hit Tulsa pretty hard and pretty low with a magazine piece. Describing her Tulsa layover with the cynicism that she normally displayed at the Algonquin, she poked great fun at what crude oil had produced: a crude town filled with crude people. She did not spare even her host. Waite Phillips, she said, had wasted $2 million to build an outlandish mishmash of pretentiousness blended with tastelessness. As for the rest of Tulsa—well, what could one say except that it was a "cultural Sahara"?

WHATEVER THE AMBIENCE OF THEIR PUBLIC BUILDINGS, TULSANS SPARED LITTLE IN DECORATING THEIR HOMES. PARTICULARLY FOR THE MOST AFFLUENT, HOMES REFLECTED TULSANS' FANTASIES— AND SOMETIMES THEIR ECCENTRICITIES. ABOVE, THE FOYER OF THE PARRIOTT HOME. FACING PAGE, THE CLUBROOM OF THE MABEE HOME.

Upon reading Miss Ferber's account, Waite Phillips took to bed, physically ill for several days. Other Tulsans who read it vowed never to read another word that the rude and ungrateful harpy would ever write again. If all they missed was *Cimarron,* they suffered no great loss.

Edna Ferber had a point, though. Through the 1920s, Tulsans gained fame as builders. They built a great American industry, beautiful neighborhoods of stately homes, and a towering urban skyline. In the 1930s, they had the wherewithal and the gumption to build one of the nation's few country clubs opened during that depressed decade: Southern Hills.

It was only after the Second World War that large numbers of Tulsans realized the limits of what they had built. Nearly all of it had been as private as Southern Hills and as commercial as a drilling rig. Josh Cosden's old refinery, renamed the Mid-Continent, produced abundant wealth, but no one would confuse it with art, industrial or otherwise. The Sinclair, Skelly, and other great mansions were visual monuments to personal fortunes, not public facilities devoted to civic values. Dozens of banks and corporate office buildings towered over downtown, but there was not a decent public library there or anywhere else.

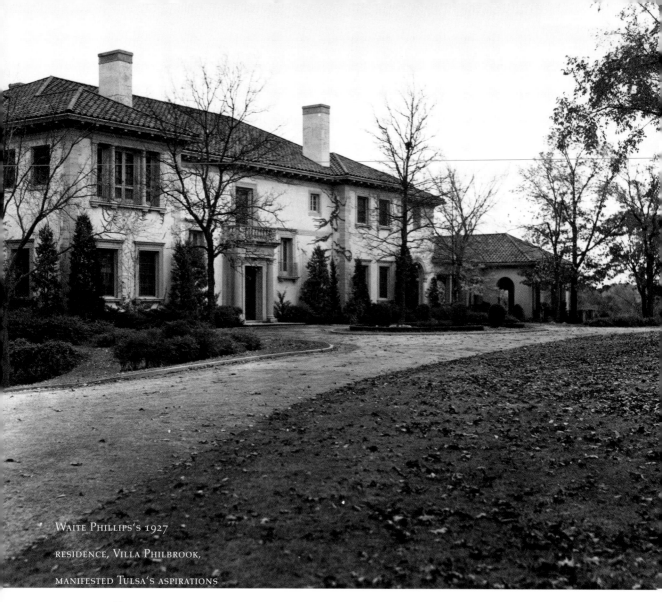

FOR ITSELF. THE STATELY RENAISSANCE REVIVAL HOME BECAME THE FOCUS OF THE CITY'S CULTURAL LIFE AFTER ITS DONATION TO TULSANS IN 1938. ALTHOUGH PHILBROOK REMAINS THE MOST VISIBLE OF PHILLIPS'S GIFTS, THE DEPTH OF HIS PHILANTHROPY TOUCHED EVERY ASPECT OF TULSA'S EDUCATIONAL, SOCIAL, AND CULTURAL ARENAS.

The industrial spurt and the collective effort inspired by the war may have helped underscore the difference between Tulsa's commercial achievement and its cultural barrenness. At least, they did for Russell Rhodes, who told the chamber of commerce in 1948 that

> In our section of the country it is not difficult for any city to become larger and to experience growth in commercial and industrial activities. This will happen almost without planning and with a minimum of effort.

> The real goal, however, is not necessarily a bigger city, but a better city—a completely balanced city, where the development of the cultural, educational, and religious phases of the community are recognized as being co-

equal with industrial development, trade area expansion, and rising skylines.

To much of an earlier generation of the city's commercial elite, such talk would have amounted either to platitudes or to heresy, but this was a new generation and a new elite. Some were children of pioneer oilmen, the generally poorly educated men who had muscled their way to the top. The second generation was privileged. Many of its boys toned their muscles not in the mud of oil fields but on the grassy playing fields of exclusive prep schools. Quite a few went on to the best schooling that money could buy, at Harvard, Yale, Stanford, and the like. They returned to Tulsa with acquired tastes for a more cosmopolitan culture.

Joining them were engineers, geologists, attorneys, accountants, and research scientists—the well-paid and expensively educated professionals recruited to service the maturing oil industry and the emerging aeronautics companies. By the 1950s, Tulsa had enough lawyers and accountants to fill pages of the phone book and was home to more engineers and scientists per capita than any city in America. Some joined the chamber of commerce. Others joined other associations, for Tulsa was coming to have not one but many elites. They came from all over. They came to build a Tulsa more like Chicago, Boston, or San Francisco than an overgrown Coweta, Bixby, or Sapulpa.

Now comfortable with their wealth, even some among the pioneering generation were ready to exchange their old roles as captains of industry for new ones as patrons of the arts. One was the oilman that Edna Ferber had outraged so unfairly. Waite Phillips deserved better, and Tulsa rarely did better than it did in Waite Phillips.

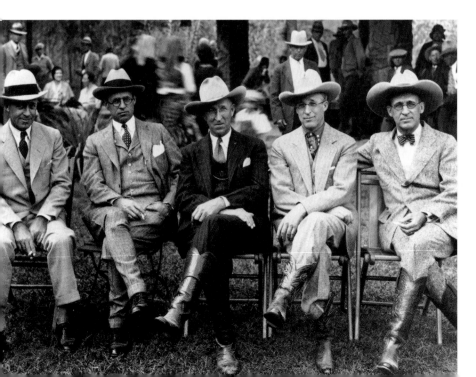

THE FIVE PHILLIPS BROTHERS POSE FOR A PHOTOGRAPH AT FRANK'S RUSTIC RETREAT, WOOLAROC. FROM LEFT: FRED, WAITE, ED, L. E., AND FRANK.

Born on a forty-acre Iowa farm in 1883, Waite Phillips was one of ten children of Lewis and Lucinda Phillips. He completed all six grades at the nearby grammar school, but his entire formal education otherwise consisted of six months' study at the Shenandoah Commercial Institute and School of Penmanship. His real education came during his teenage years, which he spent wandering the West, prospecting for gold, trapping for furs, and working for railroad construction gangs. He came to the Indian Territory and Bartlesville in 1906. His older brothers Frank and L. E. were already there and already getting rich in oil. The two helped Waite learn the ropes and set him up in the business. (They also helped a fourth Phillips brother, Ed, launch a lucrative banking career in Okmulgee.) Frank, of course, went on to establish the Bartlesville-based Phillips Petroleum Company, the one of Phillips 66 fame. His younger brother chose Tulsa to locate the Waite Phillips Company. By 1926, it had made him a millionaire forty times over.

Waite Phillips had precious little formal education and none at all in architecture or the arts, but he knew people who did, and he was smart enough and rich enough to hire them. In Jesse Claude Nichols and Edward Buehler Delk, he hired the best there was. Nichols already had established an international reputation for urban design by turning some old rock quarries into Kansas City's famed Country Club district, one of the Midwest's first planned residential areas. At its heart was an old hog farm reborn as Country Club Plaza, the nation's first suburban shopping center and a work of physical splendor. Edward Buehler Delk was the architect who built it.

In 1926, Phillips put Nichols and Delk to work on twenty-three acres of hilly land cut by gently flowing Crow Creek. Many months and $597,000 later, they had moved the creek and completed Villa Philbrook. Surrounding it were landscaped gardens that cost another $129,000. Furnishings brought the total to $1,191,000. It was quite a bit below the $2 million that Miss Ferber figured, and her aesthetics were no better than her arithmetic. The estate at 2727 South Rockford Road was an imaginative but beautifully integrated modern expression of a classic Florentine villa. Villa Philbrook was perhaps the state's most magnificent private residence.

Waite Phillips, his wife, Genevieve, and their children, Helen Jane and Elliott, lived there twelve years. In 1938, Waite Phillips gave the mansion to the city for the express purpose that it be used as an art museum. The city also received the grounds for use "as a public park and botanical garden containing plants indigenous to the Southwest." To maintain and fund both, he threw in another piece of property, the Beacon Building, a nine-story, high-rent office building on Boulder Avenue.

The children grown, Phillips and his wife moved to California, where no one thought to call them "Okies." Philbrook remained their gift to Tulsa. With generous support from Tulsans and the continuing income from the Beacon, the Philbrook Art Center became one of the premier art institutions of post–World War II America. It held an internationally known collection of Italian Renaissance paintings and entire galleries devoted to both classical and modern art. Class instruction, dance recitals, chamber-music performances, even film viewings—all of these made it a unique urban resource. It also added immeasurably to Tulsa's stature, maybe even its atmosphere. One of its early directors, Robert M. Church, left San Francisco to manage Philbrook, declaring that his reason for coming to Tulsa was "because there's a more cosmopolitan attitude here."

Waite Phillips's benefaction helped transform Tulsa's reputation as an artistic Sahara. The gift of another early oilman made Tulsa a mecca.

Thomas Gilcrease inherited his one-eighth Creek blood from his mother. She and his white father raised the boy in a log cabin near Eufaula in the old Creek nation. His formal schooling came at the feet of Creek poet Alexander Posey, who taught at a little cabin in the rolling Creek hills. As Creek citizens, Gilcrease and his mother each received a 160-acre allotment. His was located near the Arkansas River, about two-and-one-half miles from the little village of Kiefer. It turned out to be atop the Glenn Pool field, the world's "richest little oil field." Thomas Gilcrease was only fourteen when the first well came in, but it made him rich. He became richer when thirty-two more wells began producing on his land over the next twelve years. Soon he was trading leases, exploring for oil, and producing it himself under the corporate name of the Gilcrease Oil Company. He hit oil in Oklahoma, East Texas, California—almost everywhere he tried. Making money turned out to be just about the easiest thing in the world for him.

If anything came easier, it was spending money. With some of his very first oil income, young Thomas Gilcrease walked into the Hotel Tulsa, passed by the gaggles of wildcatters and boom chasers, and bought his first painting, Ridgeway Knight's *Rural Courtship*. The next Christmas, in 1913, he bought the land that would provide his home: acres of softly undulating Osage prairie that overlooked Tulsa from the northwest. Over the next twenty years, his two marriages dissolved (the first to his childhood sweetheart Belle Harlow, the second to Norma Smallwood, Tulsa's 1926 Miss America), but two things remained constant: his capacity for making money and his passion for spending it. The latter was a passion with a purpose: to amass the art, documents, books, and artifacts that recorded the history of his country and its people, including his and his mother's Native American ancestors.

He bought not just pieces but entire collections. In 1944, he spent a quarter-million to buy a group of Charles Russell's and Frederic Remington's paintings from the estate of Dr. Phillip Cole. After World War II, he purchased the entire set of documents that had traveled the country as the American Freedom Foundation's "Freedom Train." The set included Paul Revere's appointment as messenger for the Massachusetts Committee of Safety and Thomas Jefferson's letter of July 1, 1776, in which he outlined his thoughts as he prepared to write the Declaration of Independence. Along the way, Thomas Gilcrease accumulated more than two hundred thousand separate items, the greatest collection of Americana ever assembled by a private individual. In 1949, he opened a museum next to his sandstone house in the Osage hills to share with Tulsans just a fraction of his treasures.

Mayo Hotel, Tulsa, Okla.—52

PHILBROOK ART CENTER
ROCKFORD ROAD, TULSA
THE FINEST ART CENTER
IN THE SOUTHWEST

HOME LOANS
SEE
HOME FEDERAL

190   T U L S A !

INVESTMENTS INSURED
UP TO $5000 BY U.S. GOVERNMENT AGENCY

PHILTOWER BUILDING, TULSA, OKLA.

He was art rich and oil poor by 1954, when creditors demanded his immediate payment of $2,250,000. His only asset worth anything like that was the collection, and its value lay in keeping it intact. One could almost see the rich private universities and the great national galleries circling over the Osage hills. That was when Alfred Aaronson happened to take his wife by for one last look at the treasures before they probably would leave Tulsa forever. Spotting a well-dressed man whom he never had met, Aaronson thought to ask him if he was Tom Gilcrease. He was, and the conversation that followed turned out to be as important to Tulsa's history as anything said since Harry C. Hall had told the Frisco engineer where to place his depot.

The son of a pioneer oilman, Alfred Aaronson had gone into oil himself before moving into banking, investments, and real estate. Then sixty-one years old and blessed with more money than he ever could spend, Aaronson was ready to give the rest of his life enriching the city. After Thomas Gilcrease told him that it was true—he would have to sell the collection and move it from Tulsa—Alfred Aaronson approached Mayor L. C. Clark with an idea. The mayor listened and agreed; he would call a special election for a bond issue to pay Gilcrease's debt by purchasing the entire collection for the city of Tulsa. The only condition was that Aaronson would have to pay the cost of the election, $10,700. He and some friends paid it, Aaronson put together a "Keep Gilcrease in Tulsa Committee" to back it, and voters approved the bonds by a three-to-one ratio. With the collection, Tulsa also received one-half interest in Gilcrease's East Texas oil holdings as an endowment.

Never has a city bought so much for so little. After Thomas Gilcrease's death in 1962, the family gave the city his home and the surrounding grounds, and the oil income alone soon repaid a good portion of the original indebtedness. Subsequent remodelings multiplied the size of the original museum and allowed it to attract thousands of visitors per year. They came from all over the world, but they came to one place: Tulsa, Oklahoma. Perched on a hill overlooking downtown Tulsa, the city-owned Thomas Gilcrease Institute of American History and Art offered them more than five thousand paintings and pieces of sculpture, a research library of thirty thousand volumes, a massive collection of documents that dated to the voyages of Christopher Columbus, and ten thousand artifacts, some as much as thirty-five hundred years old. Economists calculated that its economic impact upon Tulsa was as great as if it were a multimillion-dollar plant carrying a sizable annual payroll. What the economists could not measure was its worth. It was and is literally priceless.

In the 1950s, it was as though Tulsans set out deliberately to silence Edna Ferber's still-stinging rebuke. They irrigated the so-called Sahara with enough art and culture to drown her and any other big-city smart alecks. Even private companies made their contribution, most notably Tulsa's First National Bank. The well-oiled bank moved into six million dollars' worth of new quarters in 1950 and decided to spend another $25,000 to decorate its lobby with an original mural. Four well-known artists, ranging from the sage-and-pony school through abstract modernists, entered the competition with proposed designs to earn the fee.

While a jury dominated by museum directors judged the entries, Tulsans examined the four offerings, which were displayed at Philbrook. Overwhelmingly, the public favored Peter Hurd's proposal. It was one that an art critic might have euphemistically labeled "representational." The professional's choice was Fred Conway's offering. It was, to say the least, very unrepresentational.

Seen from afar, it seemed to be an abstract design of great patches amid rippling ribbons of color. From about fifty feet, it assumed the form of a heroic pageant of pioneers rushing from left to right. Viewed closer, it looked like cartoons cut and pasted helter-skelter. Close-up, the figures consisted of a few farmers, pioneer mothers, and sturdy workers sprinkled among a host of grifters, grafters, gamblers, deadbeats, dandies, and prostitutes, spiced with a few crooked politicians, fat bankers, and leering undertakers. The bank paid Conway his fee, installed the finished mural, and endured the befuddled musings of its customers. "We been huntin' twenty minutes," one fellow allegedly said of himself and family, "but we cain't find Will Rogers nowheres in it."

Tulsans liked to tell that story on themselves. Another they enjoyed was about the time Burch Mayo (as in the Mayo Hotel, which his father had built in 1925) took on the job of heading up a committee to create a symphony orchestra. Hoping to pry $5,000 out of an old-time oilman, Mayo promised that its premier performance would feature Beethoven's Fifth and be dedicated to him. "I never heard of Beethoven's Fifth, Burch" the old fellow was supposed to have said, "but I'll be happy with Old Grand-dad's fifth." He thereupon wrote out his check, and anytime the Philharmonic needed a few thousand, all Mayo had to do was send the grizzled patron another tissue-wrapped bottle of Kentucky's finest.

Apparently there were others who preferred Beethoven's Fifth even to Old Grand-dad. In 1949, the city lured H. Arthur Brown away from El Paso, where he had assembled that city's regionally prominent orchestra. A Juilliard graduate, Brown found in Tulsa special opportunities, and he made the most of them. Because he realized that it would be hard to attract outstanding musicians for a season limited to twelve concerts, he approached the University of Tulsa and the city's commercial elite and worked out a set of arrangements. The gas company endowed a university chair for the teaching of violin, and other companies put up money for other chairs. The university then appointed the artists that the orchestra needed to the positions, enriching both the school and the city.

In no time at all, Brown assembled a first-rate orchestra of eighty pieces. Its success was assured in 1950 on the night that the First National Bank dedicated its new building. The bank erected a special platform, rented searchlights to pierce the night skies, and presented Tulsa with its new symphony. Twenty-five thousand Tulsans crowded Boston Avenue that night. "I guess it was Tulsa's finest hour," recalled one gentleman old enough to remember when hogs had wallowed in the same street. "I know I damn well cried."

Even before the Second World War, Tulsa already had a sizable musical reputation, but that music was hardly of the symphonic persuasion. Bob Wills had perfected a legendary blend of music called western swing at two Tulsa sites that thereby acquired as much fame as Nashville's WSM and Ryman Auditorium. KVOO—"the Voice of Oklahoma"—first broadcast the Wills band from its studio in the basement of the Wright Building around midnight on February 9, 1934. Within months, Bob Wills and the Texas Playboys had the prime 12:30 to 1:00 P.M. slot, blasting out fiddle tunes, breakdowns, and ballads as far as Oakland, California, over twenty-five thousand watts of power. For thirty-four years, either Bob Wills or his brother Johnnie Lee held that noontime spot and filled it with songs like "Steel Guitar Rag," "Faded Love," and the immortal "San Antonio Rose." The Wills brothers used it to build audiences for almost nightly dances that their bands played across the entire American Southwest. None attracted more of the faithful than those held at the Tulsa site that the Playboys first hired on New Year's night of 1935: Cain's Dancing Academy.

What some regarded as a higher form of music and dance came to Tulsa in a remarkable seven-year period through the efforts of a few remarkable people. In 1949, the same year that Burch Mayo and others put together the Philharmonic, Maude Lorton organized the Tulsa Opera Club. The widow of the *Tulsa World*'s publisher, Eugene Lorton, she had sung and coached opera in San Francisco before arriving in Tulsa to marry the young newspaperman whom she had met in California. Chairing the opera club's finance committee, she and her friends raised enough money to hire a professional artistic director, Ralph Sassano, who had coached stars of the Metropolitan Opera, and to mount lavish productions, beginning with *La Traviata.*

Seven years later, on December 15, 1956, Temple Israel's Miller Auditorium staged what the *World* referred to as "the premiere appearance of the Tulsa Civic Ballet, starring Moscelyne Larkin and Roman Jasinski." The two featured performers, husband and wife, had met as dancers with the famed Ballet Russe de Monte Carlo. They made their home where Moscelyne Larkin had grown up and learned to dance. Back in Larkin's Tulsa home, they became the guiding lights of Tulsa Ballet Theatre, one of the nation's most acclaimed dance companies. Over the next forty years, the company would tour in thirty states and be honored by *Dance Magazine* as a singular American treasure in 1988.

While some second-generation Tulsans and other newly arrived Tulsans worked to repair the city's cultural image, others from both categories found more mundane but no less important causes. Many of the women among them found a natural home in an organization that had been in Tulsa since 1925: the League of Women Voters. By the late 1940s, the league had some four hundred members and a solid record of

achievement. During the depression, the Tulsa league had forced the municipal government to improve the city's milk supply and persuaded the legislature to establish the state's first juvenile court. Thoroughly nonpartisan but effectively organized, the Tulsa league had earned the respect of both political parties; the city, county, and state governments; and the local business community, which contributed two-thirds of its annual budget.

In 1947, it found a forceful advocate for a new issue. Employing the odd-sounding journalistic practices of the day, the *Ladies Home Journal* identified the first as "Mrs. Raymond Feldman, a young housewife from Illinois with a law degree." Nancy Feldman did have a law degree (from the University of Chicago), and she also was a trained sociologist. When she came to Tulsa with her husband, she was impressed with the city's supply of doctors, modern hospitals, and overall cleanliness. Joining the league and agreeing to direct one of its study groups, she learned what lay beneath

Photo by
WALTER MADSON
'37
TULSA

When he put up the building on North Main Street, Tate Brady admitted that he had no idea how it would be used. His best guess was that it likely would become a garage. Neither he nor anyone else would have guessed its ultimate role and significance, as shown here: Bob Wills and the Texas Playboys on stage at the "Mother Church" of western swing, Cain's Dancing Academy.

that surface cleanliness. What she and her group found was an appalling situation that the league turned into a fighting issue.

For all of its private wealth, Tulsa spent less on public health than any of sixty American cities of comparable size. The city health department had had no director for at least two years, and the underpaid and overworked staff was in a state of demoralized chaos. Not coincidentally, Tulsa was one of the few American cities still plagued by diphtheria. Every year, the disease struck a fearful death toll among Tulsa's children, and it helped push Tulsa's infant mortality rate to one of the nation's highest. Tuberculosis was a rampant problem, but 40 percent of its victims were not even hospitalized.

Armed with that information, Feldman and other league volunteers alerted every local civic group they could find about what they called "Our Shame." They found allies in the Parent-Teacher Association, the Federated Women's Clubs, the Council of Jewish Women, the Council of Social Agencies, and the Tulsa Chamber of Commerce. With printed brochures and striking charts, Nancy Feldman and others delivered seventy-four talks all over the city, addressing more than four thousand of their fellow citizens directly. At the end of each presentation, the speakers passed out postcards, preaddressed to city hall, to every member of the audience. In one week, city officials received more than four hundred of the cards—enough to act.

Surrounded by league and civic-club members, the mayor and city commission voted to hire a qualified director. They also raised the position's salary from $5,600 to $10,000 per year (more than the mayor received), added more nurses and other professional staff members, increased their salaries, and consolidated the city and county health departments. Finally, they approved a $172,000 public-health budget. The figure was at last in line with the recommendations of the United States Department of Public Health.

Such policy decisions were vitally important, even if their effects were not immediately visible. The reverse may have been the case for other official actions of the era. Starting in 1950, the city began widening and resurfacing its major streets. Peoria and Lewis Avenues were widened from eighteen feet to forty-four and also stretched southward past Thirty-sixth Street into what was still open countryside. The city

widened Fifteenth Street into a four-lane boulevard and planted its dividing median with flowering trees. The latter was part of a concerted and well-publicized "City Beautiful" campaign. Another element began in 1953, when Tulsa received national attention as it started flushing and sweeping 352 miles of its residential streets. Some sections, of course, received more beautifying than others. The most favored were cleaned every night, the less favored every fourth night, the outlying districts once every six weeks, Greenwood not at all.

Tulsa was hardly alone in such unevenhanded policies. Few other cities did better; many did not do as well. Very few cities anywhere in the country, however, could match Tulsa's commitment to beautification by botany. Particularly after World War II, garden clubs sprouted in Tulsa as fast as the crabgrass and chickweed that so maddened homeowners. Nearly every city had similar clubs, just as they had similar weeds. What no other city had was an $80,000 mansion purchased by the municipal government and turned into an official agency, the Tulsa Garden Center. Located at 2415 South Peoria, the former Snedden home was a twenty-room mansion of "modified Italian Renaissance" style. It included a library to hold sixteen hundred books on everything from insects to patio plans and an open ballroom capable of serving the three thousand Tulsans who visited the center for its annual two-day flower shows. The seven-and-one-half-acre surrounding grounds included a fountain, sunken garden, and large conservatory. Still, there was room left for a municipally owned rose garden planted with ninety-five hundred rose bushes in almost as many varieties.

The Tulsa Garden Center was unique. Tulsa's public library was only extraordinary. It had not always been that way—at least not in any positive sense. At the end of World War II, the Tulsa library still occupied the cramped quarters that Andrew Carnegie had provided it during the First World War. Since then, the city's population had almost quintupled, but the library had added neither a single inch nor very many books. The city was also much larger physically, but not one of the five existing branch libraries was south of Fifteenth Street, the edge of settlement in Carnegie's day. For nearly fifty years, librarians and other specialists protested, at first quietly and ineffectively. Over time, protests rose above the librarians' whisper level, but their effectiveness improved not at all.

In 1960, stronger voices joined the choir. None was stronger than Alfred Aaronson's. Fresh from his triumph in securing the Gilcrease collection for Tulsans, Aaronson agreed to serve as the first chairman of the new Tulsa City-County Library Commission. He made sure that the board members who served with him would be neither quiet nor ineffective. Every one was a civic leader, and every one was a worker. Their work was to get a new library designed, approved, funded, and built.

It took only two years for Aaronson and his board to do the hard part. After an intense campaign to educate both the public and their officials, the library commission prepared for a multiquestion election. On July 1, 1962, county voters approved every part, beginning with the merger of the central library and its branches with five other

community libraries. They also approved a 1.9-mill library levy. The state's first levy explicitly for urban libraries, the tax guaranteed at least a tripling of library operational funding. Before leaving the polls, voters also approved a $3.8 million bond issue for capital construction and improvements.

It took another two years to complete the system's crowning jewel: a new downtown library. It was a beautifully designed, open, and inviting structure of 135,000 square feet. Its shelves held a good portion of the 125,000 new books purchased with the bond money. The remaining books went to one or more of twenty countywide branch libraries or seven bookmobiles. The bond issue financed construction of the seven new branch libraries and bought all of the bookmobiles. To staff the system, the library nearly doubled its number of employees.

Even more striking than the library's new physical facilities were the uses that the librarians, the library commission, and the community found for them. One entire floor of the new Central Library contained business and technical reports and reference works. These made available to Tulsa's citizens resources equal to those available to graduate students at a major university's school of business. Borrowing an idea from the Rochester Public Library, the Central Library began a series of book reviews combined with sack lunches, and many downtown workers began to look forward to the noontime "Books Sandwiched In" programs. The library system sponsored discussion groups on nearly every prominent social question, fearlessly facing even the most controversial. With state and federal grants, the library sponsored a three-part series entitled "Pride in Heritage." For many Tulsans, the series provided the first opportunity to meet and talk with their fellow citizens from the city's minority communities. The library scheduled several of those particular discussions and other public events in the Central Library's large and free-form meeting room. It was the Alfred Aaronson Auditorium.

No less than in its library, Tulsa had moved by cultural leagues in the few years after the Second World War. The postwar generation of Tulsans and the city's new residents had a range of cultural opportunities available in few American cities. They could immerse themselves in the Italian Renaissance at the Philbrook, examine the Gilcrease's copy of the first book published in the New World (Bishop Zumarraga's *Doctrine Breve* of 1544), walk through one of the nation's finest rose gardens, perhaps top the day off with a night at the opera—or at Cain's. Those inclined to read a good book had plenty to choose from at the Central Library or a branch nearby.

If asked to recommend a personal favorite, hardly any Tulsan would have suggested *Cimarron* by Edna Ferber. They may not have read it themselves, but they had no particular need to. After all, what could one say about a writer able to mistake a garden for a desert?

More THAN *Skin Deep*

The "miracle vaccine" developed by Dr. Jonas Salk eradicated polio as one of society's most feared diseases in the early 1950s. These students at Alsuma Separate School were among Tulsa's and Oklahoma's first to receive the Salk vaccine. They were, of course, separate but equal pioneers. Their school was merely separate.

THE FIRST ONE was bad enough. It happened to Helen Brown, a twenty-year-old expectant mother, and it happened on the morning of July 10, 1942. After Mrs. Brown had seen her husband, Bill, off to work, an unidentified assailant entered the couple's North Main Street home through an open window. Later that morning, neighbors discovered her and rushed Helen Brown to Saint John Hospital. The doctors could save neither her nor her unborn child. All they could do was tell the police that the killer had beaten Mrs. Brown across the face and strangled her into unconsciousness before brutally murdering her and the baby by stomping her belly. Police grilled Bill Brown for five intense hours before releasing him. County Attorney Dixie Gilmer had to admit that the authorities had no motive, no clues, and no suspect for the senseless, apparently random crime.

Within months, there were two more killings. Authorities believed that both were the work of Helen Brown's murderer. On January 14, 1943, attorney J. B. Underwood stopped by the north-side residence of his stenographer, Georgia Green. She had not come to work that day, and no one had answered his telephone calls to her home. After a neighbor let him in her duplex, Underwood discovered why. Both Georgia and her mother, Clara Luzila Stewart, lay sprawled in pools of blood. According to the medical examiner, the two had been bludgeoned by an ax and raped after their deaths.

Two years passed before the killer struck again. This

time the victim was Panta Lou Liles. The wife of an overseas soldier, the twenty-year-old worked at the Douglas bomber plant. In the early hours of March 15, 1945, someone entered her apartment at 501 North Cheyenne and killed her. Again, authorities had no suspect, only an observation: the most recent murder strikingly resembled those of Helen Brown, Georgia Green, and Clara Luzila Stewart. Had the term been in use, they might have said that there was a "serial killer" loose in Tulsa.

Over the next few months, detectives searched court records, trying to get a lead on a suspect. One among many possibilities was a thirty-three-year-old black man named Leroy Benton. Benton had begun a two-year term for rape when he was fifteen and since had worked as a porter at several Tulsa stores. It was that prior conviction, nearly twenty years old, that caught police attention and sent officers to his home next to the Greenwood brickyard. Benton was away at the time, but when a friend told him that the authorities had been looking for him, he innocently walked down to police headquarters. Without filing any charge against him and without mentioning that the Constitution guaranteed him the right to seek legal counsel, the police immediately arrested and jailed Leroy Benton.

For more than two weeks, Benton steadfastly maintained his innocence in the face of grueling interrogations. Finally, after a particularly brutal twelve-hour grilling, detectives took him to room 206 of the police station, seated him under an intense light, and began another round. The questioning was interrupted by what sounded like a lynch mob forming outside. The officer in charge then opened the door and shouted, "You keep them down there, and I will take care of this boy up here!" Leroy Benton's subsequent trial testimony—testimony never disputed by prosecutors—described what followed:

Q. What did he say when he came back after that?

A. He says to me, he said, "That is that mob; it looks like you are going to get it. We are just getting tired of fooling with you, it looks like you just want to get mobbed." He says, "Now, you come clean and tell us all about this now. You will be lucky to go to trial, and even if you do get to trial, you will probably be mobbed, and so will you [sic] attorneys."

Q. Well, after that, what did you say?

A. Well, I became afraid, and I says . . . "If I said I did it, and later on you find the real murderer, what will you do about getting me out of the penitentiary?" . . . and he said "Leroy, if such a thing does happen, I will spend the balance of my life trying to get you out of the penitentiary. I will even go to the county attorney and do all I can to get you out, if it costs me my job."

Q. Then what did you say?

A. I told him to call the county attorney.

Leroy Benton thereupon "confessed" to the crime of murdering Panta Lou Liles. As confessions go, it was a poor one. Benton was unable to relate any significant details about the crime or even describe the crime scene. Presumably because it was so patently defective, the authorities told Benton that they had to save him from another lynching and removed him to the Okmulgee jail, where they tried to extract an improved confession. Again, Benton neither could recreate the crime nor portray the scene. They then took him to Kansas City and administered a lie-detector test. There must have been results, but the police and prosecutors never disclosed any. In a final effort to secure a damning confession, they placed him in a McAlester, Oklahoma, prison cell with a black inmate. Although the state offered to commute the prisoner's death sentence to life imprisonment in exchange for an incriminating statement from Benton, the convict could do no better than the lawmen. Benton only protested his innocence. Meanwhile, the laboratories of the Federal Bureau of Investigation completed a report on the forensic evidence collected from the crime scene. None of it conclusively pointed to Benton's guilt; much of it (if presented at trial) would serve to exonerate him.

Amid raw feelings and near hysteria, the Tulsa county attorney vigorously prosecuted Leroy Benton. His most damning piece of evidence was the confession extracted by the Tulsa Police Department. Ignoring the circumstances of that confession, a jury of Tulsans convicted Leroy Benton of first-degree murder and sentenced him to life in the state prison. It took them three years, but his attorneys finally got Leroy Benton's case before the Oklahoma Criminal Court of Appeals. In a singular decision, the appellate court unanimously and disdainfully reversed the jury's verdict, freed Leroy Benton, and ordered Tulsa authorities to file no other charges against him.

Almost exactly four months later—on July 2, 1948—someone brutally killed and raped Mrs. J. B. Cole, her daughter Doris, and a visiting friend, LeVon Gabbard. The same person also raped and murdered their neighbor, Ruth Norton. All of the victims lived on North Cheyenne, near the site of the previous slayings. Police theorized that these were the work of the same killer. They did not know (and they never learned) who it was. It was not, however, Leroy Benton. Leroy Benton already had moved to Hammond, Indiana.

Leroy Benton was not Dick Rowland, and 1945 was not 1921. Many things had changed, even if it was obvious that quite a few had not. World War II planted seeds of changes, and in the postwar years, Tulsans harvested their fruit. Leroy Benton probably was one of the beneficiaries, and his experience was not unique in one respect: The changes that other Tulsans gathered and tasted were also bittersweet.

During the Second World War, hundreds of Tulsa's black men and women had their first experience as industrial workers. African-Americans found new jobs in Tulsa's defense plants. With few exceptions, all worked as common laborers or semi-skilled helpers. Because of the shortage of white labor, the oil industry and other big employers also began hiring several hundred blacks. By the war's end, Tulsa's forty-four major oil companies and four hundred smaller firms in other industries were employing black workers, many for the first time. Again, few held classifications above laborers or service employees, but at least they were classified.

The war's principal economic impact upon black Tulsa may have been indirect. The several hundred black defense workers took their paychecks back to Greenwood and spent most of their hard-earned dollars in their own community. Those dollars flowed into Greenwood along with other money spent by workers newly employed by oil or other companies. Nearly every dollar spent in Greenwood stayed in Greenwood. Some of those dollars went to black-owned clothing stores and ended up in the pay envelopes of clerks hired to handle the improved business. Some of those clerks' dollars paid black-owned dry cleaners. Some of the dry cleaners' profits bought cosmetics at black-owned drugstores. The teenagers who worked the stores' counters bought movie tickets at the Dreamland Theater or paid to hear Ernie Fields and his band. As their business grew, theaters and clubs hired new employees.

James W. Jones, owner and proprietor of Greenwood's Jones Drug

AFRICAN-AMERICAN WAR WORKERS AT THE DOUGLAS PLANT.

The result was that Greenwood's black-owned businesses reversed the depression's long downward spiral and experienced an economic rebirth. By 1945, few cities comparable to Tulsa in size had anything like its number or variety of black-run businesses. At the war's end, Greenwood contained 242 black-owned and black-operated businesses. Some represented investments as great as $45,000. Collectively, they employed about eight hundred of Greenwood's residents.

White Tulsans, few of whom ever ventured into Greenwood, scarcely noticed the community's improved economic vitality, but they could not escape at least one of its effects. It seemed that wherever two or three white women gathered, one or more was sure to complain that it was getting harder and harder to find good "help." It would have been more accurate to have said it was getting harder to find good, cheap help, but the prevailing social ethos scarcely permitted that way of looking at it.

Left, Caver's French
Cleaners and Ed
Benton's Busy Bee.
Below, a proud driver
of Mann Brothers
grocery in days when
marketing was done by
telephone. Privately
owned recreation
centers were popular
in Greenwood, largely
because official city
policy forbade blacks
access to publicly
owned facilities.
Shops, professional
offices, and hotels
remained economically
viable until
desegregation and
urban renewal
combined to deal a
deathblow to
Greenwood as a
commercial center.

Their husbands had similar conversations when they met for lunch at the their downtown clubs or over drinks at Southern Hills. Talk often turned to rumors that "those people" were organizing to demand what the federal government was calling "fair employment practices." Rarely pondered and less often expressed was any awareness that there might be anything particularly unfair about existing employment practices.

Gossip common to both genders (but to only one race) was that the black domestics had formed so-called bumper clubs. The ostensible purpose of these not-so-secret clubs was for servants to spend their days off riding buses and frequenting Tulsa's many "whites-only" public places, so they could push and bump white people, just to cause "trouble." Apparently innocent of any notion that their domestics might have something better to do on their own time, many whites believed and spread the rumor. Alerted to the danger, the ever-vigilant police department turned up no evidence that the "help"—good or otherwise—had organized either bumper or pusher clubs.

Still, all that talk was indication of the most important change that the war had brought to black Tulsa. While hundreds of men and women had gained their first taste of industrial employment, many hundreds more of Greenwood's sons

BROS.
& MKT.
Sell
R PRICE
in the Week

and daughters had worn their country's military uniforms. It was true that official policy had put them in a Jim Crow army and a Jim Crow navy, but they had served. They had fought the war that freed Europe's millions from racism. The victory won, the liberators were ready for a little liberation themselves.

There were white Tulsans who sensed directly and accurately how powerful were the consequences. One unidentified but obviously insightful white businessman put it this way to a researcher with the National Urban League:

> I am concerned over the hostility of many whites toward the Negroes.
> Many whites fail to recognize the changes in the Negro due to the war and his new concept of thinking.

Even without the war, there were black Tulsans who long since had rejected what the informant might have called the old concepts of thinking. One was an attorney who had represented Leroy Benton. His name was Amos Hall.

As one of only a dozen or so licensed attorneys in the Greenwood district, Amos Hall had a considerable legal practice. In addition to routine commercial and domestic matters, circumstances in Tulsa gave a black lawyer a wide, if rough, field for criminal practice. A single sensational crime or a publicized pattern of lesser ones could so arouse the citizenry that the police employed massive dragnets and hauled in scores of suspects innocent of anything except their presence. Given the slightest pretext, police also still made it a practice to take in blacks found in white neighborhoods after sundown.

Rarely did the authorities press formal charges against those enmeshed in dragnets or caught in the wrong parts of town. Instead, parked squad cars and Greenwood's separate station and jail provided opportunities for admonitions, sometimes of the physical variety. In a single year (1944), the city did file criminal charges against 2,521 black residents, a sizable portion of the African-American population eighteen and older. The vast majority of arrests were for minor offenses against antiliquor and antigambling ordinances or for "loitering." Such strict enforcement, unknown in white, middle-class neighborhoods, kept the police, the courts, and the attorneys occupied—at the cost of a noticeable tilting of the scales of justice.

In proceedings revealing the most skewed imbalance, Amos Hall worked to right the scales through long, involved, costly, and often frustrating advocacy. The case of Leroy Benton was merely one of these, and a little-noticed one at that. Amos Hall did, however, deserve national recognition. This black attorney from Tulsa's Greenwood district was the one who set in motion the series of cases that struck at injustice in its most systematic and pernicious form. That was legally mandated racial segregation in the public schools—the public schools of Tulsa, of Oklahoma, and (ultimately) of America.

THE SMALL HOTEL, ONE OF THE MOST
SUCCESSFUL OF GREENWOOD'S MANY
HOTELS AND ROOMING HOUSES, WAS
LEGENDARY ACROSS THE ENTIRE
SOUTHWEST'S SO-CALLED CHITLIN
CIRCUIT. BLACK BANDS AND
MUSICIANS PLAYING TULSA FILLED THE
SMALL'S ROOMS. THROUGH ITS
LOBBY PASSED ARTISTS SUCH AS NAT
"KING" COLE, DUKE ELLINGTON, AND
COUNT BASIE — THE LATTER HAVING
BEGUN HIS CAREER ON A GREENWOOD
SIDEWALK, PLAYING PIANO TO ATTRACT
AN AUDIENCE FOR HIS EMPLOYER, A
PATENT-MEDICINE SALESMAN.

Tulsa's public schools, of course, had been segregated for exactly as long as there had been public
schools. Every one of the city's 2,543 African-American students enrolled in 1945 attended one of three
all-black elementary schools, all-black Carver Junior
High School, or all-black Booker T. Washington
High School. The latter occupied one of the few
Greenwood buildings to survive the race riot, and it
had deteriorated to the point that it posed a threat to
its students' health, not to mention to their education.

Oklahoma had been the only state to enter the
union with a constitution that explicitly mandated
the separation of "colored" students from "all others." In addition, the constitution created a Jim Crow
method of school financing. White schools levied
property taxes and voted bonds on a district-by-dis-
trict basis. A "separate school fund" financed black

schools with taxes on a countywide basis. Bond issues to benefit black schools also had to win the approval of voters in the entire county. Because the constitution also required that any bond issue had to carry by at least 60 percent of the votes cast, the task was forbidding in counties with small black populations. Although Tulsa County consistently ranked with Oklahoma and Muskogee Counties as having the greatest number of black residents, its proportion of African-American voters never equaled even a tenth of the county's total. The result was that Oklahoma voters often refused bond proposals to improve black schools. An exception came just after World War II, when Tulsa County did vote a million-dollar bond issue, the bulk of it pledged to build a new, modern Booker T. Washington.

The decision may have spoken well of county voters, but it also may have reflected something other than disinterested generosity. Right after the war, the National Association for the Advancement of Colored People (NAACP) launched a frontal assault upon legally sanctioned racism in its many forms. Under the command of Thurgood Marshall, its Legal Defense Fund fired off an artillery barrage of lawsuits challenging discrimination in voting, in housing, and in education. Every suit in every jurisdiction raising every issue had the same ultimate purpose: to overturn the legal fiction of "separate but equal." First promulgated by the United States Supreme Court in its infamous 1896 decision, *Plessy v. Ferguson,* the doctrine had justified racial discrimination by pretending that governments could meet the Constitution's requirement of "equal protection of the laws" with actions that, although treating citizens differently, nonetheless treated them equally.

Under that doctrine, Oklahoma was one of seventeen states (plus the District of Columbia) that either required or permitted racially separate schools. In such jurisdictions, any claim of equal education was too ludicrous for precise measure. One could calculate only its approximate shortcomings. In every tangible regard—per pupil expenditures, teachers' salaries, value of physical plant, money spent on books and equipment—the figures were always separate but never equal.

For that reason, the NAACP directed one of its earliest rounds of lawsuits at forcing states and districts just to meet *Plessy*'s test. If whites insisted upon separate schools, they had to finance them equitably. To head off such challenges, many states and districts began to be more generous toward their minority schools. Tulsa already paid black and white teachers equally, and the money devoted to building a new Booker T. provided a defense for maintaining a separate Booker T. as well.

There was no doubt that separation remained the state's resolve. In 1941, the legislature had buttressed its segregation laws with new statutes making it a crime for an administrator to admit even one student of a different race to his or her school. A teacher likewise became criminally liable for instructing a single student of a different race. Every student who shared a classroom with any student of another race also violated the law. Each day's offense carried the penalty of a separate (but equal) fine.

If Oklahoma's officialdom thereby expected to frighten off challengers, it badly miscalculated. Within a month of V-J Day (August 16, 1945), the state NAACP assembled in McAlester and announced plans to attack Oklahoma's version of segregation at its most vulnerable point. Not even *Plessy* could protect Oklahoma's policies that denied black citizens access even to separate state schools. That was precisely the case for professional and graduate education. By law, black Oklahomans could receive higher education only at Langston University, but Langston offered no professional degrees for aspiring African-American doctors, dentists, attorneys, veterinarians, and the like. Neither did it offer graduate degrees. Heretofore, African-Americans who sought such degrees had been forced to leave their state to earn them.

Oklahoma's failure opened a window upon "separate but equal" as practiced. Forcing others to look into that window required an able and devoted litigator as well as a courageous and determined client. Tulsa provided both, one directly, the other indirectly. Amos Hall's courtroom success against injustice at all levels made him the obvious choice as the lead attorney, charged with identifying plaintiffs, initiating actions, filing papers, preparing briefs, and arguing points of Oklahoma law and procedure. As the initial plaintiff, Hall and others selected the daughter of a couple who came to Tulsa in 1918 and left it for Chickasha in 1921, when Tulsa's rioters burned their home and the little church that the husband had pastored. The church had been the North Greenwood Church of God in Christ. The couple was the Reverend Travis B. and Martha Bell Sipuel. Their daughter was a twenty-one-year-old honors graduate of Langston, Ada Lois Sipuel. Her January 1946 application to attend the all-white law school at the University of Oklahoma brought the artillery fire of black civil rights directly into the trenches of Oklahoma's justice system.

Before it was finished, the legal battle drew a battery of fire directed by some of the nation's foremost civil-rights attorneys. Thurgood Marshall himself assumed oversight and brought along his top assistants from the Legal Defense Fund, Robert Carter and James Nabritt. Marshall prepared most of the appellate work and anxiously sought to practice an art with which he had become familiar, oral argument before the United States Supreme Court. On the state's behalf, Attorney General Mac Q. Williamson and his cocounsel, acting OU law dean Maurice Merrill, liked to refer to their adversaries as "New York lawyers," a bunch of "outsiders." The terms were both irrelevant and inaccurate. Amos Hall, a Greenwood lawyer and insider if there ever was one, handled every significant detail and prepared every court brief.

The legal battle affirmed several things. One was that the mills of justice, like those of the gods, do grind slowly. The process that began with Ada Lois Sipuel's filing of an OU application consumed years of repeated hearings at the district court in Cleveland County and appeals to the state supreme court. They ended five years later, only after Marshall had his chance with two separate appearances on her behalf before the United States Supreme Court.

Justice might have moved more swiftly had the state responded with less determined resistance and less creative racism. Finally ordered by the U. S. Supreme Court to provide Miss Sipuel a legal education and to do so as soon as it did for any white student, Oklahoma created an overnight school for exactly one student: the Langston University College of Law. Placing it in the capitol's basement and hiring three part-time Oklahoma City attorneys as its entire faculty, the state pretended sincere amazement when the plaintiff refused to attend it. Oklahoma was shocked, shocked to learn that neither Miss Sipuel nor anyone else accepted it as equal to the long-established school at Norman.

When other black Oklahomans—including George W. McLaurin, a retired Langston professor—applied to the University of Oklahoma graduate school, the state reluctantly admitted them but proceeded to use chains and ropes to separate black from white students in their classrooms as well as in the library, student union, football stadium, and every other campus facility. Some observed that it was not the first time that authorities had used chains and ropes on black people.

Amos Hall and Thurgood Marshall thereupon fired off another assault, this one with McLaurin as the named plaintiff. Once more, the case went all the way to the U. S. Supreme Court. The Court used the occasion to lecture Oklahoma on the meaning of the Constitution. "Equal protection of the laws," the Court declared, required that a state not only provide black applicants higher learning but also must not segregate them once in school. The ropes and chains disappeared at OU, but a much more important question remained. The McLaurin case finally made it unavoidable.

George McLaurin heard the same lectures, read the same books, took the same exams, ate the same food, even watched the same football games as did white students. In every respect, Oklahoma accorded him a school experience perfectly identical to that of his white classmates. It was in his separation and only in his separation that the state had violated his Constitutional right to "equal protection of the laws." How, then, could any state or any school system avoid the same impermissible error if it operated entire school systems that separated the children of one race from those of another? The answer of the landmark *Brown v. Board of Education* (1954) was that it could not. There was no such thing as "separate but equal." Separate schools were inherently unequal schools. As such, they were repugnant to the American Constitution.

The decision had been a long time coming. That it came at all owed everything to the precedents established by Tulsa's Amos Hall and the daughter of a Tulsa family that had managed to see a better day coming, even in the smoke and fire of a riot a third of a century earlier.

In Tulsa, there was almost no overt resistance to the High Court's decision. Neither was there much immediate impact. Beginning with the 1955-1956 school term, the school board eliminated all reference to race in assigning pupils to schools. Instead, it redrew attendance zones to emphasize "neighborhood" schools. At the same time, the board adopted a policy that allowed students whose race was in the minority at their neighborhood schools to transfer to others in which theirs was the majority race. The consequence was that any immediate school integration became purely of the token variety.

That was so easily foreseeable that it could not have been unintentional. The neighborhoods that provided each school's enrollment may well have been as thoroughly segregated as any in America. At World War II's end, the city's black population generally remained huddled in Greenwood. Restrictive covenants still forbade blacks' owning or occupying homes across most of the city, but especially in the neighborhoods nearest Greenwood. The occasional white property owner who was willing to rent or sell to blacks usually gave up when neighbors threatened court actions to enforce the covenant and block the transaction.

Greenwood became ever more crowded and its housing stock became ever more dilapidated. In 1940, 59 percent of its housing units lacked running water, and 72 percent were not worth even $1,000. Tulsa's black community essentially had two choices, both of them poor, in the immediate postwar years. Some occupied the 250 homes still standing from those tacked together for wartime workers. The number was not large, and the segregated housing market made them more expensive than they should have been. The only other choice was to move into new subdivisions that builders were throwing up outside Tulsa's city limits. Builders made money, but the buyers were stuck in areas without electricity, gas, water, or sewer lines, and the city displayed no great urge to annex the black-occupied districts.

While fighting with Oklahoma over allowing black students' admission to its state university, NAACP attorneys also took on the entire American real estate industry. The key suit came from Saint Louis, and it provided one of the NAACP's earliest postwar victories. In the 1948 case known as *Shelley v. Kraemer,* the United States Supreme Court ruled that racially restrictive covenants could not be enforced by courts. The decision did not immediately remedy private discrimination, but it meant that third parties no longer could use the legal system to promote it.

Tulsa was one of the few cities in which the decision had little immediate impact. Even in Oklahoma City, blacks began moving into previously all-white neighborhoods almost immediately. In Tulsa, it was 1957—nearly a full decade later—before there was discernible movement of the city's black population. The reason was simple: Tulsa lending companies generally refused blacks mortgage money to buy property in white neighborhoods. In fact, the first black families able to get home loans borrowed through lenders in Oklahoma City. Once these families broke the psychological barrier, the financial barrier cracked too.

Economics and geography, as much as anything else, established the patterns of the resulting relocation. Black income improved significantly during the fifties but still remained too low to permit any significant migration into south Tulsa's pricier neighborhoods. A skein of railroad tracks and an industrial district immediately east of the existing black area defined a barrier in that direction. The population, therefore, shifted north and west, generally north of Pine Street and west toward Cincinnati.

Consider the tract bounded roughly by Pine on the south, Peoria on the east, Apache on the north, and Cincinnati on the west. In 1950, blacks occupied only sixty-four of the more than one thousand housing units in the area, and nearly all of those lay in the extreme southeast corner, the area bordering Greenwood. Ten years later, 802 of the neighborhood's 1,198 housing units (67 percent) had black residents. All but a few score of those had arrived within the previous thirty-six months.

The neighborhood had changed decidedly—with decided consequence for the neighborhood school. With the addition of the area lying to its west across Cincinnati and the Reservoir Hill district at its north, this was the community served by one of Tulsa's largest and most prestigious elementary schools: "Big John" Burroughs. Before the *Brown* decision, Burroughs had been all-white by overt policy. Just after *Brown,* the neighborhood-school strategy left it all-white except for a few token black students. At the end of the 1956-1957 school year, Burroughs' enrollment of about one thousand included exactly seven African-American children. A year later, black enrollment reached sixty-five, a small proportion, to be sure, but enough to indicate the beginnings of major demographic change.

To some, the change was not only significant but frightening. During the 1957-1958 school year, occasional cross burnings lit night skies in the area. Terrorists dynamited one home newly purchased by blacks. No one ever identified the responsible parties, and most of the area's white population expressed disgust and shame at what had happened. Ironically, the principal effect may have been to increase the neigh-

Tulsa skyline, 1927.

borhood's black population. The violence encouraged "white flight" out of a neighborhood perceived as unsafe.

There were other inducements as well. Not least of them was some realtors' practice of spreading fearful rumors that encouraged white property owners to list homes to sell quickly and sell cheaply before they became surrounded by blacks and their values disappeared. As rumors go, this one was terribly effective because this one was self-fulfilling. Every new "For Sale" sign spawned dozens of others. Homeowners panicked lest they become the last white family in the neighborhood.

For Burroughs Elementary School, the effect was a swift increase in black enrollment. The sixty-five black students enrolled in May of 1958 grew to nearly three hundred by February of 1959—roughly 30 percent of school enrollment. School officials addressed the rapidly changing situation with what amounted to no policy at all. The school's Parent-Teacher Association had no black members and could muster only three affirmative votes (out of thirty) on the question of having black homeroom mothers. Burroughs (like every other Tulsa school) continued to have a segregated faculty; all of its teachers were white. Superintendent Charles Mason proclaimed that any problem at Burroughs was one of real estate, not education, and that the school system would treat it like any other Tulsa school. Other than that, the educational leadership only tried to calm parents' concerns by projecting that Burroughs' black enrollment would stay at about 30 percent for the 1959-1960 academic year.

Anxious white parents filled Burroughs's massive front playground on the first

day of school in 1959. Most were there to count the number of black children filing through the big front doors to begin the school year. Before noon, no one really had to wait for the school system's final tally: Burroughs had an enrollment 52 percent white and 48 percent black. At least one mother already had made her decision. As one of her friends described it, she

THE BURROUGHS

PLAYGROUND, AFTER

THE SCHOOL HAD

BEEN "INTEGRATED."

COURTESY TULSA

PUBLIC SCHOOLS.

> went over to school right after enrollment took place and in the grade her child was in, the white children were in a minority, and she saw what looked to her like a whole sea of black faces and she absolutely went to pieces. She became hysterical. . . . This was the breaking point for her. They moved so they were in another school district.

As it turned out, school officials were more than receptive to this woman's alarm. Tulsa Public Schools permitted children to transfer from the neighborhood schools, but only under well-defined circumstances. One was for health reasons. If a child's parents and physician declared that his or her health would be impaired by attending the neighborhood school, the superintendent's office would authorize transfer to another school. During the first weeks of the fall of 1959, a blizzard of written requests fell upon Mason's desk, as parents colluded with doctors to claim that their children's health, usually their emotional health, was endangered by their presence in a school that was nearly half-black. Understanding and sympathetic school officials routinely and promptly passed out transfers.

It did not take long. On September 25, 1959, the school system issued a press release to announce that it had moved enough white children from Burroughs to make it a majority-black school. That was the news. The statement's point, however, was to remind parents that, since their children now comprised the minority, white children were eligible for transfers on the majority-to-minority basis. In fact, school officials carefully instructed parents how to take advantage of the policy, suggested other schools they might prefer, and provided precise numbers showing the racial composition of each alternative, two of which were still all-white. The formula amounted to a step-by-step recipe for segregation.

Most of those who wanted out got out. Not quite a year later, the school opened the 1960-1961 school year with an enrollment that was 85 percent black. Burroughs began the 1961-1962 year with 954 students, only 28 of which (less than 3 percent) were white. What had been an all-white school had become, for all practical purposes, an all-black one.

Within seven years, what Amos Hall and others had fought so hard to achieve had come—and gone. First Burroughs, then Emerson Elementary, then other northside schools resegregated. The neighborhoods that surrounded them went the same way, as hundreds of white families made the choice that the unnamed white mother had made upon visiting her child's classroom on the first day of school, 1959. Most of those families who fled lost money, but they were willing to pay a steep price to live in another part of Tulsa.

Their black fellow Tulsans finally had more choice of better housing. Once more, though, it usually was housing in all- or nearly all-black neighborhoods. Once more, their children went to all- or nearly all-black schools. That was the price they paid to live in their part of Tulsa.

Both Tulsa's white families and Tulsa's black families paid heavy prices, but the city that was home to both paid a greater one. For all the changes that had come, Tulsa remained a city in which race, like beauty, was more than skin deep.

Palaces of Illusion

THE AKDAR THEATER

THE RITZ THEATER HAD UNIFORMED USHERS
TO SHOW MOVIEGOERS TO THEIR SEATS.

The Delman

WILL ROGERS THEATER

THE MAJESTIC

THE PLAZA

THE ORPHEUM

Convention Hall

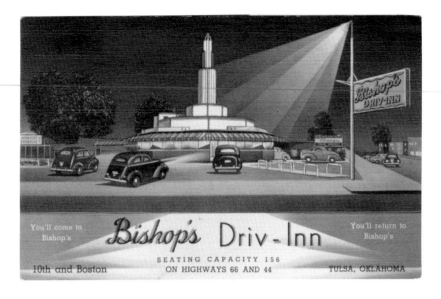

PRECEDING PAGES:
GRETCHEN HARALSON
CAPTURED THE ESSENCE OF A
COMFORTABLE FIFTIES FAMILY
IN THIS PHOTO OF DR. AND
MRS. EUGENE LEWIS AND
THEIR CHILDREN. BELOW,
BASEBALL FROM THE TULSA
OILERS 1963 SEASON. PEPPER
MARTIN, A NATIVE
OKLAHOMAN, COACHED THE
OILERS, AND GROVER
RESINGER WAS THEIR
MANAGER. ABOVE, WHEN
BISHOP'S DRIV-INN OPENED,
ITS LOCATION AT TENTH AND
BOSTON WAS CONSIDERED
SOUTH TULSA.

For such a reputedly democratic people, Americans are much given to rankings. Neither Tulsans nor Oklahomans are exceptions. The state's fans of the University of Oklahoma football team are particularly renowned for their chants that the Sooners are Number One—and notorious for a glumness that enshrouds them should the team fall below that level or (horror of horrors!) drop out of the rankings altogether. More sophisticated Tulsans might pretend to be above such as that, but one can imagine even their joy in 1972 when *Fortune* magazine told the nation that Tulsa was the second best of the country's fifty largest cities.

tulsa
TOMORROW

TULSA METROPOLITAN AREA PLANNING COMMISSION

Seattle, Washington, ranked higher, but Tulsa outpaced Dallas (in the twentieth spot), Los Angeles (twenty-second), New York (thirty-second), and Chicago (forty-eighth).

The magazine's overall rankings rested upon a seemingly firm and objective basis: a statistical analysis of each city's separate scores on twenty-four qualities of contemporary urban life. In such categories as its robbery rate (third lowest of the fifty), overall personal health (second best), rate of homeownership (third highest), and measurable air quality (fourth best), Tulsa consistently ranked at or near the very top. Those were the kind of qualities that gave Tulsa its high standing—even if *Fortune* declared that Tulsa's merits "may surprise most people who don't live there." Those who did live there, however, found their hometown pride justly affirmed.

If Tulsans did not break out in a chant that "We're Number Two," neither did they swell up in glumness. Any swelling was purely of the pride variety, and the local attitude was closer to smugness than glumness. In short order, the city found itself the beneficiary of an even more impressive title. Those who were supposed to know such things officially designated Tulsa an "All-American City." If less imaginative than "the Magic City" and less impressive than "the Oil Capital of the World," Tulsa's newest title did have one thing to recommend it. It was true.

In the post–World War II years, Tulsa became an All-American city in several ways. Delivered from its dependence upon a single, regional industry, its modern economy began broadening into a fair reflection of the entire nation's. Luck was no more responsible for that than it was for the city's original emergence. Tulsans and others deliberately made it that way, even if they did not always reckon on all of the consequences. Like the nation's economy, Tulsa's moved and swayed to great currents that swept from coast to coast until they eventually encircled the globe. There was irony here, for Tulsans (and Americans) had achieved an economic success that lashed it to new forms of international interdependence.

Many of those economic changes assumed physical expressions, a manufacturing plant with worldwide sales here, an office building for an international corporation there, not to mention a huge concrete-lined river running from Tulsa's doorstep toward the sea. The city's skyline regularly rose, and its borders steadily stretched. The horizontal growth was by far the more important. Other concrete rivers, these carrying swarms of cars on the land's surface, carried Tulsans to new jobs, new homes—and to new problems. These were not Tulsa's alone, since nearly every American city of comparable size had similar experiences and confronted similar problems.

If Tulsa did have a singular claim, it lay in its early and innovative attempts to address those problems. A comprehensive metropolitan development plan and a creative scheme to integrate its public schools attracted the national attention that helped earn Tulsa its designation as an All-American City. Tulsans rightly took pride in that in the 1970s.

More than two decades later, that pride remained. What remained too were the issues and tensions that their award-winning efforts had left unresolved. Again, there was irony. It seemed that Tulsans' much-admired designs had only worsened them.

If so, Tulsans deserved no shame. Theirs may not have been America's best city, but neither was Tulsa its worst. The issues, the tensions, the plans, the successes, and the failures—all of these were part of Tulsa's history in precisely the same measure that they also were part of America's history. Whatever else Tulsans had done or ever would do, they had not yet and would not ever escape their own history.

What they had done and always would do was much more than that. They had contributed to America's history, and they would continue to do so. In that respect, Tulsa's future would resemble its past. Tulsans would keep on adding their own measure to the sum of America's hopes, of its dreams, of its successes, and of its failures. In doing so, they would make both Tulsa's history and America's too. It could be no other way. After all, Tulsa was an All-American City.

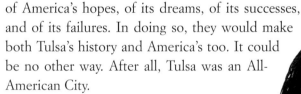

When aviator Amelia Earhart landed her autogyro at Tulsa Municipal Airport in 1932, the city's commercial future augured to depend entirely upon modern air transport. Ironically, much of its economic development eventually came to rely upon the oldest form of commercial traffic: river barges.

Damnation and Benefaction

WHEN THE RAIN first started falling on May 7, 1943, drought-weary Oklahomans regarded it as something of a godsend. The rain fell steadily through the next day, and they counted their needs fulfilled and thanked the Almighty. But it continued on, falling hard and ceaselessly through the ninth, the tenth, into the eleventh of May. By then the apparent blessing had become an obvious tribulation, and benediction had turned to blasphemy. Twenty-four inches had fallen on Muskogee; Tulsa had received twenty. In each, the five-day total was more than might reasonably have been expected for an entire year. Tulsa experienced minor flooding, but the Arkansas River, fed by rain-swollen streams below Tulsa, leaped its banks at Muskogee before cresting at 38.3 feet, one-and-one-half feet above any previous level known.

Two days later, on May 13, the rain began again. It lasted a week before finally breaking. The Arkansas rose to 48.2 feet this time and flowed as much as 700,000 cubic feet of water every second. Up and down the river, from above Tulsa to Pine Bluff, Arkansas, and beyond, the river had its way. Swirling waters colored by the rich topsoil of two states washed out bridges, ruined highways, toppled oil derricks, dislocated holding tanks, destroyed crops, inundated fields, drowned livestock, flooded downtowns, ravaged homes, and wrecked lives. It took three years just to survey the damage and calculate the cost. The final figures were 1,448,400 acres (nearly 2,300 square miles) of land flooded, $31,130,300 in property destroyed, and 26 known killed.

On the afternoon of the first clear day, Don McBride, a water expert with the Oklahoma Planning and Resources Board, drafted a memorandum outlining the disaster's known dimensions and delivered it to the Governor's Mansion that night. The governor who read it was Robert Samuel Kerr. The next morning, Kerr and McBride drove to Tulsa, where they met Colonel Francis "Babe" Wilson, director of the U. S. Army Corps of Engineers' Tulsa District. Wilson already had requisitioned a government plane from the corps's Denver office. The three—Don McBride, Governor Kerr, and Colonel Wilson—spent the next two hours in the air, nearly mute as they surveyed the devastation beneath them. There are people who knew Bob Kerr who say that those were the two most important hours in the man's whole life. There also are Tulsans who say that they were the two most important hours in the city's entire history.

What Bob Kerr saw during those two hours was his political future. Joseph Howell, a longtime *Tulsa Tribune* reporter and Kerr watcher, remembers Kerr's saying that "here was a ready made issue which no one in politics was using and which he could make his exclusively." What Tulsans gained was a powerful advocate, one destined to grow far more powerful, for a notion that had been tossed around for nearly forty years: navigation of the Arkansas River.

Those who knew the river in its normal state might charitably have pronounced the idea fanciful. Cynics would have called it crazy. For much of the year, the Arkansas was less a free-flowing river than a vast sand bed scarring the face of northeastern Oklahoma. In the hot summer months, there were times when Tulsans could walk across it, jumping from sandbar to sandbar, scarcely getting their shoes wet. There were other times, though, when the river repaid those who would mock it so. Between 1907 and 1961, it flooded Tulsa's low-lying neighborhoods fifty times.

Either way, the Arkansas was no obvious candidate as a dependable waterway. Even an Oklahoman, United States Congressman A. S. "Mike" Monroney, told his colleagues on the House Rivers and Harbors Committee that "nine out of ten Oklahoma citizens would be willing to appropriate money to pave the Arkansas River," but neither they nor he thought it sensible to do anything else with it. According to the Fifth District representative, any money spent to render it navigable amounted to a "gigantic pork barrel boondoggle."

In politics, one man's boondoggle is often another man's breadbasket, one man's fantasy another's vision. On both counts, Mike Monroney more than met his match in Tulsa's Newton R. Graham. A longtime chamber director and banker, Graham took charge of the Tulsa Clearing House Association in 1934. The job gave him a secure and sizable income. More important, it freed his time for Graham's one true mission: building support for river navigation of the Arkansas. Wherever two or three would gather together, there he would be also, preaching the gospel of navigating the Arkansas. Any Tulsa club or group that needed a speaker and a presentation could find the first in Newt Graham and the second in Tulsa's glorious future once it was

opened to waterborne commerce. Oklahoma's many commercial clubs and professional organizations heard him so often that many of their members thought he must be a member himself. Every assembly of boosters of every river in every state found him there, actively pushing the case for the Arkansas. In countless trips to Washington, he made his face, his voice, and his vision known in congressional offices and committee rooms. He tirelessly enlisted support; assembled data; and constructed charts, maps, and graphs of cheaper freight rates, projected tonnage, and other benefits.

In time, people began to refer to Newt Graham as the "Admiral of the Arkansas," and he wore the title proudly. Colonel Wilson later told the story of how he had arrived in Tulsa in 1942, his plate already heaped high with war-related orders from Washington. The army already had directed him to build five flying schools, transform four municipal airports to military uses, construct an entire air base at Enid, build a bombing run on the Great Salt Plains, and erect several camps for prisoners of war. According to Wilson, he had not been in his new office ten minutes when Newt Graham burst in, shook his hand, and instructed the colonel on his mission: "I'm sure glad you are going to be here to help us get navigation for the Arkansas."

The disastrous floods of May 1943 gave Newt Graham his most valuable ally of all. Before entering politics, Kerr had been an oilman. A millionaire many times over, he brought to the governorship a determination to lift the state from the lingering depression and rebuild it as a modern commonwealth. In the roiling waters of the 1943 flood, Kerr saw a way to do that. An interlocked series of giant, multipurpose dams would make the Arkansas navigable all the way to the Mississippi and from there to the sea. The rebuilt river would lower the freight rates that long had stifled Oklahoma's commerce. Farmers could ship their crops, oilmen their products,

THE TULSA PORT OF CATOOSA IN 1975, FOUR YEARS AFTER ITS FORMAL OPENING AS A $2 BILLION PUBLICLY FUNDED PROJECT PROMISING COMMERCIAL REBIRTH AND REGIONAL ECONOMIC DEVELOPMENT.

and manufacturers their goods cheaply and globally. Raw materials would flood Oklahoma and finished products would flow from it. Dams and reservoirs would protect Oklahoma's farms and communities from floods and preserve the state's waters against droughts. They would provide its people new forms of recreation, cheap sources of power, and the basis for reclaiming the tired land. In every way, Oklahoma would exchange its outworn past for a bright, shining, unlimited future. On all of that, there was complete and absolute agreement between Governor Kerr and Admiral Graham.

Kerr provided Newt Graham some very heavy artillery. It was among his fellow Tulsans, however, that he found the troops necessary to win his campaign. In 1946, Congress prepared to write its first major postwar rivers and harbors bill. After approaching the city's elite of oilmen, merchants, bankers, manufacturers, and attorneys, Graham persuaded the chamber to host a dinner for them at the Mayo Hotel. In a rousing address, he spelled out the question for Tulsa in terms that Tulsans understood:

> Unless we tell our story vividly and in detail we cannot hope for success. If this is to be done, Tulsa must do it. Muskogee and Fort Smith are, after all, small second-class cities and while Little Rock is a good sized city, it yet is a lazy southern town, strong on desire but slow in performance. All of them will follow—none of them will lead. Having drilled this hole to the top of the deep formation, is Tulsa willing to bring in the well?

The answer was never in doubt. The people assembled that evening did not leave the Mayo until they had pledged $80,000 to fund the new Arkansas Basin Development Association (ABDA). The assembly picked Newt Graham to be its president. He surrounded himself with vice presidents culled from Tulsa's most powerful elite: merchants John Dunkin, Gary Vandever, and Maurice Sanditen; oilman Charles Klein; steelmaker N. R. Patterson; and Russell Rhodes, general manager of the Tulsa Chamber of Commerce.

An army of nearly 120 ABDA representatives and other businesspeople from Oklahoma and Arkansas invaded Washington in May of 1946 for hearings scheduled by the House Rivers and Harbors Committee. Don McBride and others testified as expert witnesses. Newt Graham produced Corps of Engineers figures to demonstrate that every dollar spent on Arkansas projects would yield $1.08 of definable benefits. A slide presentation laid open the "neglected riches" of the Arkansas basin to the committee; every member also received a specially bound copy of the photographs, charts, and text of the exhibit. Back home, the chamber of commerce kept a chartered plane on standby in case Graham might need any other materials or witnesses.

All of that work paid off in the Rivers and Harbors Act of 1946. The act authorized the construction of twenty-eight multipurpose dams and reservoirs, twenty-three navigation locks and dams, twenty local flood-protection works, and a nine-foot-deep channel running from the Mississippi up the Arkansas, then through the Verdigris River to the little hamlet of Catoosa, a few miles east of Tulsa. Catoosa's elevation was a hundred feet lower than Tulsa's, and to carry the project the rest of the way would have required another fourteen locks and dams.

Tulsa could live with the difference. The problem was that the 1946 act merely authorized the long-anticipated project. Actual construction would require annual appropriations to build a dam at a time and to do it on a year-by-year basis. That would require considerable, sustained political leverage.

Reenter Bob Kerr. After his election to the United States Senate in 1948, Robert S. Kerr did not so much arrive in Washington as he descended upon it. Within months, journalists were marveling about the "Big Boom from Oklahoma," the one they described as the Senate's loudest—and richest—man. They might have added its smartest and most determined too. As soon as Kerr hit the Capitol, he allied himself with John McClellan, Arkansas's powerful senator and champion of the river's downstream development. Kerr also demanded (and received) a seat on the Senate Public Works Committee. The post allowed him to keep tabs on competing undertakings. As opportunity arose, he also picked up support for his project from senators needing a hand with their own. Thus, Texans later found powerful help in placing the National Aeronautics and Space Administration complex in Houston, the Southwest discovered an ally for the Central Arizona Project, the upper Midwest counted on a friend for the Saint Lawrence Seaway, and the Pacific Northwest had a patron for Hell's Canyon Reservoir. In every case, the regions' senators repaid the Oklahoman in spades, in particular, the gilded variety used ceremonially to break ground along the Arkansas.

Kerr next persuaded President Harry Truman to order federal agencies to cooperate in comprehensive planning for the Arkansas, White, and Red River basins as a single entity. Combining the three into one, Kerr instantly transformed the corps' projected 1 to 1.08 cost/benefit ratio for the Arkansas alone into a much more salable 1 to 1.20 for the combined basins. He also thereby united Oklahoma's and Arkansas's interest in one river to the desires of states home to the other two. Those states were Missouri, Kansas, Colorado, New Mexico, Texas, and Louisiana. Their senators (who constituted one-sixth of the Senate's membership) thus became a single political bloc merged behind his leadership.

A united Oklahoma was very much part of that bloc. Mike Monroney joined

Kerr in the Senate in 1951, still steadfastly opposing the senior senator's pet project. In 1955, a year before Monroney was due to run for reelection, Tulsa's Newt Graham, Verser Hicks, and Joe Jarboe flew to Washington to meet with Monroney and explain some political facts to him. The facts turned upon just how important Tulsa campaign money would be for a successful second election and just what Tulsa expected in return. The Tulsans witnessed to the senator, laid hands upon him, and made him a believer then and there. A born-again and well-funded Mike Monroney did win a second term in 1956 and took a seat on the Senate Appropriations Committee's Subcommittee on Public Works. There, he did missionary work on behalf of funding the Arkansas project through to completion.

On the Capitol's other side, Page Belcher, the Republican congressman who represented Tulsa, proved to be a loyal ally to Kerr on the city's behalf. Ranking high among the Republicans sitting on the House Agriculture Committee, Belcher could deliver as many as sixty votes for the Arkansas project. The votes were those of conservative Republicans representing farm states. They might not have known that there even was an Arkansas River in Oklahoma, but they did know that favorable treatment for their constituents' crop, storage, and credit needs could use the goodwill of the congressman from Oklahoma's First District.

All of that political firepower would have been misdirected (if fired at all) had it not been for the active involvement of the ABDA, the Tulsa Chamber of Commerce, and area business leaders—until his death, coordinated by the indefatigable Admiral of the Arkansas, Newt Graham. As the ABDA once wrote in a newsletter:

> The Arkansas project is as far along as it is today because it has the support of a great many of the commercial and industrial leaders of this area. Without such support you could not have the bi-partisan, non-political backing of the entire Oklahoma congressional delegation. Political office holders do not guide the thinking of such men on matters of local economic concern, but instead they let the thinking of the business community they represent guide them.

Tulsa's business community did more than think, however. Following the Tulsa chamber's lead, voters in Tulsa and Rogers Counties (the jurisdiction that included Catoosa) passed a $2.5 million bond issue in 1964 to purchase 1,750 acres and begin construction of an industrial park near the waterway's eventual terminus. Subsequent bond issues, again prepared by the chamber, added another $21.2 million in taxpayer dollars.

The project took years to complete, too many years for either Newt Graham or Bob Kerr to see it finished. Graham died in 1957. Kerr died on January 1, 1963. It was eight years and fifty-one days later when the first barge, bearing 650 tons of newsprint, arrived at the Tulsa Port of Catoosa. In the seventeen years since Congress first had

In the new postwar economy, Douglas stayed strong on a steady diet of defense contracts. Spartan Aircraft retooled its facilities to build Spartan Travel Trailers for an increasingly mobile American public.

authorized the project and in the thirty-three since Newt Graham had become its apostle, the Corps of Engineers had built dozens of locks, dams, and reservoirs—enough in Oklahoma alone to give the state more miles of shoreline than the Atlantic and Gulf coasts combined. The corps also had stabilized and channeled 448 miles of river, 398 of the Arkansas, 50 of the Verdigris. Christened the McClellan-Kerr Arkansas River Navigation System, the project had a cost exceeded only by the Panama Canal and the Apollo moon-landing program as a civil-works project. American taxpayers had spent $1.2 billion to give Tulsa a window on the sea.

And what did Tulsa see through that window? Every year after its opening, the system recorded higher levels of traffic than the year before. By the end of July 1997, a total of more than 37 million tons of freight had shipped out of the Tulsa Port of Catoosa. Floods did not end (in 1986, Tulsa suffered severe damage from the vengeful Arkansas), but their severity and frequency greatly lessened. Entire communities arose to serve the needs of fishermen, campers, and tourists for beer, bait, snacks, and doodads. In some cases, these communities were more populous than those they replaced, the older ones that disappeared under impounded waters. Rarely, however, were they as attractive, since countless old brick buildings and homes had been replaced by prefabricated gas stations, trailer parks, and second homes. Aesthetics aside, there remained those who regarded the project and its astounding price tag as examples of modern politics at its most provincial and most wasteful.

The fact is that even professional economists have been reluctant to put a value on the project's worth to Tulsa and northeastern Oklahoma. That Congress has not since funded even one huge water-authorization bill may indicate policy makers' skepticism about the returns on the public's dollars. Maybe preconverted Mike Monroney and later critics were right; maybe the project did amount to pork-barrel politics on a scale awesome both in daring and in execution. The late Senator Kerr's retort bears remembering. "Let Washington wags make their jokes about the federal pork barrel," Kerr liked to say, but "the Oklahoma congressional delegation is happy to be bringing home the bacon."

Plenty of bacon did come home. The fact is that a good (if indeterminable) share of more than a billion dollars was spent, some for wages of Tulsa and eastern Oklahoma workers, some for services of Tulsa and eastern Oklahoma contractors, some for materials from Tulsa and eastern Oklahoma suppliers. That was a lot of bacon, and it helped fatten modern Tulsa's economy.

Of course, the city's economy had hardly been on starvation rations anyway. Borrowing from Mark Twain, reports of another round of depression for Tulsa after 1945 proved to be greatly exaggerated. Aircraft production ceased completely for a time, but the much-anticipated and much-dreaded post–World War II collapse never came. Considerable pent-up consumer demand provided much of the explanation. War workers drew upon their savings accounts, servicemen and their families spent their allotments, and countless citizens cashed in their war bonds. All became consumers hurrying to buy goods scarce, if available at all, during the war. J. Paul Getty knew what he was doing when he declared (before departing for Saudi Arabia) that Spartan Aircraft would produce not airplanes but travel homes, refrigerators, and heaters after the war. Other Tulsa firms did well enough in the new consumer market that the city experienced an astonishing 9 percent employment growth in 1946.

Once unleashed, consumer demand helped summon Tulsa's continuing industrial development like a benevolent sorcerer's apprentice. The real magic came via the greatest consumer of all: the United States government. Expectations that government would shrink to its prewar and predepression size turned out to be no more accurate than those predicting massive postwar unemployment. Instead, government in the late forties and beyond maintained nearly all of the New Deal's domestic programs and expanded those most popular with the middle class. More important, the end of war marked not the end of military spending but its swift and phenomenal growth. Repackaged as "defense spending" and justified by the need to protect the entire "Free World," World War II's millions of military dollars became the cold war's billions. Tulsa employers and Tulsa employees got a good share of that.

Spartan's School of Aeronautics was an early beneficiary. While the manufacturing division's foray into civilian consumer goods failed, the school prospered from the

Tulsa—the Center of A

FROM ITS EARLY DAYS, TULSA HAD THOUGHT OF ITSELF AT THE CENTER, THE HUB—ALL ROADS LEAD TO TULSA. WITH THE ADVENT OF COMMERCIAL FLIGHT, THE IDEA WENT AIRBORNE, AS ILLUSTRATED BY THIS MAP FROM A 1945 ISSUE OF *Tulsa Spirit.*

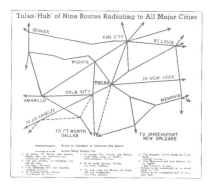

moment that it won the contract to train officers and enlisted men to maintain the army's growing fleet of observation planes and helicopters. Starting in January 1952, the school trained more than eight hundred officers and men, the same eight hundred who then opened and staffed the new army school that took over the training. Their departure only eased Spartan's next task: training two thousand mechanics for the air force during the Korean War. Thereafter, the school stayed financially fit under a steady diet of U. S. contracts, sweetened by those with America's "Free World" allies, including the new state of Israel.

Douglas Aircraft profited even more from the hot bath of spending prescribed to fight the cold war. The last of its war work done, the Tulsa plant closed in June of 1946. Within less than five years, it was open and humming again. Douglas was back to work building bombers. This time it was the B-47 Stratojet, the first jet-powered heavy bomber in the American arsenal and the first one able to deliver nuclear bombs to any target on earth. The Tulsa plant turned out 250 before the orders ended in 1956. Earth's inhabitants could be grateful that not one bomber had dropped one bomb, and Tulsa's residents could also be grateful for the $301 million that Douglas had paid out as wages and the $53 million spent with 1,711 local subcontractors.

Those figures did nothing but improve. One reason was that Douglas stayed busy on bombers. Its mechanics overhauled and modified the existing B-47s until the last one was replaced in 1966. By then, they also were busy with its replacement, the giant B-52 intercontinental bomber. Equipped with either atomic or hydrogen weaponry, the B-52 long served as the nuclear spear point for the Strategic Air Command. Only the developing missile system could rival it; but for that too, Tulsa workers stayed busy, first on the Nike system, then with Thor missiles, and finally on the Minuteman system. In different config-

ation in the Southwest

urations, the latter two missiles also were the workhorses of the Gemini and Apollo space programs, and Tulsa's Douglas workers made their contributions to both, capped by the latter's successful series of moon landings.

The Tulsa workers who helped put Neil Armstrong and others on the moon were the descendant's of the Second World War's mechanics, including quite a few local versions of "Rosie the Riveter." They were also the product of considerable evolution. As late as 1951, Douglas's ratio of hourly production workers to its skilled technicians and highly educated engineers was 10.5 to 1. The ratio of the mid-1960s had dropped to 3.5 to 1. Average wages reflected the difference, climbing by more than 500 percent over the same years.

Douglas's 1967 merger with McDonnell Aircraft Company did nothing to reverse either trend. It was one of those transactions in which both parties gained by strengthening each other. Hardly a disinterested third party, Tulsa may have gained even more than either. Able to compete even more effectively for even more contracts, the combination promised Tulsans steady work at wages undreamed of by Rosie and the guys.

Part of the new McDonnell Douglas's competition was with another Tulsa firm bidding against it for Tulsa labor. North American Aviation arrived in Tulsa in 1962 and hired eighteen people. Five years later, the figure was four thousand. To get them, North American had to pay more than $30 million in annual wages. To keep them busy, the company also had to spend another $3.3 with 272 Tulsa subcontractors and suppliers. The money bought North American a major share in government military and space contracts as well as civilian work on Boeing's new "jumbo jet," the 747.

On the civilian side, American Airlines took over Douglas's vacated wartime maintenance facilities on January 10, 1946. Within eleven months, American was employing fifteen hundred Tulsans and had spent $2 million in Tulsa on capital improvements, with another $2.5 already under contract. By 1950, American had concentrated all maintenance operations for its entire fleet to Tulsa and was running an annual payroll in excess of $8 million.

The emergence of jet-powered civilian aircraft in the 1960s lifted the Tulsa operation onto another higher and more rewarding plateau. Tulsans not only assumed the high-paying jobs of maintaining the new fan-jet engines (as well as the airframes attached to them) but also converted American's existing turbojet engines to fan-jets. In addition, they did the same for Trans World Airlines under TWA's contract with American. With such work orders, American was Tulsa's largest employer by the mid-1960s. To pick a single year (1967), American Airlines employed forty-five hundred Tulsans, paid them $36 million, and spent more than $15 million with local companies that supplied everything from paper clips to heavy industrial machinery.

Of course, Tulsa had plenty of potential vendors for the paper clips. Perhaps surprisingly, it had quite a few local firms that could supply sophisticated tools as well. If American needed a winch to lift a jet engine or move it down the maintenance line, it looked no farther than Tulsa. Ramsey Winch Company, Tulsa Winch Incorporated, and Braden Winch manufactured 90 percent of all commercial winches sold in the United States (a market already worth more than $17 million by 1964) and over half of those used in the world. A company that needed a custom-built, heavy-duty, all-terrain truck to move any piece of equipment anywhere on earth could try Tulsa's Industrial Vehicles International. If I.V.I. was swamped with orders (and it usually was), a buyer could go over to the site of Getty's old Spartan plant. Crane Carrier Company had taken over the facility to fabricate trucks for custom uses. How about a heat exchanger? Any firm needing one had to go to Tulsa. Nearly all of them used anywhere in the world were manufactured there.

The cumulative effects were massive and early felt. By the early 1970s, Tulsa was easily the state's leader in manufacturing, employing a quarter again as many workers as did the otherwise much larger Oklahoma City. Compared to the capital city, Tulsa's companies also were involved in heavier industry, which consumed more than twice as much industrial power. In 1973, Tulsa manufacturer's paid out $386,276,000 in annual payrolls to 42,543 workers. Of these, 10,924 had been hired since 1969 in new or expanded plants.

Tulsa's postwar economy may have looked like a sorcerer's apprentice turning out manufacturing jobs, but there was no magic to it. Just as when Tulsa was calling itself "the Magic City," its post–World War II economic development was the product of leadership, not legerdemain. As before, leadership's most powerful lever lay in the city's chamber of commerce. The chamber and its members who worked so closely with Senator Kerr to bring navigation to the Arkansas discovered that they had just as important a friend in Senator Monroney. His early apostasy on the Arkansas aside, Monroney was a stout champion of postwar economic development, particularly as it involved aviation. Legislation that bore his name contributed hundreds of millions of federal dollars to the nation's airports, including quite a few million to Tulsa's. Supplemented by local bond money produced by the chamber's efforts, the money provided irresistible bait for firms like McDonnell Douglas, North American, and American Airlines.

More generally, the chamber and city government virtually combined the former's economic-development efforts and the latter's policy-making role as it affected the city's economy. What might be described as a private-public partnership found expression in a series of trust authorities. They permitted Tulsans to overcome many of the barriers to the exercise of strictly public authority erected in the Oklahoma Constitution of 1907. The city thus made use of its tax-exempt status and powers of condemnation through influence sharing. It even turned over a portion of its taxing powers to fund such chamber-inspired operations as the public Economic Development Commission with its private shadow, Industries for Tulsa, Incorporated. Even if such arrangements might have been troubling for democratic purists, they did pay off economically. In a single year (1985), the Tulsa Industrial Authority spent more than $57 million on new or growing industries, and Industries for Tulsa sold corporations 492 acres of land taken by the city to build the 1,320-acre Cherokee Industrial Park.

The other principal reason for Tulsa's modern economic development was a legacy of its earlier status as Oil Capital of the World. The major oil producers began to relocate their headquarters in the 1950s. Houston, Texas, the beneficiary of much of the movement, took to bragging that it was Tulsa's rightful heir as the oil capital. Even Tulsa's own residents no longer seriously could maintain that their city dominated oil—or that oil dominated Tulsa. Nonetheless, Tulsa took away more than greasy britches from its days of sitting in oil's seat of power.

Dozens of small producers still operated out of Tulsa, and in the 1970s a big one joined them. It was Cities Service, Henry Doherty's old company, which relocated its New York offices to Tulsa. Far more typical and far more important, though, were Tulsa's continuing oil-related companies. They may not have produced oil themselves, but their products made it possible for others to find and extract it.

Reading and Bates, a worldwide leader in offshore drilling, stayed in Tulsa, moved into Josh Cosden's old Boston Avenue building, and fully restored and modernized it with another thirty-two floors. The old Williams Brothers Company, a pipeline outfit that had worked with the likes of Doherty and Cosden, became the new Williams Companies. It operated pipelines around the globe even as it expanded into agricultural chemicals and turned rusting pipelines into conduits for fiber-optic communications. Gerald Westby's Seismograph Service Corporation provided the instruments and expertise to locate oil wherever it might hide itself. It also ran one of ten Tulsa-based petroleum research laboratories, each staffed by engineers and technicians who honed the cutting edge of oil-related technology.

Other Tulsa companies provided tools to extract oil everywhere from Alaska's frigid North Slope to Saudi Arabia's sizzling sands. C-E NATCO evolved from its old business of building holding tanks to a new one providing scores of products for land and offshore drilling as well as chemical processing. Unit Rig and Equipment turned out tons of drilling equipment and the vehicles to move it. The Byron Jackson Company provided the pumps to get oil out of the ground, and Flintco could build an entire power plant to use it.

In other instances, manufacturers of the most modern consumer goods could trace their origins to the city's pioneering days in the oil fields. If a family bought a new Ford Explorer from the Doenges brothers or Fred Jones, its attached winch that pulled the family's fishing boat from Keystone's waters almost certainly was built by one of three Tulsa companies. No one would have been surprised to learn that each of the three began by producing winches to haul oil-field equipment out of Oklahoma's muds. There might be surprise, however, to learn that the family's Zebco fishing reels were made by a Tulsa company that once specialized in producing "torpedoes" for oil drilling. Its name? The Zero Hour Bomb Company.

Under its old name, producing its old product, Zero probably would have bombed out in recent years. Without the pun, an awful lot of oil companies did. Inspired originally by the Arabs' oil boycott sparked by their Six Day War with Israel and thereafter sustained by the Organization of Petroleum Exporting Countries' (OPEC's) manipulation of crude-oil prices, many an oil firm soared high in the late seventies. So many out-of-state workers flocked into what they still thought was the oil capital that the chamber's executive director, Clyde Cole, had to warn them publicly not to come to Tulsa looking for work—there was not enough to go around.

The OPEC cartel broke ranks in the early eighties, crude prices plunged, and the oil companies that had risen so fast fell even faster. With its many oil-related firms, Tulsa took something of a hit. It was nothing compared to that which decked Houston. If Houston had assumed Tulsa's old title, it paid heavily for it. The big-talking south Texas city suddenly quieted down, muffled under the weight of massive unemployment, a nearly bankrupt public treasury, and an imploded real estate market.

Tulsa had it better because Tulsa had come to have it differently. Insulated from the grandest effects of either the boom or the bust, Tulsa's economy shadowed not Houston's but all of America's. As had been true for nearly the entire post-1945 period, Tulsa's income and employment figures went up just a little faster and little higher than did the nation's during the good years. During the bad, income slowed and employment fell just a little later and a little less than America's.

Zebco kept producing and selling reels. The world kept buying winches built in Tulsa, Oklahoma. Flintco kept buying and using structural steel. American Airlines' planes kept flying. McDonnell Douglas and North American workers kept active. Barges kept loading and unloading at the Arkansas port.

Houston should have done so well. But, then, Houston was just the oil capital. Tulsa was an All-American City.

THE *Downtowner* SERVED AS A POPULAR DIRECTORY OF URBAN ATTRACTIONS. EVERY COVER FEATURED A TULSA SECRETARY, SALESCLERK, OR WAITRESS MOMENTARILY GLAMORIZED INTO THE IDEAL OF SOPHISTICATED AMERICAN WOMANHOOD.

DEPRESSED TRACKS

BOULDER AVE.

CAMERON ST.

MAIN ST.

DEPRESSED TRACKS

DETROIT AVE.

CINCINNATI AVE.

PUBLIC LIBRARY
COUNTY BUILDING
FEDERAL BUILDING

THE PLAZA
THE UNION STATION

MUNICIPAL AUDITORIUM
MUNICIPAL BUILDING
HALL OF RECORDS

THE CIVIC CENTER

"THE *Best-laid* Plans"

THE PATTON BROTHERS, Dan and Gus, were on to something. When they laid out Tulsa's original street grid and numbered its east-west streets from First Street on out, the pattern was neither brilliant nor innovative. Their alphabetical arrangement of the avenues east and west of Main and their naming them for cities on appropriate sides of the Mississippi—that was a little bit of both. Even someone passing through could find Cincinnati (two blocks east of Main, between Boston and Detroit) just about as easily as she or he could

ALTHOUGH NEVER REALIZED, THE CIVIC CENTER PORTION OF THE "1924 TULSA PLAN" ENVISIONED SYMMETRICAL GROWTH CENTERED ON DOWNTOWN. THE 1953 OPENING OF UTICA SQUARE HAD NO SUCH INTENT AND NO SUCH EFFECT. SUBSEQUENT LANDSCAPED CULS-DE-SAC AND PARK AREAS GAVE A GREEN FEEL TO DEVELOPING SUBURBIA, IF AN EMPTY FEEL TO DOWNTOWN.

locate Third Street, north of the tracks, between Second and Fourth. In retrospect, the Patton boys may have qualified themselves as Tulsa's first urban planners.

Unfortunately, they also were its last for a very long time. In the absence of conscious planning, Tulsa became something like Topsey. Like her, Tulsa "just growed." Except for zoning ordinances approved in the early 1920s, the order and form of its growth depended largely upon the marketplace. Rather than develop by conscious design, Tulsa developed for private profit. Limitations tended to be those imposed by nature or the unintentional residue of other policies designed for other purposes.

Nature's most obvious encumbrance was the Arkansas. The river naturally divided Tulsa into two parts. Originally the two were separate municipalities. Even after they merged, each retained its separate flavor, almost its separate identity. Tulsa's oilmen helped that along considerably when they placed their refineries along the Arkansas's west bank. Thereafter, the west side was destined to grow as a distinctive working-class area.

Socially and economically separated from the east side, it also remained physically isolated from it. One decent early bridge replaced the toll bridge so honored in city legend ("You Said We Couldn't Do It, But We Did"), but it took the Great Depression and the New Deal's public-works programs to provide a second, at Twenty-first Street, in the 1930s. Federal and state highway planners finally created the third in the early fifties, when they placed one at Fifty-first Street as part of the modern interstate highway system.

East of the river, policy decisions helped shape the city's long-term growth, even if the decisions had other, more immediate goals. The racial separation of Tulsa's population resulted from choices both deliberate and insidious. Whether enforced by municipal ordinance, by restrictive covenants, by discriminatory lending practices, or promoted by school-board practices, segregation was public policy. Once in place, that policy had effects both powerful and long-lasting, at least as powerful and far longer-lasting than the official policy itself. No one could claim that the outcome was either natural or neutral.

Other policy choices, not geography, had more long-range consequences for Tulsa's entire north side. In 1930, when the city elected not to connect streets or to extend utility lines into Dr. Samuel Kennedy's proposed development of "The Osage," the municipal government made a choice. The rancorous Dr. Kennedy made a choice too. He directed that his property, nearly ten square miles of land lying right at Tulsa's northwestern doorstep, could not be sold for development within twenty years of his own death. The two negatives generated a third. The good doctor lived a long time, until his seventy-seventh year, 1941. Up to then and for twenty years thereafter, Tulsa simply could not develop toward its northwest. Many of Dr. Kennedy's good deeds were buried with him, but his spite was not interred with his bones.

Whether wise or foolish at the time, the city government that rejected Dr. Kennedy's plan in 1930 almost certainly did not anticipate that it thereby was putting

The Spavinaw Water Project

Incredible Growth Forces Tulsa to Spend $8,000,000 and Go Sixty Miles for Pure Water--Water in Abundance

EARLY DECISIONS WOULD DRAW THE MAP OF TULSA FOR GENERATIONS: THE SPAVINAW WATER PROJECT, THE DECISION TO BUILD AN INTERNATIONAL AIRPORT, THE EXCLUSION OF THE OSAGE WHICH BLOCKED NORTHWEST DEVELOPMENT, ALL COALESCED VISIBLY IN THE SHAPE, DEMOGRAPHICS, AND LOCATION OF TULSA NEIGHBORHOODS.

THERE is an old saying, "We never miss the water until the well goes dry," which was brought forcibly to the attention of the citizens of Tulsa and the entire southern portion of the United States in the year 1925, when a drought unprecedented in the history of the south, was brought to a close by the rains which occurred throughout the south beginning about September 12.

Those who have followed the history of this drought know that southern California, Arizona, New Mexico, Texas, Oklahoma, Arkansas, Tennessee, Georgia, South Carolina and Alabama have experienced a drought unknown to the oldest inhabitants of these states, and when the governors of Georgia and Alabama proclaimed a day of prayer that the drought might be broken in their states, it brought to the attention of the citizenship of Oklahoma, and Tulsa in particular, the wonderful advantage that they had obtained by securing, in the month of October, 1924, an adequate supply of mountain water for the city of Tulsa.

Why Tulsa Went to Spavinaw

During the last ten years the tremendous development of the southwest has been one of the outstanding features of our national growth and development, not only of industrial and agricultural importance, but record-making in the matter of civic achievements.

Oklahoma has been the center of development, and Tulsa one of the fastest growing cities. Its population has risen from 18,900 in 1910, to approximately 130,-000 in 1925. The cause of this remarkable increase has been the fact that it is the center of the Mid-Continent oil fields around which the entire activity of the southwest has centered, and to the spirit

By CYRUS S. AVERY
Member Non-Partisan Water Commission
Chairman State Highway Commission

of the citizens who have looked ahead and visualized the future of Oklahoma.

The water problem had been one of the hardest which the city had to solve, owing to the fact that it had no adequate supply except the Arkansas river, the quality of which was extremely bad, for the Arkansas is one of the hardest, saltiest and muddiest rivers in the southwest. Tulsa became a city in spite of Arkansas river water. The whole city purchased its drinking water in five-gallon bottles. For some months of the year, the water was not fit for any use whatever on account of its mud content, which sometimes becomes even too heavy for the modern filter plant which was built in 1918, and which under ordinary circumstances, would handle the purification of the water in an efficient manner.

About a decade ago, when Tulsa's population figures began to increase by leaps and bounds, the builders of this city saw that good water was to be an imperative necessity. Up in the Ozark mountains, 60 miles to the northeast, were clear, sparkling streams of cold, soft water and one of the most beautiful of these was the Spavinaw. Certain far-sighted citizens began to talk of the possibility of bringing this water to the city, and various plans were suggested.

Recommended by Goethals

In 1921, a charter amendment, a non-partisan water commission was appointed, consisting of four members, two to be elected every two years and the water commissioner of the city to be the chairman. This commission invited George W. Goethals to come to Tulsa and look over the

situation and recommended a source of supply. His recommendation was for the Spavinaw source, if a preliminary survey showed this to be a feasible plan and within the financial reach of the city of Tulsa. This survey was carried out in the summer of 1921, by the Holway Engineering company of Tulsa, after a bond issue of $250,000 had been voted for this purpose.

The report of the survey presented a gravity plan for bringing the Spavinaw water to Tulsa and stated the cost would be about $6,800,000 In November of the same year, a bond issue for that amount was voted five-to-one. This was one of the largest per capita bond issues for water supply ever carried in this country.

In April, 1922, W. R. Holway of Tulsa and J. D. Trammel were retained as engineers and Dabney H. Maury of Chicago as consulting engineer and work was immediately started on the final surveys and preparation of plans and specifications. On October 11, 1922, eleven contracts were let. Later, six more were let and $700,000 additional in bonds were voted.

In February, 1924, the contractors for the laying of the concrete pipe abandoned their contract and the work was completed by the city under the direction of W. R. Holway for the water commission. A rather unusual thing was accomplished here, for the contractor's superintendents and foreman were replaced with men from the engineer's organization and the whole work was carried to a successful completion so that on October 29, 1924—a few days over two years from the letting of the first contract—Spavinaw water flowed by gravity a distance of 60 miles into the city of Tulsa at the rate of 28 million gallons per day.

(Continued on Page 40)

Spavinaw Lake, Source of Tulsa's Water Supply

a barrier around Tulsa's northwest quadrant or that it would remain impenetrable for two generations. Neither did Tulsa deliberately block off expansion into its own northeast, but it did with two obstructions, both the unforeseen consequences of otherwise enlightened decisions.

The first was the resolve to build the mighty Spavinaw water system in the 1920s. Created when Tulsa was not much more than a really big boomtown, the Spavinaw project guaranteed that the city would become a city. Particularly with its post–World War II expansions, Spavinaw freed Tulsa to develop without any real fear that it would reach limits imposed by thirst. A second decision—the decision to build a first-class, modern airport—had similar long-term benefits. The airport's construction and steady expansion provided the magneto to ignite economic diversification. The industries drawn to it guaranteed that the city would grow even as its identification with the oil industry faded.

Their benefits aside, both decisions had massive, unintended consequences for Tulsa's physical development. To impound Spavinaw's flow, the city bought a huge tract of land to the northeast. Part of the land provided space for Spavinaw's necessary reservoir and waterworks. The remainder became the sprawling Mohawk Park. Near it lay the airport. Requiring immense space for facilities, runways, and flight clearance, it was a job-creating genie but land-consuming monster. With Mohawk Park and the airport properties, Tulsa inadvertently had restricted residential and mercantile development in much of its northeastern quadrant. Only a fraction of the area could be developed residentially; its population would be predominantly working-class.

Whether naturally, deliberately, or incidentally, the Tulsa that emerged from the Second World War was socially segmented and physically malformed. The lines of class were nearly as perceptible as those of race. West and northeast Tulsa were white working-class, north Tulsa black, east Tulsa middle-class, south Tulsa white and prosperous, northwest Tulsa vacant. Unlike a normal, healthy cell with its nucleus comfortably working away near the middle, Tulsa's central core, its downtown business district, jammed up against the northwest before the prairie took over. The center of population and the center of wealth lay well to downtown's south and east.

However odd, the arrangement worked well enough through the Second World War. Thereafter came a series of circumstances so disruptive of normal growth that their effect was almost catastrophic. Most were changes of nationwide dimensions, and Tulsa, like other American cities, had to deal with their consequences.

Spreading into every corner and layer of society, the automobile carried prewar America into its uncertain future. Tulsa became one of many cities in which the number of personal vehicles climbed upward toward the number of licensed drivers. To manage the traffic, federal and state highway planners spent billions of dollars on giant expressway systems that linked and transformed America's cities. Tulsa was one.

The new highways moved a lot of cars and moved them quickly. Unfortunately, they provided no place to leave them when they were idle and empty. Multistory parking garages and vast fields covered with asphalt provided some answer, however ungainly. Series of shopping centers with their vast parking lots gave Americans and Tulsans another solution. Shoppers seized upon them, sometimes less for their prices or range of services than for their hospitality to the shoppers' vehicles. Successive shopping centers became ever larger and ever farther removed from the cities' historic centers, particularly in Tulsa, where the residential and commercial center was already distant from the geographical center.

Whether disguised as a village square or glorified into a modern

temple to sanctify the money changers, the new shopping centers were expressions both of the automobile's impact and of the new American religion of consumption. In the latter regard, Tulsans were hardly the only Americans with tastes defined by the national media or satisfied by national retail chains. To some degree, the bond that united them was less allegiance to the city or to their neighborhoods than it was their shared identity with the places that they shopped and the things they consumed.

In all of these ways, the automobile transformed everything it touched, and it touched everything in postwar America, Tulsa included. The city's contribution lay in

its efforts to address the changes. Unique neither in the challenges nor in the responses, Tulsa was hardly singular with the consequences. As elsewhere, Tulsa's efforts were not entirely successful. As elsewhere, they occasionally were counterproductive.

The same Dan Patton of the brother team that had laid out Tulsa's original street grid was an early champion of Tulsa's eventual expressway system. A Republican elected as the city's mayor during the great GOP landslide of 1928, Patton served a single term and thereafter became city engineer. At World War II's end, he and fellow Republican Mayor Lee Price worked out a plan to loop the central business district with a four-lane, limited-access highway. The $6.7 million project would uproot more than 550 families to connect eventually to thirty-six thousand miles of interstate expressways in the planning stages in Washington and Oklahoma City.

Politics undid Patton and Price's plans. Mayor Price's fellow Republican nominees in the 1948 election refused to endorse the project. One—Joseph R. McGraw—publicly broke and ran in the other direction. The Democratic mayoral nominee was Roy Lundy, a Tulsa investor of the old school. Ridiculing the absurdity of building a "highway on stilts" (his term for the elevated interchanges), Lundy swore that he would "go up or . . . down on this expressway [issue]." Up he went, taking nearly the entire Democratic slate with him. So clear was the lesson that nearly a decade passed before officials dared offer voters a bond issue for expressway construction. Passed in late 1957, the package funded Tulsa's so-called Inner Dispersal Loop. By election time, it had the attraction of pulling together seven other expressways already under way and financed by federal and state moneys.

The individual expressways generated their own share of controversy. Some came from disinterested parties who questioned either the expense or the wisdom (or both) of certain projects. The most notable instance involved the projected Mingo Valley Expressway. Many argued that the highway was certain to attract developers out into far east Tulsa. The developers would lay their concrete, change the face of the land, and make their money. The new business proprietors, homeowners, and the city itself would pay dearly with increased and regular flooding along Mingo Creek and its many tributaries. This prophecy's pinpoint accuracy underscores its curious lack of effect. What may explain things was that it affected no immediately interested party—except for the developers.

Other critics of other projects were parties at interest. The interest was considerable among those whose property stood to be condemned or might be greatly devalued by a new expressway. Plans for every expressway generated such groups. Building each highway would dislocate hundreds of families. Their completion would leave others stranded in homes looking out upon rivers of concrete, the rivers' sounds not the gentle gurgles of flowing water but the unending racket of screaming traffic. In only one instance, however, did the critics' influence equal their concerns.

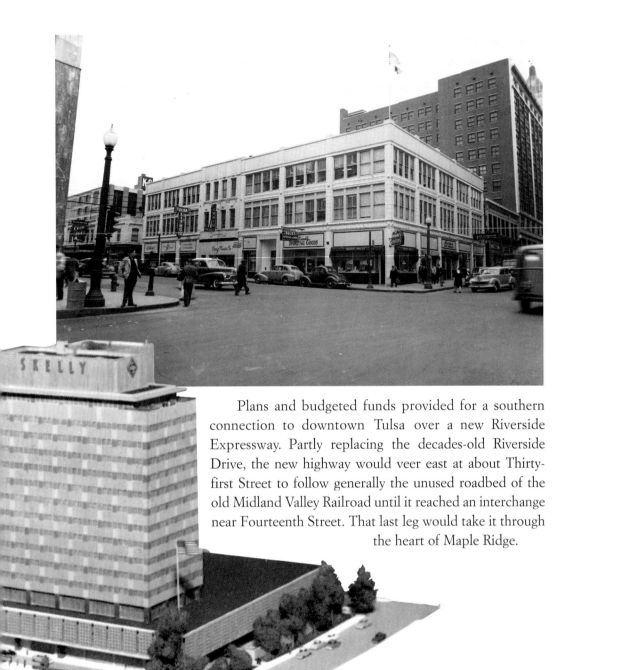

Plans and budgeted funds provided for a southern connection to downtown Tulsa over a new Riverside Expressway. Partly replacing the decades-old Riverside Drive, the new highway would veer east at about Thirty-first Street to follow generally the unused roadbed of the old Midland Valley Railroad until it reached an interchange near Fourteenth Street. That last leg would take it through the heart of Maple Ridge.

In the 1940s, downtown Tulsa was still the city's commercial heart. By the 1960s, even high-rise office buildings such as the new Skelly Building at Fifteenth and Boulder, whose model is shown here, were pushing southward.

The estimated seventeen hundred families living in Maple Ridge raised a howl of protest. Theirs was not the only neighborhood protesting or howling in the 1970s. It was, however, a neighborhood that included a good number of attorneys, engineers, and architects. It had families with money, time, and perseverance to make their resistance effective.

Even before the surveyors could set their stakes, something calling itself the Maple Ridge Association appeared, raised $4,000 at its first meeting, and discovered that its neighborhood was a historic national treasure on the order of New York's Greenwich Village or Washington's Georgetown. A newsletter followed to alert Maple Ridgers both to their special heritage and to every opportunity to preserve it. Thereafter, hardly a single public meeting with an agenda that included a variant of the verb *to develop* or the noun *highway* was without a contingent from Maple Ridge. Working the phones and knocking on doors (often doors just down the street), the not-so-plain folk of Maple Ridge sought help from their friends and neighbors in the legislature, and importuned their friends and neighbors with the chamber of commerce to back off. Ultimately, they prevailed, through the efforts of their friends and neighbors in the legal community who secured injunctive relief. They even persuaded the National Park Service to declare the entire neighborhood a historic site and thereby save it from future development. Not even Greenwich Village or Georgetown had that distinction.

Neither did west Tulsa and Greenwood. The Skelly Bypass (later designated Interstate 44) pinned west Tulsa against a concrete barrier between its Fifty-first Street bridge and the road's bend to reach the new Turner Turnpike. The Red Fork Expressway (to become part of Interstate 244) then dealt west Tulsa a felling blow by consuming hundreds of its homes and utterly dislocating its once-thriving commercial district along Southwest Boulevard. The northern side of the Inner Dispersal Loop and the Osage and Cherokee Expressways (the latter U. S. 75 North) established a concrete box canyon that bound much of the population of the old Greenwood district. One could argue that both west Tulsa and Greenwood had at least as much historical significance as did Maple Ridge, but the National Park Service didn't see it that way.

Even without a handy southern route from downtown, Tulsans still found plenty of ways out. When the so-called Okmulgee Beeline (U. S. 75 South) opened in 1958, Tulsa's southside neighbor, Glenpool, nudged toward the new four-lane and experienced its first boom since the Sue Bland No. 1. Communities that considered themselves blessed to be along the northbound routes became all but unrecognizable to their old inhabitants. Those off the new superhighways considered themselves blessed just to keep their own residents. The Broken Arrow Expressway (U. S. 64 and S. H. 51) awakened the sleepy little town that shared its name. The highway also opened every one of its many Tulsa exits to commercial and residential development. The expressway that bore Bill Skelly's name created an unsightly mass of new construction along both its flanks. Its own exits at or near the county's old section lines (Peoria, Lewis, Harvard, Yale, Sheridan, Memorial, Mingo, and Garnett) opened evenly spaced doors for strip development. Quiet country lanes became crowded traffic arteries clogged with freestanding buildings, many lit by neon and each somehow uglier than the others. Successive strips drew their trade from neighborhoods which sprang up on what recently had been farms and grazing lands.

At the roads' other end, Tulsa's downtown felt the commercial effect. In May 1952, the city opened its first modern shopping center, at Utica Square. In addition to convenience and compactness, the fashionable center offered consumers the new three most important things in urban mercantile real estate: parking, parking, and parking. One of the first to read accurately the handwriting on its own downtown walls was Sears. In 1955, the giant retailer moved out to occupy a new building nearly dwarfed by its surrounding parking lot at Twenty-first and Yale.

Whether because they were more optimistic or less prescient or only because they lacked Sears's mountain of investment capital, most remaining downtown merchants tried to fight back. In 1956, they formed Downtown Tulsa Unlimited (DTU). Hoping to hang onto their trade with a so-called park-and-shop plan, the more than a hundred downtown retailers allied under DTU worked out arrangements to validate parking tickets issued by forty-five private parking lots or garages. The plan barely slowed the inevitable. Within seven years, many of DTU's original members and downtown Tulsa's oldest stores were packing up to move to the new Southland Shopping Center, then under construction at Forty-first and Yale.

Downtown Tulsa survived, prospered even, but not as a retail center. New office buildings arose with some regularity. Some housed local elements of national firms, many with major roles in the city's history. Texaco and Gulf were examples. Oneok, the holding company that had acquired Oklahoma Natural Gas, moved the company out of its beautiful

art deco property on Boston Avenue and into a new, flattened ellipse around the corner. Banks kept building. For a time, Fourth National Bank's new structure was downtown's tallest building, until the new First National Bank tower took the record. The massive new structure built for the Bank of Oklahoma (a direct descendant of the old Exchange National) eventually eclipsed both. There were still jobs and money aplenty downtown. The difference was that the jobholders tended to live far away and tended to spend their money far away too.

The creative planning that helped save downtown Tulsa came neither too little nor too late—but just barely. To a remarkable degree, that it came at all was the product of one of the city's most remarkable mayors: James Maxwell. Originally elected mayor in 1958 as a thirty-one-year-old Democrat, Maxwell was known first as Tulsa's "Boy Mayor." He eventually acquired other nicknames, nearly all of them honorable, as he became one of only three mayors (H. F. Newblock had been the first and Robert LaFortune would be the third) to serve the city for four terms.

Never marrying, Maxwell ran a florist shop with his father before entering politics. His work with the local chapter of the United States Junior Chamber of Commerce introduced him to most of the community, and he was responsible for its national headquarters' coming to Tulsa under a new name, the U. S. Jaycees. Maxwell's first campaign promised effectiveness and cooperation in place of retiring Mayor George Norvell's genial ineptness and the city commission's internal feuding. Working sixteen-hour days, Mayor Maxwell fulfilled both halves of that promise for the next two years and for the six that followed. For generations of Tulsans to come, Jim Maxwell's vision as mayor shaped the city that they would see and love.

In his first year as mayor, Maxwell persuaded the public to approve $7.2 million in bonds to build a new civic center. Over the next five years, he got another $24 million to construct an entire complex that covered twelve city blocks and provided modernized, architecturally integrated city and county office buildings. Prominent among the new structures was the new city-county Central Library. With the library's archangel, Alfred Aaronson, Maxwell also found the money to modernize and enlarge Thomas Gilcrease's original museum.

MAIN MALL, BEGUN IN 1964, WAS A MAJOR STEP TOWARD DOWNTOWN TULSA'S REDEVELOPMENT. *TULSA TRIBUNE* COLUMNIST ROGER DEVLIN, MAYOR JAMES MAXWELL, AND ROBERT VASSAR RAISED THE STANDARD IN THE FORM OF A NEW STREET SIGN AT ITS INAUGURATION. RIGHT, THE MAXWELL FLOWER HOUSE AT 305 SOUTH BOSTON AVENUE.

Appointing new members to the Tulsa Metropolitan Area Planning Commission (TMAPC), Maxwell kicked it into gear. The commission had been founded in 1953 but frozen in controversy since. Under his watchful eye, the TMAPC developed the city's first master plan in 1960. In keeping with its recommendations, Maxwell oversaw the acquisition and development of new parklands and led the city to annex more than one hundred square miles of adjacent territory in 1966. He also began the process that led eventually to a downtown pedestrian mall.

With county officials, Maxwell built a $3.5 million International Petroleum Exposition Building on the fairgrounds—and even suspended his impeccable taste when the county placed the notoriously tacky Golden Driller statue at its front door. Never mind: By the time Republican James Hewgley stunningly upset him in 1966, Jim Maxwell had established a permanent legacy of lasting importance, even beauty.

Tulsa's downtown was only one of the city's older areas rebuilt under Maxwell and his successors. Later administrations were able to carry on the work through an agency that dated to the Boy Mayor's first year in office. That was the Tulsa Urban Renewal Authority (TURA). Authorized by a state law of 1959 and generously funded thereafter with federal grants, TURA became the city's principal planning tool. Through the 1960s, it used its power of eminent domain (and 42.4 million federal dollars) to acquire sites that the city government defined as "blighted." TURA then either rehabilitated them or cleared them for sale to private investors prepared to redevelop the areas.

Not one to hide its candle under a bushel, TURA (renamed the Tulsa Development Authority in 1985) could point to solid achievements. Taken singly or collectively, they did not make Tulsa a heavenly city, but they did change the city's physical face. TURA bulldozed shacks, diners, and beer joints just south of the new civic center to make room for the new, four-hundred-room Doubletree Hotel as well as a prime residential complex, Center Plaza. Across the river from downtown, TURA maneuverings led to a modern, stylish apartment complex

MAYOR MAXWELL IN MOTION: URBAN DEVELOPMENT REQUIRED STATE COOPERATION AND
FEDERAL FUNDING. MAXWELL COUNTED ON BOTH, PARTLY THROUGH THE EFFORTS OF SENATOR
(AND FORMER GOVERNOR) J. HOWARD EDMONDSON, VICE PRESIDENT LYNDON B. JOHNSON AND
SENATOR MIKE MONRONEY SHOWN WITH MAXWELL AT LEFT. ABOVE, MAXWELL GREETED 1959'S
MISS AMERICA, MARY ANN MOBLEY (FIFTH FROM LEFT) AND THE CONTEST'S SECOND RUNNER-UP,
ANITA BRYANT, MISS OKLAHOMA AND GRADUATE OF TULSA'S WILL ROGERS HIGH SCHOOL
(SECOND FROM RIGHT).

known as West Port. The authority leveled most of the old Greenwood district to make room for the Heritage Hills neighborhood, including Jordan Plaza, a development sponsored by the First Baptist Church of North Tulsa to house the elderly. TURA's Greenwood acquisitions also made possible construction of the University Center at Tulsa, which brought publicly funded bachelor's and master's degree programs to Tulsa for the first time. Renamed Rogers University in 1996, the college sat only a duck pond away from another urban renewal product, the Greenwood Cultural Center.

But not all TURA's best plans worked out. Decades after the first bulldozers belched to life in Greenwood, most of its old residential area remained empty, and its former residents were victims of a movable ghetto. The eight tony neighborhoods planned to occupy the twenty-eight acres surrounding Center Plaza never appeared. Instead, its residents had an unobstructed view of at least sixteen lanes of concrete expressways and their incessant traffic. Having changed hands, Center Plaza itself acquired garish pink paint. The new owners hoped to recoup a portion of their investment by selling off its units as affordable condos.

Similarly, the much-ballyhooed commercial redevelopment of Greenwood's old business district amounted to little more than an expensive face-lift for the one block of buildings left between Archer Street and the overpass for the northern leg of the Inner

SHERIDAN VILLAGE

SHOPPING CENTER,

BELOW, OPENED IN

1954.

Dispersal Loop. The area's single significant occupant was the *Oklahoma Eagle*. Run by Greenwood's Goodwin family, the newspaper was the one surviving black-owned voice for what once had been called the "Negro Wall Street of America." The *Eagle*'s narrow escape from financial ruin in 1996 was a signal (should any have been needed) not of Greenwood's redevelopment but of its ruination.

It took years, decades even, for most of those shortcomings to rise to the surface. As they lay concealed in the 1960s and 1970s, the apparent success of immediate, neighborhood planning only encouraged the city to extend the concept. Rather than attack one blighted neighborhood at a time, Tulsa would plan for the long-range future of the entire city. The grandest, fullest, and most articulate expression of that heady ambition came from the TMAPC in 1972. Its name was Vision 2000.

The plan seemed to have everything going for it: a receptive city government under Mayor Robert LaFortune, the stout support of the chamber of commerce, enthusiastic local media coverage, even a team of professional city planners. The urban consultants hired for a background study had not been in Tulsa long before grasping what resident policy makers already recognized as the city's chief problem. Their term for it was Tulsa's "expanding unidirectional (southeastern) sprawl." Declaring that southeastern Tulsa already was on the verge of becoming a "city within a city," the consultants noted that "much of Tulsa's population, wealth and affluence" then centered in the region bounded by Twenty-first and Forty-first Streets between Harvard and Sheridan. Moreover, there were abundant signs that, left unchecked, the sprawl would move farther south and east, accelerate its pace, and add immeasurably to the city's nagging social and economic problems.

To great publicity, Vision 2000 rejected that established pattern and potential future in favor of "balanced growth." The final report included nineteen specific areas of policy recommendations, some divided into as many as five subfields. Their purpose was to restrain the southern and eastern drift and encourage the revitalization of Tulsa's western, central, and northern regions. Hardly anyone objected to the report. But then, hardly anyone read it either. Hardly anyone objected to the overall goal. But then, no one was in a position to achieve it either. The fate of what the planners regarded at the time as two hopeful signs measured the prospect for balanced growth—and, perhaps, for Tulsa's destiny as well.

The first was the so-called Williams Center Complex. The project received national acclaim as a stunning model for private-public partnership. The swiftly expanding and recently renamed Williams Companies needed office space. It also had money available through its Wall Street bankers, Lehman Brothers. The city needed a performing-arts center, a first-class retail complex, and other facilities to hold downtown together, particularly after the office workers got off work. The city's assets included the ability to receive federal grant money and the power to condemn any property it needed.

The resulting match seemed made in heaven. On land secured and cleared by TURA, Williams put up the state's tallest office tower, landscaped a small urban park, built two parking garages, matched city and privately raised funds to build a Performing Arts Center, and lured the Westin Corporation to put in a 450-room luxury hotel. Uniting all of it was the Williams Companies' own shopping gallery, which included gourmet restaurants, specialty shops, a first-run movie theater, and one of the city's very finest clothing stores—all overlooking a commercial ice rink. If anything could bring Tulsans back downtown after 5:00 P.M., surely this was it. If anything could reverse the city's southern and eastern flight, maybe this could.

Except it could not. Neither could it lure Tulsans back downtown after work. The office tower emptied at five o'clock. The park was a nice patch of green but not much else. The parking facilities became one of the few dependable places to park a car on a workday, dependable because they were rarely full. The Performing Arts Center attracted crowds for special events, but they had to be special events. Westin eventually sold the hotel, and its quality dipped below the five-star level. One by one, the gallery's shops abandoned it. The movie theater hung on for a while, specializing in art films that not many wanted to see. It closed because not many was not enough. Even the ice rink failed. Its ice melted, and its Zamboni disappeared to parts unknown.

All of that was happening just about the same time that hope was draining from a second project: Gilcrease Hills. In 1968, twenty-seven years after Dr. Samuel Kennedy's death and seven years after the expiration of his prohibition of development, Tulsa's Tandy Industries formed the Gilcrease Hills Development Corporation (GHDC) and opened an engineering office to plan the development of the southeastern corner of what Dr. Kennedy had called The Osage. Acting with California and Atlanta investors, GHDC acquired 1,634 acres of land and set about creating Tulsa's first fully planned community.

It opened on August 12, 1971. Susan Supernaw, Tulsa's reigning Miss Oklahoma, welcomed the thousands of visitors entering the project at its landscaped waterfall. The guests toured the tree-lined boulevards; inspected architecturally designed homes available to middle- and upper-income buyers; and noted the bicycle paths, stables, skeet range, and the $150,000 Swim and Racket Club. Within a year, Gilcrease Hills had sold a good portion of the three hundred homes projected for its first year and seemed well on its way to meeting the expectation of seventy-five hundred sales within five to seven years.

It was the urban experts hired for the Vision 2000 project who noted the single disturbing statistic: 68 percent of the first year's buyers were young, childless couples or older families with children past school age. Those groups represented nothing like that proportion among Tulsa's potential home buyers. Where were the families typical of the bulk of Tulsa's housing market, the ones that would make or break Gilcrease Hills: young families with school-age children? Like Sherlock Holmes's discovery of a clue in the dog that did not bark, the scarcity of those buyers should have been a powerful sign that something was awry.

It did not take Sherlock Holmes to know what it was. Gilcrease Hills was an integrated community bordering a predominantly black one. The developers made it a point to welcome any family who wanted—and who could afford—a home there. Most of its white buyers knew that and shared its developers' liberal attitudes. Many openly declared that they had chosen Gilcrease Hills to expose their children to those of another race. They doubtlessly were sincere in wanting their children to play with African-Americans in one another's expensive homes or on their well-maintained lawns. The developers encouraged these noble sentiments by refusing to participate in federal programs to subsidize homeownership for the poor. They had to, they said, to maintain the neighborhood's "educational quality."

The problem was that Gilcrease Hills had no educational quality to maintain; it had no schools. Its residents' children were assigned to Pershing and Lombard Elementaries, Roosevelt Junior High, or Central High School. None was particularly noted for its educational quality—at least not on the high side. Except for Central (which was in steep decline since its glory days), all were located in older, semiblighted areas south of the development. Their decaying, fortresslike buildings and crowded classrooms were packed disproportionately with poor and minority children. However nice their children's black, middle-class playmates, poor and minority kids were not the youngsters that very many well-off white families intended to be their children's schoolmates.

To its credit, Tulsa's official leadership tried to turn the tide. For the only time in its history, Tulsa Public Schools freed a neighborhood to disannex itself. In the fall of

1973, Gilcrease Hills opened its own independent school, Academy Central, to serve kindergarten trhough eighth grade. Every surrounding school district (including Tulsa) agreed to open its high schools to the older students. The Tulsa Utility Board cooperated with the developers to extend and improve the neighborhood's water and sewer system. In 1978, the city of Tulsa formally annexed Gilcrease Hills, thereby assuring its residents police and fire protection. In short, Tulsa's public institutions did nearly everything in their power to assure Gilcrease Hills's success as a planned, close-in, integrated community.

All of it was to little effect. Outside investors pulled out in 1974. By the end of 1976, the developers had sold only 450 housing units—precisely 6 percent of their original projections. Thereafter, runaway inflation and record interest rates tore the bottom out of Tulsa's real estate market. Much of the rest of the city recovered in good order—but not Gilcrease Hills. Property values tended to inch upward, if they went upward at all. Many realtors refused even to list or show its properties. The community took on a run-down look, odd given its age and tragic given its original expectations. Even nature seemed to conspire against it. On May 28, 1987, fire begun by lightning reduced the Swim and Racket Club to ashes.

Fire and lightning, of course, were not the root causes of these problems. Neither did flames gut the shopping gallery of the Williams Center. For that matter, it was not nature that left Greenwood's old residential districts vacant or its commercial spots underused. Whether they admitted it or not, many Tulsans knew exactly what the problem was. One who did acknowledge it was Joseph Williams, the Yale-educated president of the Williams Companies, who had tried—and failed—to reverse his beloved city's mindless sprawl. Perhaps only a man of his stature and experience could say it so bluntly, but say it he did:

> Racism is still the number one problem in Tulsa. . . . It has distorted our growth patterns and in fact is the real reason that the goal for balanced growth for our community is not being realized.

If Joe Williams was right—if a later generation of Tulsans had compounded the sins of their fathers—all of Tulsa paid a steep price. What the Vision 2000 planners had feared was precisely what happened. North Tulsa's residential areas slid downward. Displaced by Greenwood's "renovation" (if such it was), many black families used their urban renewal relocation moneys for down payments on white-owned homes. The prior owners took their money and ran, often down an east- or southbound expressway toward moderately priced neighborhoods in far east Tulsa or Broken Arrow. Joining them were many blue-collar workers who were victims of the aircraft industry's shift toward highly skilled and educated technicians. Adding to the exodus were the white families who were victims chiefly of their own fears, fears that their homes had lost their values and that their neighborhoods had become unsafe. So many whites fled their homes that those fears assumed a self-fulfilling capacity. As repossessions and outright abandonments spread across whole sections of north Tulsa, property values did depreciate and neighborhoods did decay.

In the city's south and east, multifamily housing units and new neighborhoods sprang up to profit from the flight and to fuel Tulsa's accelerating urban sprawl. Buyers had their choice of new homes in every price range, running all the way from government-subsidized houses in far east Tulsa to luxurious homes in deep south Tulsa. Within a few years, the center of Tulsa's population and economy moved farther south and east of where it had been, even as recently as 1972. In fact, the area between Twenty-first and Forty-first Streets and Harvard and Sheridan itself went

SEVENTY-FIRST AND MEMORIAL NORTHEAST CORNER.

into a sharp commercial decline. New residential developments undercut its housing market. New shopping centers pulled away its trade. By the mid-1990s, the once-prestigious Southroads Mall, across from Southland at Forty-first and Yale, sat vacant, its once-crammed parking lot pocked with chuckholes.

More than likely, the center's old customers were trading at another mall—this one farther south and farther east. When Woodland Hills Mall opened at Seventy-first and Memorial in the 1970s, some of its nearest neighbors were meadowlarks and ground squirrels. The birds and mammals swiftly went the way of their habitat, however. Retail shops, fast-food joints, and discount stores replaced their nests and dens. What had been their songs and chirrups became the sounds of traffic echoing against concrete walls. The beauty of nature's rolling hills gave way to rows of neon displays and heaps of undistinguished architecture—if one could so dignify the buildings thrown up overnight.

The city's sprawl spread havoc everywhere. City engineers and construction crews no sooner widened an existing street than they had to go back again, this time to add even more lanes, turning bays, and complex traffic signals. Commuting time stretched longer and longer; tempers got shorter and shorter. Money that might have been spent to maintain the city's decaying infrastructure or to upgrade services in north or west Tulsa went instead to playing catch-up with the developers. Business profits that heretofore had stayed in the community now padded the portfolios of distant investors in national or even international retail chains. The Tulsans who served their customers may have spent their wages at home, but those often were wages of the bread-and-butter variety, at or just above the minimum set by law. The gravy often stayed not in Tulsa but flowed to New York, California, Europe, or Japan.

Of course, there were local beneficiaries of all that sprawl. School districts were the most notable. Whatever the worth of meadowlarks or ground squirrels, their nests and dens did not amount to much on the property-tax rolls for funding local schools. High-density residential areas and multimillion-dollar retail centers gave the public schools a luxury of abundance.

The problem was that neither the tax dollars nor the abundance fell upon Tulsa's schools. When Mayor Maxwell annexed a hundred square miles of nearly vacant land in the sixties, there were those who doubted his judgment, but no one put up much resistance. It was Tulsa Public Schools that got the rebuff. Old, country school districts with historically tiny enrollments stubbornly refused to submit to annexation or to adjust their district lines, which dated, in some cases, to the horse-and-buggy age. The effects in the car-and-expressway age were almost immediately visible. Between 1968 and 1974, Tulsa's schools lost 14,136 students, almost a fifth of their total enrollment. Over half of those gone ended up in the schools of Broken Arrow, Jenks, or Union, which experienced growth rates of 69, 137, and 349 percent respectively.

That was merely the beginning. From a peak of more than eighty thousand students in the 1960s, Tulsa's school enrollment dropped by more than half over the next three decades. Suburban schools grew astoundingly, with both Union and Jenks predicting that their school population would soon pass Tulsa's. The school enrollment of the Jenks district already greatly exceeded the town's population. As for Union—there was no town of Union, just a lot of schools that got bigger every year.

Those districts' bound and constricted big-city neighbor began to close and sell off its underused school properties. One of the first to go was Mason High School, which had cost $4 million to build only a few years earlier. As the system closed some schools, consolidated others, and shifted attendance zones to maintain enrollments in others, it added to neighborhood instability. Some of the affected families became so disaffected that they joined the exodus.

Meanwhile, the suburban districts could hardly put up schools fast enough. Exploding property-tax collections gave them the money to do so—and more. The Broken Arrow and Jenks systems bought the latest in pedagogical equipment, including computers. Blessed to have Woodland Hills Mall and the Seventy-first Street shopping district included in its tax base, Union bought computers by the truckload and still had enough left over to light and carpet its new football stadium too. In Tulsa, though, voters rejected successive bond issues devoted merely to maintaining the district's decaying buildings.

The real dimensions of the problem transcended enrollment figures and educational gadgetry. To a remarkable degree, Tulsa disproportionately lost the kind of families who had originally contributed so much to making its public schools work: the young, middle- and upper-middle-class families who were most involved in their children's schooling—the ones who served on homeroom committees, who volunteered in school offices and classrooms, who organized fund-raisers, who campaigned for bond issues to improve their schools. Of course, Tulsa still had them everywhere, quite a few in its most stable neighborhoods. Some doubted, however, if it had enough of them. No one could deny that it had less than its former share of them.

No one had planned it that way. For that matter, no one had planned to turn downtown over to the homeless at nightfall. No one had planned for north Tulsa to remain a depressed near ghetto. No one had planned to scatter the city's commerce along a series of ugly strips. No one had planned to place the city's most vibrant commercial district and its most prestigious neighborhoods beyond the reach of its public schools. On the contrary: Every plan consciously made had warned that these things might happen, and every plan had aimed to avoid them.

Still, they all had happened. For all the planning, for all the homage paid to balanced growth, Tulsa, like many other American cities, had sprawled to the degree that its physical form imperiled its own continuing health. Physicians surveying the situation might have thought to use a metaphor like cancer to diagnose it. It was the poets, though, who best understood it. In particular, there was Scotland's Robert Burns, who long since had pondered the fate of plans made by mice and men—and, for that matter, by Tulsans too.

Shane Culpepper

Two, Three, *Many Tulsas*

WHEN THE POLICE arrested her in 1978, she was an unlikely looking criminal. The charges they filed against her were nothing short of astonishing. Worn down by years, her thinning hair tucked beneath a curly brown wig, she was barely ambulatory. Her eyesight and hearing had faded so badly that she had to hire a cab-driver to take her to her February trial. As the meter ran on his parked taxi, the driver stayed by her wheelchair during the proceedings. When the nine-man and three-woman jury returned after nearly two hours' deliberation, she heard neither the jury foreman declare her guilty nor Judge Raymond Graham pronounce her sentence. For those, she had to turn to the cabdriver, who still waited so faithfully.

"Guilty!" the cabby shouted into her ear.

"I know that," the old woman answered. "What about the bond?"

This time, there was no bond to be posted and forgotten. Time had finally caught up with Pauline Lambert. At age eighty-seven, she had received a thousand-dollar fine and a three-year prison term for prostitution.

Once, there must have been many like her. The fourth of eight children born to a west Tennessee cotton farmer, she dropped out of school after the ninth grade to work in the fields. She joined the Methodist Church and taught Sunday school for three years before meeting William Lambert, a coal miner, at an ice cream social. She followed him from the shafts of Kentucky to the pits of Wyoming, until his lungs gave out and he died after nine years of marriage.

Thereafter, she supported herself and six kids, earning four dollars a week by selling ribbons in a Tennessee dry-goods store. It was a traveling customer who told her that she could do much better running a "boardinghouse" near the Oklahoma oil fields. In 1936, she came to 326½ East First Street, Tulsa, Oklahoma, and opened the May Rooms. In sentencing her, Judge Graham said from the bench that Pauline Lambert owned and ran Tulsa's oldest continuing business proprietorship, one that had operated forty-two years from the same location.

Presumably her enterprise was unaffiliated with the chamber of commerce and went unlisted in booster guides to the city, but neither was it purely one of ill repute. Pauline Lambert never drank, never smoked, never set foot in a bar during her entire life. During the hard times of the Great Depression, she often went without eating to feed her own children or her sister's four, whom she also was supporting with the income from the May Rooms.

Business picked up in the forties and fifties. Employing six to eight "girls" full time, her May Rooms provided a service esteemed by coaches and alumni to reward winning high school football teams. Everyone knew that she took good care of her girls, and that she was a legendary soft touch for everything from down-and-outers to widows of police officers killed in the line of duty. The newspaper quoted the sentiments of one local judge, Richard Armstrong, who declared that "some of the founding fathers of our city grew up under her tutelage."

By the 1970s, those days were as far behind Pauline as her own youth. After the expressway system ended passenger train service at the nearby Union Depot, she lost a steady flow of out-of-town customers. The "Rideshy," a moving brothel so named because its permanent telephone line was accessed by punching R-I-D-E-S-H-Y on a push-button phone, captured much of the local trade. The "girls" had left, replaced by what she called two or three "old tomatoes," and she could get them only irregular business.

It may have been her dulled senses that let her be trapped in the police department's "sting" operation. When she hired a young, female undercover police officer, assigned her to a customer, and accepted fifteen dollars as her share of the fee for service, officers finally had Pauline Lambert cornered. Her attorneys filed appeals and began nearly five years of delays and hearings. Neither they nor any of the judges ruling upon them had any idea of how meaningless they were.

In February 1979, Judge Armstrong himself ignored Pauline Lambert's services to the city fathers to declare the May Rooms a public nuisance and ordered the doors padlocked. Deprived both of her business and her home, Pauline Lambert checked herself into the Four Seasons Nursing Home on March 6, 1979. Seven months later, she went to Saint John Medical Center. Pauline Lambert died there on October 31, 1979. Listing the cause of death as heart disease, the death certificate bore the name that she had not used since her childhood on the flat, dark soil of Tennessee: Clara Palmer.

It was probably for that reason that her death went unnoticed for four years, until 1983, when her bondsman and attorneys discovered it after Presiding Judge Clifford Hopper ordered them to present her for final sentencing. Her last delay and appeal had been exhausted, but Pauline Lambert managed to outfox the law one last time—and that from her grave. A greatly embarrassed Judge Hopper dismissed the charges against her. Instead, he, other judges, and veteran attorneys offered impromptu tributes to her near legendary status.

She had escaped justice but not history. In fact, Pauline Lambert was a reminder of Tulsa's history. Long before her May Rooms, First Street had been the site of brothels visited by the likes of the Doolin and Dalton gangs. Through the city's entire history, it was the chief street that generations of politicians and moral reformers had vowed to "clean up." No one had—not until urban renewal.

In the seventies, bulldozers leveled most of the area across the street from the May Rooms, clearing land for the intended site of the new state-funded Tulsa Junior College. The college eventually chose instead to buy and renovate the old Sinclair Building at Tenth and Main. That building and its name were, of course, more respectable pieces of Tulsa's history. For that matter, its location was too. It was at the edge of the Patton brothers' initial survey of the original Tulsa townsite.

Tulsans, it seemed, could escape their history no more than could Pauline Lambert. That included a lot of history that they may not have known about. In 1973, when the city gave itself a diamond anniversary gift in the form of a glittering River Parks system, its centerpiece was a low-water dam across the Arkansas where a new pedestrian bridge spanned the river. A few Tulsans may have known that the reconstructed bridge earlier had carried the locomotives and cars of the Midland Valley Railroad. Not many, however, realized that the Midland Valley had selected the crossing back in 1904, when it had rerouted its line to earn the $15,000 bonus put up by the old Tulsa Commercial Club. Standing on that bridge, Tulsans were sharing a piece of the history that had turned a cow town into a metropolis, for the arrival of the Midland Valley had helped assure the city's future.

Many Tulsans realized that the new jogging and biking trail running east and north of the bridge took them along the old Midland Valley right-of-way. Very few—if any—knew that when they used its asphalt surface they also were crossing the allotment assigned Wehiley Neharkey: the allotment that included the Creeks' ceremonial grounds, the allotment so swiftly seized by developers. For that matter, few realized that the streamlined, new concrete bridge that carried thousands of their cars daily over the Arkansas as part of Interstate 244 rested near the site of Tulsa's first toll bridge, the one built by three daring citizens and emblazoned with their boast: "You Said We Couldn't Do It, But We Did."

It was not that Tulsans were oblivious to their history and certainly not that they were ashamed of it. On the contrary: they often acted with commendable resolve to

preserve and to honor it. The ancient oak that had sheltered the original Creek settlers and had defined the spiritual center of the Lochapoka community continued to grow through a variety of owners. At one time or another, these included the Sinclair brothers (Harry and Earl), oilman Charles B. Peters (whose wife lovingly watered it), and the Oral Roberts Evangelistic Association (which demolished the old Sinclair mansion but preserved the tree).

In 1967, Texas businessman J. Paul Little bought the property and approached the city to rezone the land for heavy commercial use. Fearful that the Texan would dispatch chain-saw gangs to sacrifice the Council Oak for a parking lot, protesters besieged the Tulsa Metropolitan Area Planning Commission. Among them were the Girl Scouts, long since expanded to include black scouts and black troop leaders. The scouts presented petitions bearing signatures of eight thousand enraged Tulsans.

The city thereupon began negotiations that ended in 1974 with the dedication of Tulsa's newest but most historic municipal park, Creek Council Oak Park. Two years later, the National Park Service placed the still healthy tree on its National Register

THE SIDEWALKS AND TREE-LINED STREETS OF MAPLE RIDGE ATTRACT YOUNG FAMILIES OF THE 1990S TO THE GRACIOUS HOMES BUILT BY THE OIL BARONS MORE THAN SEVENTY YEARS AGO.

of Historic Places. By then, developers also had completed a series of tasteful town houses that bordered the tree's site, just as Lochapoka's communal buildings had done nearly one-and-one-half centuries earlier.

The park came early enough to preserve the historic oak. Time nearly ran out before Tulsans rescued another site significant to their earliest history. Among the little land excluded from the allotment process had been Indian cemeteries. None was more meaningful to Tulsa's beginnings than that of the Perrymans. From the original Perryman's arrival in the west (Benjamin Perryman's in 1828) through the remainder of the city's Native American experience, the Perrymans had played major roles.

JEAN DENNISON

JEAN DENNISON

Some had married into the Lochapoka community. Others had been missionaries serving two denominations and countless believers. Perrymans had fought in both armies during the Civil War and had joined Opothle Yahola's flight to Kansas. Perrymans had ranched land that covered nearly all of the modern city. Perrymans had built the area's first mansion and its first real store. Perrymans maintained the original post office, the first to use the name Tulsa. Perrymans also had died and been buried in their private cemetery. It rested northeast of the first post office, on Perryman land.

The city's street system and residential growth finally caught up with the cemetery in the 1930s and 1940s. The cemetery became an isolated island situated amid fine homes. Over time, many of its neighbors probably began to ignore it. Most who drove past it on the corner of Thirty-second Street and Utica Avenue likely never noticed it or, if they did, wondered what it was. Vandals destroyed or carried off at least nineteen headstones and toppled or broke another seven. When the city widened Utica Avenue, street crews destroyed several graves. Eventually, it looked less like a cemetery than a weed-choked field.

It was not until the 1990s that a private association, the Tulsa Historical Society, secured title to the cemetery and give it the care that it so richly deserved and had so disgracefully lacked. With donated funds and labor, the society cleaned the grounds, restored as many original markers as possible, and enclosed the entire property with a stately iron fence. If only a minority of shoppers heading to or from fashionable Utica Square had any idea of the Perrymans' contributions to their city's history, at least they knew that the family merited a special cemetery gracefully kept and solemnly preserved.

Historically significant commercial properties also reminded Tulsans of their own past. Wrecking balls and planned implosions wiped out many of the city's landmark sites. Among the prime casualties were the Hotel Tulsa and the Daniel Building. The first had been the Oil Capital's luxury palace, the second its first skyscraper. Other commercial properties not only survived but acquired new lives.

The Union Depot, which opened in 1931 and saw thousands of tearful families send their sons off to two wars, nearly fell into ruins after the last passenger train passed through

OPENED AS BELLEVIEW SCHOOL IN 1910, LINCOLN ELEMENTARY SCHOOL AT FIFTEENTH AND PEORIA WAS WHERE THOUSANDS OF TULSANS BEGAN THEIR EDUCATIONS. IN THE 1990S, THE VACANT BUILDINGS WERE PURCHASED FROM THE SCHOOL DISTRICT AND RENOVATED TO BECOME A CENTER FOR SMALL SHOPS AND RESTAURANTS LIKE JASON'S DELI, RIGHT.

Tulsa. Its windows smashed, its art deco architecture befouled with grime and graffiti, it often glowed during winter nights with fires lit to warm the homeless. Private investors restored most of its exterior splendor and successfully converted its interior into studios and office suites.

A few blocks west and north, new owners restored the old Cain's Dancing Academy. They carefully polished the hardwood floor, still resting on springs to lighten dancers' feet, found and posted old broadsides announcing play dates for Bob Wills and the Texas Playboys, and welcomed a new generation of boot-scooters. A mile or so south, other investors completely gutted the old Warehouse Market building, leaving nothing standing but a thin skin of brick and terra-cotta artwork. They then fleshed out the structure with imaginatively designed shops.

Some entire commercial districts enjoyed a similar renascence. Whittier Square, opened in pre–World War I days as the city's first suburb, overcame both age and a modern expressway's gouging of its side to capitalize upon the value of its charm. Whittier offered something so old to Tulsans that it was almost new: a variety of independently owned stores, many run by the children or grandchildren of their founders. Just as stubbornly self-reliant as their ancestors, they kept up a trade nearly as lively as in the old days, when Ferguson's Bakery came up with something new for Tulsans—sliced bread.

The area along Fifteenth Street as it ran east from Peoria Avenue shed decades of slowly accumulating seediness to enjoy a revitalization as the Cherry Street shopping district. The name was supposed to reflect the street's historical appellation. It sounded more modern and more upbeat than the name actually used for the district when it was a World War I–era shopping area: Alhambra. Farther south on Peoria, the Brookside area recaptured the novelty of its early post–World War II years by mixing a few older and established businesses with a host of new and innovative ones.

In both Cherry Street and Brookside, local merchants offered specialty items (including Tulsa-brewed beer) that shoppers were unlikely to find on the rows of shelves lining the discount houses and chain stores at the expressways' outer reaches. Remarkably, retailers in both areas maintained a lively trade with almost no use of mass, electronic (and loud) advertising. They relied and thrived instead on techniques better suited to the days of their original success: handbills posted on telephone and light poles and the indispensable word of mouth. What was most remarkable of all was that a steady stream of customers walked, actually walked, down several blocks of sidewalks. Leaving their cars far behind, they stopped perhaps to purchase an antique lamp, a fresh-baked pastry, a piece of Mexican pottery, or a frozen yogurt. One would have thought that Tulsans were discovering in their oldest shopping areas the greatest thing since sliced bread.

What they were discovering, of course, was their own history—even if it was sweetened with nostalgia. There were times, though, when Tulsans' encounter with history delivered a bitter flavor. Their city had more than one history, and Tulsans regularly encountered the two, three, many Tulsas shaped by those histories.

There was the Tulsa that celebrated its history in the Creek Council Oak Park. There also was another Tulsa, one that bore another, larger history, but that particular Tulsa was little noticed. Although Tulsa was founded as a Native American community, the modern city's Indian population was historically small and nearly invisible. From statehood onward, census takers listed only a small minority of Tulsans—between 3 and 5 percent—as Indians. Thomas Gilcrease was hardly the only prominent Tulsan or oilman of Native American ancestry, but neither was he typical. Most chose the comforting shelter of rural communities, many with great concentrations of other Indians. Often near Tulsa—about a third of Oklahoma's huge Indian population lived within fifty miles of the city—they were seldom part of it. Those who lived in Tulsa were usually isolated from its social, political, and economic mainstreams.

Several circumstances multiplied Tulsa's Indian numbers but barely reduced that dividing line. In the 1950s, the federal government launched a well-intended but ill-conceived policy of "termination." Wanting to end long and debilitating patterns of dependency, the government designated ten American cities as "relocation centers" for native peoples. The idea was to remove Indians from reservations and rural backwaters and force their full assimilation into urban America. Tulsa was one of the ten cities, and it received a stream of Indians from western states, immigrants in their own country. Even more came from the poverty-stricken areas of northeastern and western Oklahoma, where Native American unemployment ran as high as 80 percent.

By the time of the 1970 census, only sprawling Los Angeles, California, had a greater number of Indian residents, and no American city—Los Angeles included—had a greater percentage concentration. Both remained facts to be recorded in the 1980 and 1990 censuses. What also remained facts were that Native Americans' poverty rate was three times and unemployment rate ten times the levels of the general population's. Indian housing was poor and concentrated as semighettos in west and north Tulsa's transitional neighborhoods. In a city hooked on cars, 70 percent of Tulsa's Native American families did not own an automobile. Such numbers measured a history of a Tulsa that few knew and none celebrated.

African-Americans had accompanied the Creeks on their western migrations, some as slaves, others as free people, yet others arbitrarily designated as Indians themselves. Not many Tulsans may have known that particular history, but quite a few knew some of the events that punctuated its aftermath. The 1921 race riot was a subject rarely discussed but never forgotten on either side of Tulsa's color line. The line itself, although moving, was another inescapable fact that made more than one Tulsa. The white flight that set in during the 1960s soared through succeeding decades with no apex in sight. Thirty-five of the thirty-six neighborhoods lying nearest downtown Tulsa lost population between 1980 and 1990, and demographers projected that nearly half of Tulsa County's population growth between 1980 and 2010 would occur not in Tulsa but in Broken Arrow.

JEAN DENNISON

The city's black population crossed Cincinnati Avenue, spreading westward until it ran up against the barrier of the Osage Expressway. It also stretched north and northeast, often into neighborhoods still warm from fleeing white families. Rare was any significant movement of African-Americans to the city's south side, its southeast, or to the suburbs surrounding Tulsa. The little there was was often a consequence of federal housing programs that subsidized homeownership and rents, and those programs fed as much resentment as they did integration.

Such patterns were, of course, neither new nor accidental. On the contrary: they were continuing expressions of Tulsa's generally poor record of race relations. However brightly illuminated by a single tragedy like the 1921 riot, the record included thousands of unlit private acts as well as long shadows cast by public policies on housing, schooling, and employment. The policies were exactly the kind that might land a city and its institutions in court.

They did. Racially segregated public schools had been impermissible since 1954, but the Tulsa system initially did little to correct its past injustices and much to further them. Every year, more and more north-side schools became all- or nearly all-black, despite (sometimes because of) the school board's constant shifting of attendance zones. It was 1968 before the school board reversed its old minority-to-majority

ABOVE, LINCOLN SCHOOL IS NOW LINCOLN PLAZA. FACING PAGE, WAREHOUSE MARKET AT ELEVENTH AND ELGIN IS NOW LYON'S INDIAN STORE AND MAZZIO'S PIZZA. BY PRESERVING SOME OF TULSA'S UNIQUE ARCHITECTURE FOR 1990S SHOPS, ENTREPRENEURS ARE HELPING TO REVITALIZE OLDER NEIGHBORHOODS NEAR DOWNTOWN.

transfer policy to permit students to contribute to integration by leaving schools in which theirs was the majority race. The results were negligible. No more than a token number of blacks—and almost no whites—left their neighborhood schools to join the minority population at schools across town.

Meanwhile, the district continued to assign only white principals to the north side's new predominantly black schools, but not a single black principal headed a single school that had not been designated as black prior to 1954. The central administration employed only one African-American, and it told her to work with slow learners. Two credit unions—one black, one white—served school employees, maybe equally, certainly separately.

Such continuing practices provided a broad and deep base for the United States Justice Department's 1968 lawsuit against the Tulsa Public Schools. The district fought back for two years, ultimately defending itself before the Tenth United States Circuit Court. Its judges found Tulsa's practices indefensible. Declaring that they "constituted a system of state-imposed and state-preserved segregation," the court ordered the Tulsa school board to come up with an acceptable plan to correct injustices and establish a "unitary" public school system. To ensure compliance, it also placed the Tulsa Public Schools under the direct oversight of United States District Judge Fred Daugherty.

It took a while, but the school board had a plan at the start of the 1971-1972 school year. Part of it involved the familiar juggling of attendance zones. What was new was the closing of Carver Junior High School, the assignment of its students to seven other junior highs, and the creation of something called a Metro Learning Center, sort of a school within a school, at Booker T. Washington. In Washington, the Justice Department pronounced the plan acceptable.

African-Americans in Tulsa did not.

BUILT IN THE 1940S, THE BROOK THEATER WELCOMED MOVIEGOERS AND STAGE PRODUCTIONS FOR YEARS. TODAY, REVAMPED AS A RESTAURANT, IT WELCOMES LATE-NIGHT DINERS IN THE BROOKSIDE DISTRICT.

With a passion as strong as it was accurate, black Tulsans charged that the righting of injustice in the city's schools fell most heavily upon them, the victims of the injustice. Several black families pulled their children from the public schools and placed them in a new Carver Freedom School. Booker T. Washington's black students boycotted classes. Protest marches, prayer rallies, and sit-ins greeted school officials whenever they met.

In the middle of the controversy, the *Tulsa Tribune* received a letter from a surprising source: Dr. John Hope Franklin. A Harvard-trained professor of history at the University of Chicago, Franklin was one of the nation's most esteemed men of letters and learning. He also may have been the foremost product of Tulsa's public schools. His thoughts bear quoting at length:

JEAN DENNISON

I graduated from Booker T. Washington High School in 1931. Even now I recall how inferior our school was to Central High School and how we who went on to college and graduate school had to make up for the deficiencies created by a separate but unequal school system. It is almost inconceivable that 40 years later the educational leaders of Tulsa could be engaged in an enterprise that, in some ways, is even worse. They seek to destroy institutions that deserve to live. They seek to undermine the few sources of pride that a whole group of people have. They seek to meet their legal obligations by contrivances that reveal no appreciation for the principles of equity and justice.

The new policy fails to perceive the undeniable fact that as Negro teachers were, at times, compelled to make bricks without straw, they did not abandon the principles of dignity and decency that, in the long run, may well prove to be the salvation of the world as well as Tulsa. It would indeed be a meaningful experience for white Tulsa if it closed some of the white junior high schools and enrolled students in schools like Carver. . . . The white students would discover what it means to live in a world where dignity and self-respect and a commitment to equality are more important in the elevation of the human spirit than racial isolation and the oil-rich fat of the land to which so many have become accustomed.

The patent unfairness of the situation, whether so eloquently expressed in Professor Franklin's letter or so dramatically expressed in local mass actions, had an effect. The effect was not on the school board, which voted to hold tight. The effect was on average Tulsa families, some white, some black, all determined to find a just solution. Meeting initially in one another's homes, they began to devise plans to reopen Carver, to restore Washington, and to redeem Tulsa's public schools. Plain people, they had a plain solution: integrate the affected schools on a voluntary basis.

The idea had a firm basis in experience. At the time—the fall of 1971—Tulsa maintained exactly one successfully integrated public school. It was at "Big John" Burroughs, the once all-white school at the foot of Reservoir Hill. Several families had persuaded the school board to experiment with an open-design elementary school attached to the larger and traditionally structured Burroughs. Moreover, they promised to send their own children to such a school. School officials rushed prefab buildings to the campus, remodeled and equipped them, and recruited and trained teachers. When Burroughs Little School, as it was called, opened in November 1971, it enrolled seventy-nine black and ninety-eight white pupils. Well before the school year's end, it was a model of educational excellence as well as interracial harmony.

With the Burroughs example before them and committed parents behind them, school administrators readied Carver for reopening and Booker T. Washington for full integration in the fall of 1973. Curriculum specialists designed new programs for both schools, and school officials approached the district's top teachers to volunteer. Teams of parents, teachers, and schoolchildren visited every junior high and high school in the city to recruit students. Individual families scheduled coffees in their homes and arranged meetings in their churches for interested parents and children.

Carver reopened in 1973 with an enrollment of 150 white and 100 black students. Washington had about 1,100 students, half of them white, half of them black. Planned and steady expansions brought Carver's total enrollment to 500 and its racial mix to 50/50 by 1981. Washington had to cap its enrollment at 1,200 and place scores of families on waiting lists to attend what was widely perceived to be Tulsa's finest public high school. Thereafter, both schools thrived, and the district steadily refashioned more schools as successful "magnets" to attract voluntary integration. Satisfied, the Justice Department dropped its suit, and the federal district court relinquished its oversight in 1983.

No one believed that Tulsa had solved all of its racial problems, not even those centered in its public schools. The honor and attention that the nation gave Tulsa for its successful integration probably said more about the nation than it did about the integration. Tulsa had avoided ugly protests, open violence, and unseemly disruptions over court-ordered "busing." Alas, it had done it by moving a lot of black kids (by bus, no less) to previously white schools and by getting a few white kids to attend formerly black ones. Unnoticed amid all the external praise and the internal self-congratulation was the fact that 33,290 white students had chosen to leave the district altogether between 1968 and 1981 and that nearly a fifth of Tulsa's black students yet attended schools that were at least 90 percent black. Still, there were elements of decency and dignity there—if not enough to save Tulsa, enough at least to give it hope.

The same lesson came from another of Tulsa's encounters with its racial history. When Tulsa adopted the city-commission form of government in its 1908 charter, it was at the cutting edge of municipal reform. That edge grew rusty and dull over the years. Even its friends confessed that Tulsa's government worked despite its form rather than because of it. The charter's critics had more detailed arguments: that it promoted divisiveness in city affairs, that it fostered separate empire building rather than coherent policy making, that it encouraged neither administrative expertise nor legislative capability, and that it denied the mayor necessary executive authority. Many also noticed that it resulted in unbroken rule by an upper-middle-class white elite that generally lived in a few prime neighborhoods. Over the years, independent study groups uniformly recommended the charter's overhaul, and civic organizations ranging from the League of Women Voters to the National Association for the Advancement of Colored People (NAACP) urged its outright replacement. Popular and effective statesmen like Democratic Mayor James Maxwell and Republican Mayor Robert LaFortune agreed.

Several times, Tulsans voted to reform their charter; every time, they refused to do so. The circumstances varied, but the pattern was always the same: nearly everyone acknowledged the need for change, but no one could assemble a majority agreed on what the change should be.

The NAACP did not have to assemble a majority. All it had to do was file a lawsuit and convince a federal judge that Tulsa's form of government had done effectively and consistently precisely what it had been designed to do—deprive minorities of a fair chance for representation within municipal government. If so, it would violate the federal Voting Rights Act of 1965.

NAACP attorneys from the national office, aided by both black and white Tulsa lawyers and citizens, began to assemble the case law for such a suit. They had much from which to choose. Several courts already had overturned many cities' practices (such as citywide rather than ward-based elections) that were integral to Tulsa's form of government. They also began to assemble the history to back their claim that the results were discriminatory. For that too they had much to choose—more than seven decades' worth of history, in fact.

NANCY GODSEY

TWO, THREE, MANY TULSAS 287

Tulsans avoided a courtroom encounter with that history. With a Damoclean sword hanging over their collective head, civic groups, the chamber of commerce, both political parties, and nearly every other interest group imaginable fashioned a new, modernized city charter, replaced the old commission government with a strong mayor/city-council form, provided for council election by separate wards, and mustered the votes to get it passed. Rodger Randle, the last mayor to serve under the old charter, became the first to be elected under the new one. Working-class west Tulsa and African-American north Tulsa finally got the representation so long denied them once they were able to elect their own council members ward by ward. As in the case of its school system, Tulsans had not overcome their different histories. But they had confronted them, and they had addressed them responsibly.

That was the point. Tulsans never could unwrite the histories that had made their many Tulsas. Not even the threat or the power of the federal judiciary could do that. The best Tulsans could do was to transcend those histories, and the best of them did.

Native Americans, finding allies in the business community's chamber of commerce and the social-service network of the Tulsa Metropolitan Ministry (TMM), founded a Native American Coalition. Run by Indians themselves, the coalition referred many of Tulsa's heretofore forgotten and invisible first citizens to dozens of social agencies. Those agencies offered counseling, health care, job placement, and temporary financial assistance. Native Americans helping Native Americans, it was also Tulsans reaching out to other Tulsans.

More generally, the chamber of commerce stretched beyond the pure economic-development focus of its counterparts throughout America to reach toward improving north- and west-side schools and encouraging child-care services for the city's large number of single mothers. No one questioned what chamber old-timers like Robert McFarlin or Colonel Clarence Douglas would have thought about such an agenda. But no one particularly cared either.

On its part, TMM's little moneys and boundless energies cast the seeds that would grow to become the Residents' Services Department for the Tulsa Housing Authority and the Community Sentencing Program of the Oklahoma Department of Corrections. It also spawned a variety of citizen-action groups like Western Neighbors, which revitalized both the depressed economy and the fatalistic psychology of the Tulsa too long regarded as a stepchild. In its own right, TMM opened a day center for the homeless and named it for Henry and Anne Zarrow, members of one of Tulsa's oldest and most philanthropic families. No one had to wonder what the founders of the many faiths represented in TMM would have thought. TMM's members exercised their different faiths through common service.

Anyone who wondered what Dan Allen thought or what Dan Allen believed had only to ask—or just get close enough to hear him, unasked. A saint who swore like a sailor, Dan Allen left the Catholic priesthood in 1973 to head Neighbor for Neighbor (NFN), the organization that he had founded while at Saint Jude's Church three years earlier. "It was time for me to put up or shut up," he said of his decision, except Dan Allen never quite managed to shut up.

Who comprised Tulsa's finest families? Dan Allen said that it was the poor, both black and white, who were his north Tulsa neighbors: "They live so close to authentic human needs and authentic human wants and aspirations." Where were Tulsa's worst ghettos? Dan Allen said that they were in Tulsa's highest-priced neighborhoods, the ones packed with rich people who went to the same schools, joined the same clubs, attended the same churches, and thereby damned themselves to the luxurious hell of social isolation.

Dan Allen's words sometimes got him in trouble, but no one disputed the worth of what he did. Neighbor for Neighbor's budget was in excess of $400,000 annually, three-quarters from individuals, one-quarter from businesses and churches, not a cent from government at any level. With only nine paid staff members (but 260 unpaid volunteers), 98 percent of its funds went directly to serve up to 33,000 Tulsans per year. Seventy percent of its clients were the "working poor," those who worked irregularly or for minimum wages. To receive aid, they filed no documents, submitted to no interviews, opened their homes to no prying social workers. All they had to do was say they could use some help.

The help they got included access to NFN's health clinic, which each month distributed $50,000 worth of drugs obtained as free samples from pharmaceutical companies and another $7,000 worth bought outright. An optometric branch examined eyes, wrote prescriptions, and dispensed glasses at a flat fee of $25. NFN's food store amounted to a small supermarket that distributed food to 1,430 people monthly, some using cash, others vouchers. Its legal clinic helped 386 clients a month cut through the legal hassles to which the poor fell victim. At one time or another, NFN even operated its own gas station (which provided clients jobs), a car-repair garage (which got donated junkers in running shape), and a real estate office (which bought and rehabilitated repossessed homes for resale to the homeless).

When Dan Allen died of a brain tumor on November 12, 1995, it was these deeds, not Dan Allen's words, that Tulsans remembered. He had put up.

Cynthia Lowry Descher had too. Over her kitchen table, she and some neighbors founded the Tulsa Task Force for Battered Women. The year was 1976, and spousal abuse still was a subject for quiet whispers rather than vocal advocacy. For a time, the task force operated out of her home. The phone rang day and night, most calls followed by a quick trip to pick up a beaten woman and her children and get them to a safe place. So many angry husbands and boyfriends threatened her that she took to using her maiden name to protect her family. Nothing she could do would protect herself from the pain of attending the funerals of some of the women whom she had tried to help.

Twenty years later, the task force had become the Domestic Violence Intervention Services (DVIS). Supported in part by the United Way since 1979, DVIS sensitized physicians, prosecutors, and judges to the horrors of spousal abuse. Its trained advocates accompanied clients to court dates and testified on their behalves. Professional counselors worked with the abused, the abusers, and their children to restore families where possible. Where not, DVIS offered temporary shelter in sixty small but comfortable apartments. Nearly every one was full nearly every day.

Like the parents who brought effective integration to the city's schools, hundreds of Tulsans worked with the Native American Coalition, the Tulsa Metropolitan Ministry, Neighbor for Neighbor, or Domestic Violence Intervention Services. They saw a Tulsa that could be one city with one history. Like the city's earliest pioneers, they were building bridges, bridges arising from faith, bridges stretching out to every part of every Tulsa.

Sometimes they failed. Beneath the modern city's real bridges, dozens and scores of people made homes. Others found what little shelter there was in the shadows of the few buildings left standing after urban renewal. Many gathered within sight of Pauline Lambert's old May Rooms. It was the part of town that most Tulsans called "skid row," inhabited by human beings they dismissed as "winos" and "bums." Police Officer Robert E. Fagan called them something different. To Bob Fagan, they were "my people."

They were his because he was theirs. A onetime alcoholic, Fagan had joined Alcoholics Anonymous and had been sober for ten years when a *Tulsa Tribune* reporter accompanied him on patrol. Fagan did not speak much that night about his winning police-officer-of-the-year honors after he had faced down a heavily armed criminal who had just shot two other officers. Instead, he talked about his disease and "his people" who suffered from it too. From time to time, the cop and the reporter stopped to check on a drunk and take him or her to a shelter. Most of the time, they just drove through the skid-row district, their driving interrupted with smiles, waves, and a little bantering with Fagan's people. "I try to treat them with dignity," he told the reporter, "I don't write them off. I believe in miracles."

The reporter got his story, and Tulsans learned a lot about one of their city's finest when they read the *Tulsa Tribune* on Valentine's Day 1981. Maybe they learned a little about his people and their particular Tulsa too.

Seven months later, Officer Fagan's name appeared again in Tulsa newspapers. On the night of September 22, 1981, Bob Fagan parked his cruiser in the police garage, pulled out his service revolver, and fired a shot through his chest. His fellow officers who rushed to his car found him dead, a suicide note carefully placed beside him. It spoke of his personal battles. "Alcohol has begun to plague my life again—very gently at first, but it is becoming more of a monster again," the note said. Mostly, though, it spoke of his pain in dealing with a Tulsa that few Tulsans acknowledged. "I foresee no relief for my people—I'm too weak to help them anymore," Bob Fagan had written just before he unholstered his .38 police special.

Many Tulsans attended Robert Fagan's funeral. His police friends were there, including his closest one, Chief Harry Stege. There also were a lot of Tulsans that Bob Fagan had never met, and some he would not have recognized. The latter included a few freshly bathed, freshly shaved, and freshly clothed men. Their fellow inhabitants of skid row had chosen them to represent the many of Bob Fagan's people who could not be there. They were Tulsans showing all of Tulsa how much Officer Fagan had meant to their common city.

Perhaps for a later observance, some historian will repeat Bob Fagan's story—and Cynthia Lowry Descher's and Dan Allen's—and add to them other stories of other Tulsans not yet born.

If Tulsa is lucky, that historian will record that its people entered the second century of their city's history as others had its first. They saw a Tulsa still rich with opportunity. The pioneer generation that opened cattle trails, lured railroads, and built oil pipelines had been succeeded by a later generation. That one had built an avenue to the sea, sent shuttles to the moon, and turned rusting old pipelines into conduits for fiber-optic communication. That generation had bequeathed to succeeding generations a whole history to be appreciated and to be carried forward. Like all the pioneers before them, the pioneers of Tulsa's second century were builders too. They even kept building bridges, never resting until they built one city with one history.

THE SUNDAY-SCHOOL CLASS OF BESSIE
MAE AND LAURA BELLE HOLMES,
FEBRUARY 1908.

Tulsa's Children

A bridge across time . . .

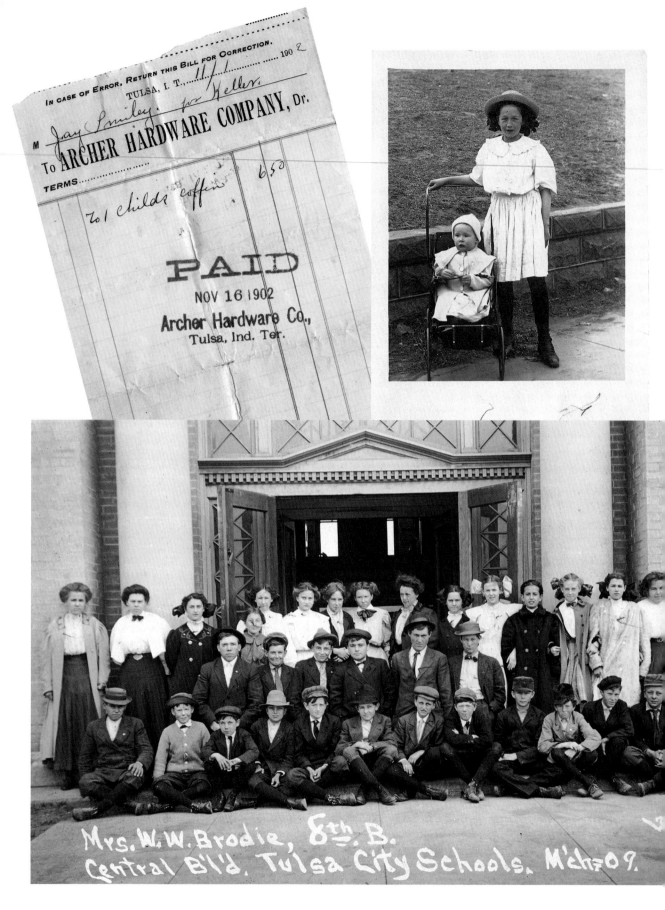

Mrs. W. W. Brodie, 8th. B.
Central B'l'd. Tulsa City Schools, M'ch 09.

Bess McAlester (Cog)
2. Mary Nicholson
3 Mary Fewell
4 Dencie Stebbins (Darnell)

5 Gayle Pehos (Miller)
6. Louise Berry (Walker)
7 Bess Rushmore (Grove)
8. Beth Fewell
9 Frances Smith

10 Edna Ruggles (Marrs)
11 Zella Bynum

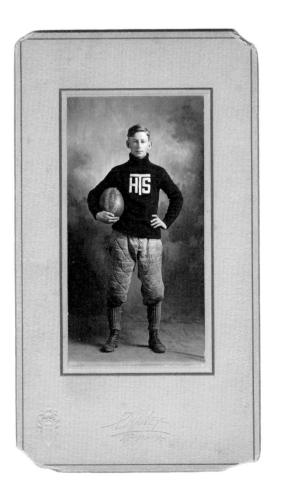

Facing page, Helen and Robert Rushmore in front of the future site of Central High School on Cincinnati between Fifth and Sixth Streets; Mrs. W. W. Brodie's eighth-grade class, gathered at the entrance to Tulsa's second school in 1910; above, club members of the BBB Club—the "Bashful, Beautiful Bachelors"—in 1907; a Tulsa High School football player, ca. 1900.

DOROTHY L. TAYLOR'S CLASS GROUP PERFORMS *THE SONG OF HIAWATHA* AT LEE SCHOOL IN FEBRUARY 1931

TULSA CENTRAL HIGH SCHOOL IN 1957

Irving School

N.W
Taulman
Tulsa '49

TULSA PUBLIC SCHOOL STUDENTS DRAMATIZE THE
EXPERIENCE OF INTEGRATION.

PROLOGUE

13 "never to quench it again": quoted in Grant Foreman, *Indian Removal: The Emigration of the Five Civilized Tribes* (Norman: University of Oklahoma Press, 1932), p. 140.

14 to govern themselves": treaty in Charles J. Kappler, ed., *Indian Affairs, Laws and Treaties* (57 Cong., 1 sess., Sen. Doc. No 452), II (Washington: Government Printing Office), cited in Foreman, p. 111.

14 "under the influence that existed": Foreman, p. 112.

16 "who can but respect him for it?": quoted in Foreman, p. 153.

16 pay for its own rebellion: Angie Debo, *The Road to Disappearance* (Norman: University of Oklahoma Press, 1941), pp. 102-103.

16 reached the West alive: ibid., p. 103.

17 the beginning of the new: Angie Debo, *Tulsa: From Creek Town to Oil Capital* (Norman: University of Oklahoma Press, 1943) p. 14.

CHAPTER ONE

26 "very wild and superstitious": The Reverend J. Ross Ramsey, quoted in Debo, *Tulsa*, p. 21.

27 including slave quarters: John Bartlett Meserve, "The Perrymans," *Chronicles of Oklahoma* (June 1937), pp. 166-184.

27 under the pastorate of James Perryman, Lewis's brother: Debo, *Tulsa*, p. 20.

28 they executed them all, men, women, and children: Robert W. Trepp to the Tulsa Committee on the Centennial of the City Charter, May 1, 1996, letter in author's possession.

28 camp on the Neosho (or Grand) River: Debo, *Tulsa*, pp. 24-31.

30 bounty given for personal subsistence: ibid., p. 39.

30 to the Sac and Fox agency and back: Lon R. Stansbury Interview, Indian-Pioneer Papers, Oklahoma Historical Society, Oklahoma City, Oklahoma; hereafter cited as Indian-Pioneer Papers.

31 "relations with whites were liberal": Hall, quoted in Effie S. Jackson's Memoirs of J. M. Hall, Indian-Pioneer Papers.

CHAPTER TWO

36 in the entire Creek nation: Debo, *Road to Disappearance,* p. 286.

42 the big spread in Osage country: Norman A. Graebner, "The Public Land Policy of the Five Civilized Tribes," *Chronicles of Oklahoma* (Summer 1945), pp. 110-111.

42 where real power already lay: D. O. Gillis Interview, Indian-Pioneeer Papers.

48 names like Sinclair (Harry and Earl) and Roberts (Oral): Land Records, Office of the Tulsa County Clerk, Tulsa, Oklahoma.

49 Indians two generations earlier: Angie Debo, *And Still the Waters Run: The Betrayal of the Five Civilized Tribes* (Princeton, N. J.: Princeton University Press, 1940), chapters 3, 4, and 5.

CHAPTER THREE

56 the quality of leadership: *Tulsa World,* Chamber of Commerce Special Issue, 1952.

57 some incredibly so: *Tulsa World,* November 7, 1949.

59 his original home: Miami, Florida: *Courtney Ann and Glen Vaughn-Roberson, City in the Osage Hills: Tulsa, Oklahoma* (Boulder,

Colorado: Pruett Publishing Company, 1984), pp. 73, 80.

67 He promised to clean up the city: R. M. McClintock, "Tulsa: The Story of Achievement," *Tulsa Tribune,* July 31, 1924, pp. 78-80.

67 Dispute surrounds the details of the previous six weeks: Carl Coke Rister, *Oil! Titan of the Southwest* (Norman: University of Oklahoma Press, 1949); cf. Fred Clinton, *First Oil and Gas Well in Tulsa County* (Oklahoma City: Oklahoma Historical Society, 1952).

67 "one of the vilest spots in the area": quoted in Kenny A. Franks, *The Oklahoma Petroleum Industry* (Norman: University of Oklahoma Press, 1980), p. 30.

INTRODUCTION, PART TWO

83 the annual meeting of the Tulsa Chamber of Commerce: Herbert Feis, "Tulsa," *The Survey: A Journal of Constructive Philanthropy* (October 1, 1923), pp. 18-24, quotations at pp. 19 ("White"), 22 (cf. New York), and 54 ("friendliness").

CHAPTER FOUR

86 a steady fifteen hundred barrels per day: Franks, *The Oklahoma Petroleum Industry*, p. 42.

89 its own domain: McClintock, "Tulsa," pp. 33-34.

90 no scars upon the city: Daniel Yergin, *The Prize: The Epic Quest for Oil, Money, and Power* (New York: Simon and Schuster, 1991), p. 128.

90 adding to Tulsa's refining capacity: McClintock, "Tulsa," pp. 11-12, 58-59.

91 Tulsa provided his throne: *Tulsa Spirit* (October 1917), pp 6-7.

91 a prince's golden crown: Clarence B. Douglas, *The History of Tulsa, Oklahoma* (Chicago: Clarke Press, 1921), I: 136-38.

91 their numbers, not their success: McClintock, "Tulsa," p.68.

92 two princes named Sinclair: Sinclair Oil and Gas Company, *A Great Name in Oil: Sinclair through Fifty Years* (New York: McGraw-Hill, 1966), p. 2.

92 title said it all—loudly: Roberta Ironside, *An Adventure Called Skelly: A History of Skelly Oil Company through Fifty Years* (New York: Appleton-Century-Crofts, 1970), pp 10-11.

95 rooms 810, 811, and 812 of the Daniel Building: Robert Gregory, *Oil in Oklahoma* (Muskogee: Leake Industries, Inc., 1976), p. 7.

96 its entire population: *Tulsa Spirit* (April 1920 and June 1920).

99 Robert McFarlin, representing McMan: McClintock, "Tulsa," pp. 37-38.

100 "new men on the scene": Douglas, *History of Tulsa,* I: 538.

102 "$10,000,000 to $15,000,000": *Tulsa Spirit* (March 1918).

107 Nonpartisan, it also was nonelected.: McClintock, "Tulsa," pp. 63, 99-100.

107 oilmen from around the world: *Tulsa Spirit* (July 1928); Donald Meyer Barnum, "International Petroleum Exposition, 1923-1940," master's thesis, University of Tulsa, 1968.

108 markers used on all federal highways: *Tulsa Spirit* (January 1927).

108 oil originating in the United States: *Tulsa Spirit* (January 1928).

CHAPTER FIVE

114 to reach into their own city: McClintock, "Tulsa," pp. 72-73.

115 hardly a single male enrolled: Douglas, *History of Tulsa,* I: 315-339. Other Tulsans served as conscripts in units consisting entirely of draftees.

115 "victory the same way": Yergin, pp. 167-183; Curzon, quoted in Albert Raymond Parker, "Life and Labor in the Mid-continent Oil

Fields, 1859-1945," Ph.D. diss., University of Oklahoma, 1951, p. 82.

115 secretary of the Tulsa Chamber of Commerce: McClintock, "Tulsa," pp. 76, 97; *Tulsa Spirit* (March 1918).

117 second place with $10.6 million: Douglas, History of Tulsa, I: 415-427; *Tulsa Spirit* (December 1918).

117 generously, if not freely: McClintock, "Tulsa,"pp. 92, 95.

118 "in this city and in this vicinity": Douglas, *History of Tulsa*, I: 468.

118 whom the Knights nearly hanged: McClintock, "Tulsa," p. 92.

118 when they produced their cards: McClintock, "Tulsa," pp. 92-93.

118 what Douglas called "Reds": Douglas, *History of Tulsa,* I: 468-473.

119 as they did during World War I: Parker, "Life and Labor," pp. 41-43, 72-73.

122 who had defended the men at their trial: Nigel Sellers, "Wobblies in the Oil Fields," in Davis D. Joyce, *"An Oklahoma I Had Never Seen Before": Alternative Views of Oklahoma History* (Norman: University of Oklahoma Press, 1994), pp. 129-144.

123 during those years: U. S. Department of Commerce, Bureau of the Census, Special Census of Tulsa County, Oklahoma, January 15, 1919 (Washington: Government Printing Office, 1919).

123 and one black library: Scott Ellsworth, *Death in a Promised Land: The Tulsa Race Riot of 1921* (Baton Rouge: Louisiana State University Press, 1982), p. 14.

123 on its statute books: Tulsa City Ordinances, chapter 36, sections 1336-1344 (Ordinance Number 1547); *Tulsa Democrat,* (August 5, 1916); Richard Kluger, *Simple Justice: The History of Brown v. Board of Education and Black America's Struggle for Equality* (New York: Alfred A. Knopf, 1975), pp. 134-135.

124 the state constitution: William R. Wilkinson, "A History of Negro Public Education in Tulsa, Oklahoma," master's thesis, University of Tulsa, 1954, p. 47; Ronald L. Trekell, *History of the Tulsa Police Department* (Tulsa: Tulsa Police Department, 1989); quotation from *Tulsa Daily Democrat,* (April 17, 1912).

124 join the pillaging mob: Connie Cronley, "That Ugly Day in May," *Oklahoma Monthly* (August 1976), p. 31.

127 Even now, nobody knows: "Report of the Tulsa Race Riot Disaster Relief Committee," Tulsa City-County Library, Reference Division.

128 "agitation among the negroes of [for?] social equality": "Grand Jury Report: Final Report of the Tulsa Grand Jury," reprinted in R. Halliburton Jr., *The Tulsa Race War of 1921* (San Francisco: R and E Research Associates, 1975), p. 38.

129 the Imperial Knights of the Ku Klux Klan: McClintock, "Tulsa," p. 102.

129 "Be No" blacks, Catholics, Jews, or foreigners welcomed there: Carter Blue Clark, "A History of the Ku Klux Klan in Oklahoma," Ph.D. diss., University of Oklahoma, 1976, pp. 45-47; Charles C. Alexander, *The Ku Klux Klan in the Southwest* (Lexington, Kentucky: University of Kentucky Press, 1965), pp. 44-45, 67.

130 sold cocaine, morphine, and heroin by the pound: Clark, "History of the Ku Klux Klan in Oklahoma," pp. 10-11.

131 an immoral caste they never could accept: "Membership Rolls of the Tulsa Ku Klux Klan," Ku Klux Klan Collection, Special Collections, McFarlin Library, University of Tulsa. I am indebted to Melanie Black for her careful analysis of the Klan's membership rolls.

133 martial law on the city and county of Tulsa: McAlister Coleman, "When the Troops Took Tulsa," *The Nation* (September 5, 1923), pp. 239-240.

CHAPTER SIX

135 three months shy of his fortieth birthday: Gregory, *Oil in Oklahoma,* p. 9.

136 "but not altogether easy": quoted in Yergin, p. 212.

137 a federal penitentiary: ibid., pp. 211-216, quotation at p. 216.

137 his business was Tulsa's business: McClintock, "Tulsa," p. 26; Slick, quoted in Yergin, p. 224.

138 the inevitable result: Parker, "Life and Labor," pp. 283-288.

140 greatly reduced pay scales: ibid., 298-299.

140 none had clothes: The Reverend Wilkie Clyde Clock, "Survey of West Tulsa," unpublished manuscript in author's possession.

142 women came in to scrub them: Francis Dominic Burke, "A Survey of the Negro Community of Tulsa, Oklahoma," master's thesis, University of Oklahoma, 1936, pp. 50-54, quotation at p. 54.

142 than did New York City's Harlem: ibid., pp. 68-76.

142 without regular trash pickup: ibid., pp. 22-52.

143 well-placed white families: ibid., pp. 53-68; William James Butler, *Tulsa 75: A History of Tulsa Commissioned by Mayor LaFortune* (Tulsa: Tulsa Metropolitan Chamber of Commerce, 1974), p. 73.

146 over to private parties: Oklahoma Department of State, Revised Laws of Oklahoma (Saint Paul: The Pioneer Co., 1912), p. 1159; Bobby Thomas Quinten, "The Social Impact of the Great Depression on Metropolitan Tulsa, 1929-1932," master's thesis, Oklahoma State University, 1963, pp. 7-62.

146 strong prolabor record: Quinten, pp. 63-66, 104-105.

147 So much for the deserving poor: ibid., pp. 159-160; Burke, "Negro Community of Tulsa," pp. 78-80, Girl Scout quotation at p. 89.

148 but not much else: Quinten, pp 89-90.

149 said that in 1929: Yergin, pp. 220-223, quotation at p. 228.

165 "few run-down sections": Longwell, "Where Beauty is Everybody's Business," the *Reader's Digest* (June 1957), pp. 69-71.

CHAPTER SEVEN

167 "mulish stubbornness": quoted in Gregory, *Oil in Oklahoma,* p. 14.

168 "That's the secret.": quoted in Yergin, p. 439.

169 nothing left to give—or to get: Gerald M. Lage, Ronald L. Moomaw, and Larkin Warner, *A Profile of Oklahoma Economic Development, 1950-1975* (Oklahoma City: Frontiers of Science Foundation of Oklahoma, 1977), p. 71-73; Minutes of Directors, January 5, 1943, Tulsa Chamber of Commerce, Tulsa, Oklahoma, hereafter cited as TCC Directors' Minutes.

170 Southwestern Bell Telephone or Sears, Roebuck and Company: *Tulsa Chamber of Commerce, 1942 Annual Report* (Tulsa: The Chamber, 1942), p. 31.

170 future military spending fell too: TCC Directors' Minutes, April 16, 1940, November 5, 1940; *Tulsa Spirit* (August 27, 1940).

173 caused the overcrowding in the first place: TCC Directors' Minutes, July 11, 1940; *Tulsa Spirit* (July 30, 1942).

173 Office of Priorities and Contract Distribution: *Tulsa Spirit* (January 8, 1942).

179 in excess of $185 per month: John David Hoff Jr., "A History of Tulsa International Airport," master's thesis, University of Tulsa, 1967, pp. 66-72.

180 graduates of Spartan themselves: Esther Martin Robinson, "A History of the Spartan School of Aeronautics and Spartan Aircraft

Company," master's thesis, University of Tulsa, 1983, pp. 7-57.

181 wartime's industrial expansion: *Tulsa Spirit* (September 13, 1945, April 21, 1949, February 1, 1950).

181 "methods of the 1930s": *Tulsa Spirit* (September 13, 1945).

CHAPTER EIGHT

185 no great loss: Michael Wallis, *Beyond the Hills: The Journey of Waite Phillips,* Oklahoma Trackmaker Series, Oklahoma Heritage Association (Oklahoma City: The Association, 1995), p. 223.

187 "rising skylines": Rhodes, "Blueprinting a Balanced Tulsa," *Tulsa Magazine* (August, September, October 1948), p. 27.

189 building on Boulder Avenue: Wallis, pp. 28-92, 101-169, 218-227, 280-282.

189 "more cosmopolitan attitude here": Noel Houston, "Talk about Tulsa!" *Holiday* (October 1954), p. 104.

190 Native American ancestors: Gregory, *Oil in Oklahoma,* pp. 59-69.

191 literally priceless: *Gilcrease Institute of American History and Art: A National Treasure* (n.p., n.d.); Mrs. John Ladner, "Gilcrease Collection Draws 100,000 Visitors Annually," *Tulsa Magazine* (November 4, 1965), pp. 3-7.

192 "cain't find Will Rogers nowheres in it": "Tulsa Goes Modern," *Life* (March 5, 1951), pp. 78-79; quotation from Houston, p. 105.

192 bottle of Kentucky's finest: Houston, p. 105.

193 "damn well cried": Carl Post, "Once Called a Cultural Sahara, Tulsa Now Boasts an Active Musical Life," *Musical America* (January 1, 1954), p. 33; quotation from Houston, p. 105.

193 Cain's Dancing Academy: Charles R. Townsend, *San Antonio Rose: The Life and Music of Bob Wills* (Urbana: University of Illinois Press, 1976), pp. 123, 134, 145.

193 beginning with *La Traviata:* "Mixed Fare, High Hopes," *Christian Science Monitor Magazine,* (April 8, 1950), p. 13.

193 singular American treasure in 1988: *Tulsa Sunday World* (December 15, 1996).

195 United States Department of Public Health: Margaret Hickey, "League of Women Voters in Tulsa, Oklahoma," *Ladies Home Journal* (April 1950), pp. 23, 225-226.

196 Greenwood not at all: William R. Wooten, "Paving Oklahoma's Busiest Street," *The American City* (June 1950), pp. 110-111; W. A. Beck, "As Different as Night and Day," *The American City* (October 1953), pp. 92-93.

196 almost as many varieties: Eva Stacey, "The Tulsa Garden Center," *The Flower Grower* (June 1959), pp. 59-62; Houston, p. 100.

196 effectiveness improved not at all: Ralph A. Ulvelling, "Report of a Survey of the Tulsa Library, 1950" Tulsa City-County Library Reference Collection.

197 Alfred Aaronson Auditorium: Allie Beth Martin, "Triple for Tulsa," *Library Journal* (December 1, 1964), pp. 4740-4744; Roderick G. Swartz, "Pride in Heritage: One Library's Approach," *Wilson Library Bulletin* (January 1972), pp. 431-435.

CHAPTER NINE

201 already had moved to Hammond, Indiana: *Benton v. State,* Criminal Court of Appeals of Oklahoma (February 18, 1948); Jay Robert Nash, *Encyclopedia of World Crime* (Crime Books, Inc.: Wilmett, Illinois, 1990), p. 3001.

202 at least they were classified: National Urban League, *A Study of the Social and Economic Condition of the Negro Population of Tulsa, Oklahoma* (Washington: National Urban League, 1946), p. 88.

205 either bumper or pusher clubs: ibid., p. 88.

206 "his new concept of thinking": quoted ibid.

206 scales of justice: ibid., pp. 56-60.

210 riot a third of a century earlier: Ada Lois Sipuel Fisher with Danney Goble, *A Matter of*

Black and White: The Autobiography of Ada Lois Sipuel Fisher (Norman: University of Oklahoma Press), pp. 12-150.

211 the black-occupied districts: National Urban League, *A Study of the Negro Population of Tulsa,* pp. 37-39.

211 financial barrier cracked too: Karl Thiel, "The Racially Changing Community," master's thesis, University of Oklahoma, 1962, p. 24.

212 within the previous thirty-six months: ibid.

214 "in another school district": quotation from ibid., p. 123.

215 an all-black one: ibid, pp. 69-93.

CHAPTER TEN

233 26 known killed: William A. Settle Jr., *The Dawning: A New Day for the Southwest: A History of the Tulsa District Corps of Engineers* (Tulsa: U. S. Army Corps of Engineers, Tulsa District, 1975), p. 44.

234 "make his exclusively": quoted ibid., p. 45.

234 "gigantic pork barrel boondoggle": Anne Elizabeth Phillips, "The Merchant's River of Gold: Civic Boosterism and the McClellan-Kerr Navigation System," master's thesis, University of Tulsa, 1993, p. 99, quotation at p. 88.

236 "get navigation for the Arkansas": Settle, p. 72; Phillips, pp. 43-44, quotation at p. 44.

237 "willing to bring in the well?": quoted in Phillips, pp. 84-85.

238 break ground along the Arkansas: Anne Hodges Morgan, *Robert S. Kerr: The Senate Years* (Norman: University of Oklahoma Press, 1977), p. 165.

239 "community they represent guide them": quoted in Phillips, p. 136.

241 a window on the sea: Morgan, pp. 139-174.

242 worth to Tulsa and northeastern Oklahoma: James Chien-Hua Chang, "The Impact of the McClellan-Kerr Arkansas River Navigation on the Oklahoma Economy," Ph.D. diss., Oklahoma State University, 1977.

242 "bringing home the bacon": quoted in Phillips, p. 132.

242 employment growth in 1946: *Tulsa Magazine* (January 1947), p. 11.

243 the new state of Israel: Esther Martin Robinson, pp. 89-97.

244 civilian work on Boeing's new "jumbo jet," the 747: JoAnn Boatman, "NAA," *Tulsa Magazine* (May 4, 1967), p. 5.

244 everything from paper clips to heavy industrial machinery: Kenneth Wayne McGill, "Establishment and Growth of the American Airlines Maintenance and Engineering Center, 1945-1966, Tulsa, Oklahoma," master's thesis, University of Tulsa, 1971.

245 new or expanded plants: Bruce D. Hall, "Tulsa: Winch Capital of the World," *Tulsa Magazine* (March 5, 1964), pp. 10-25.

246 Cherokee Industrial Park: "Mid-Year Report," Tulsa Metropolitan Chamber of Commerce (July 10, 1986), p. 1.

247 not enough to go around: "Job Seekers Get C-C Caution," *Tulsa* (August 12, 1982), p. 1.

247 a little later and a little less than America's: Tom Baines, "Tulsa Economy: The Long-Term View," *Tulsa* (June 1983), pp. 9-11.

CHAPTER ELEVEN

254 expressways already under way and financed by federal and state moneys: *Tulsa World,* October 31, 1991.

256 Not even Greenwich Village or Georgetown had that distinction: Bobbye

Ruth Potter, "Tulsa, Oklahoma, Properties Listed on the National Register of Historic Places," master's thesis, University of Tulsa, 1983.

257 under construction at Forty-first and Yale: "The Bid for Bucks," *Greater Tulsa Magazine* (November 5, 1959), pp 6-7; *Tulsa* (June 8, 1967), pp. 22-23.

260 lasting importance, even beauty: *Tulsa World* (October 10, 1984).

262 only a duck pond away from another urban renewal product, the Greenwood Cultural Center: *Tulsa Development Authority, The Annual Report: Thirty-five Years* (Tulsa: The Authority, 1994).

264 for Tulsa's destiny as well: Tulsa Metropolitan Area Planning Commission files, Vision 2000 planning documents, Tulsa City-County Library.

266 reduced the Swim and Racket Club to ashes: ibid.; Phyllis Braunlich, *A History of Gilcrease Hills and Surrounding Landmarks in Near Northeast Tulsa* (Tulsa: Gilcrease Home Owners Association, 1990).

266 "balanced growth for our community is not being realized": Williams, quoted in Vaughn-Roberson, *City in the Osage Hills,* p. 167.

268 growth rates of 69, 137, and 349 percent respectively: Oklahoma Advisory Committee to the United States Commission on Civil Rights, School Desegregation in Tulsa, Oklahoma (Washington: Government Printing Office, 1977), p. 20.

CHAPTER TWELVE

273 tributes to her near legendary status: Judge Richard Armstrong, quoted in *Tulsa Tribune* (December 27, 1983), in *Tribune* files, Tulsa City-County Library, Reference Division; *Tulsa Tribune* (February 15, 16, March 14, June 15, 1978; April 5, 18, 1980).

275 had done nearly one-and-one-half centuries earlier: Connie Cronley, "The Creek Council Oak," *Tulsa* (October 1980), pp. 70-72.

278 the greatest thing since sliced bread: *Tulsa Tribune* (December 7, 1977, April 29, 1976); *Tulsa World* (November 5, 1978); Steve Millburg, "Good Old Cherry Street is Back," *Southern Living* (June 1995), p. 42.

279 few knew and none celebrated: Connie Cronley, "Expressway of Tears," *Tulsa* (September 1978), pp. 22-27; *Tulsa Tribune* (June 6, 1978, December 18, 19, 20, 21, 22, 1978).

280 not in Tulsa but in Broken Arrow: Indian Nations Council of Governments, *Demographic Atlas of Tulsa County* (Tulsa: The Council, 1990), pp. 13, 86.

282 maybe equally, certainly separately: *Tulsa Tribune* (March 4, June 26, 1968)

284 "the oil-rich fat of the land to which so many have become accustomed": John Hope Franklin to the editor, *Tulsa Tribune* (August 26, 1971).

285 enough at least to give it hope: *Neither Black Nor White: A History of Integration in the Tulsa Public Schools, 1954-1983* (Tulsa: Tulsa Public Schools, 1982).

286 what the change should be: Max K. Knarr, "The Attempts at Charter Revision in Tulsa," master's thesis, University of Tulsa, 1973.

289 He had put up: *Tulsa World* (January 30, 1994, November 26, 1995).

290 full nearly every day: Domestic Violence Intervention Services: *A Celebration of Twenty Years of Service, 1976-1996* (n.p., n.d.).

MANUSCRIPT COLLECTIONS

Chapman, Leta McFarlin Collection. University of Tulsa Special Collections. McFarlin Library. University of Tulsa.

Farm Security Administration Photographs. University of Tulsa Special Collections. McFarlin Library. University of Tulsa.

Galbreath, Frank Collection. University of Tulsa Special Collections. McFarlin Library. University of Tulsa.

Indian-Pioneer Papers. Division of Manuscripts. Oklahoma Historical Society.

International Petroleum Exposition Collection. University of Tulsa Special Collections. McFarlin Library. University of Tulsa.

Kennedy, Dr. Samuel Grant Collection. University of Tulsa Special Collections. McFarlin Library. University of Tulsa.

Ku Klux Klan Collection. University of Tulsa Special Collections. McFarlin Library. University of Tulsa.

Lindsey, Lilah D. Collection. University of Tulsa Special Collections. McFarlin Library. University of Tulsa.

Minutes of the Boards of Directors Collection. Metropolitan Tulsa Chamber of Commerce.

Oklahoma Ephemera Collection. University of Tulsa Special Collections. McFarlin Library. University of Tulsa.

Port of Catoosa Collection. University of Tulsa Special Collections. McFarlin Library. University of Tulsa.

Randolph, Fred Collection. University of Tulsa Special Collections. McFarlin Library. University of Tulsa.

Settle, William Collection. University of Tulsa Special Collections. McFarlin Library. University of Tulsa.

Smith, W. W. Collection. University of Tulsa Special Collections. McFarlin Library. University of Tulsa.

Tulsa Art Deco Collection. University of Tulsa Special Collections. McFarlin Library. University of Tulsa.

Tulsa Maps Collection. University of Tulsa Special Collections. McFarlin Library. University of Tulsa.

Tulsa Race Riot Collection. University of Tulsa Special Collections. McFarlin Library. University of Tulsa.

Tulsa Women's Club Collection. University of Tulsa Special Collections. McFarlin Library. University of Tulsa.

THESES AND DISSERTATIONS

Alexander, Constance. "A History of Sand Springs." Master's thesis, University of Tulsa, 1948.

Almen, William Harned. "A History of the Theater in Tulsa from 1906 to 1928." Master's thesis, University of Tulsa, 1958.

Angelletti, Charles Edward. "Jeremiad on the Far Right: A Case Study of Billy James Hargis and His Christian Echoes National Ministry, Inc." Master's thesis, University of Tulsa, 1964.

Barnum, Donald Meyer. "International Petroleum Exposition, 1923-1940." Master's thesis, University of Tulsa, 1968.

Bradshaw, Roy B. "An Experiment with a Group of Superior Pupils in Junior High School." Master's thesis, University of Oklahoma, 1935.

Brown, Thomas Elton. "Bible-Belt Catholicism: A History of the Roman Catholic Church in Oklahoma, 1905-1945." Ph.D. diss., Oklahoma State University, 1974.

Burke, Francis Dominic. "A Survey of the Negro Community of Tulsa, Oklahoma." Master's thesis, University of Oklahoma, 1936.

Chang, James Chien-Hua. "The Impact of the McClellan-Kerr Arkansas River Navigation System on the Oklahoma Economy." Ph.D. diss., Oklahoma State University, 1977.

Clark, Carter Blue. "A History of the Ku Klux Klan in Oklahoma." Ph.D. diss., University of Oklahoma, 1976.

Cooper, Norman W. "Oklahoma in the Great Depression, 1930-1940: The Problem of Emergency Relief." Master's thesis, University of Oklahoma, 1973.

Corbett, William Paul. "Oklahoma's Highways: Indian Trails to Urban Expressways." Ph.D. diss., Oklahoma State University, 1982.

Davenport, John Stephen. "The History of Holland Hall School." Master's thesis. University of Tulsa, 1961.

DeBerry, Drue Lemuel. "The Ethos of the Oklahoma Oil Boom Frontier, 1905-1929." Master's thesis, University of Oklahoma, 1970.

Doughty, Ralph Miller. "The Mid-Continent Petroleum Corporation Strike of 1938: A Study in Oklahoma Industrial Relations." Master's thesis, University of Oklahoma, 1948.

Engles, Leo James. "A Study of Catholic Education in Oklahoma with Special Emphasis on the Diocese of Oklahoma City and Tulsa." Ed.D. diss., University of Tulsa, 1971.

Forbes, Charles G. "The Origins and Development of the Oil Industry in Oklahoma." Ph.D. diss., University of Oklahoma, 1939.

Fowler, James H. "Extralegal Suppression of Civil Liberties in Oklahoma During the First World War." Master's thesis, Oklahoma State University, 1974.

Frazier, J. Vere Jr. "History of the Glennpool Oil Field." Master's thesis, University of Oklahoma, 1961.

Gilbert, James L. "Three Sands: Oklahoma Oil Field and Community of the 1920's." Master's thesis, University of Oklahoma, 1967.

Hoff, John David Jr. "A History of Tulsa International Airport." Master's thesis, University of Tulsa, 1967.

Holland, Reid. "The Civilian Conservation Corps in Oklahoma." Master's thesis, Oklahoma State University, 1968.

_____. "Urban Frontier Leadership." Ph.D. diss., Oklahoma State University, 1971.

Howard, James A. W. "A Critical History of the Editorial Policy of the *Tulsa World* and *Tulsa Tribune* on the United Nations, 1945-1970." Master's thesis, University of Tulsa, 1972.

Hunter, Jim Ernest Jr. "A Gathering of Sects: Revivalistic Pluralism in Tulsa, Oklahoma, 1945-1985." Ph.D. diss., Southern Baptist Theological Seminary, 1986.

Jackson, Pauline P. "The Sapulpa Story to 1929." Master's thesis, University of Tulsa, 1956.

Knarr, Max K. "The Attempts at Charter Revision in Tulsa." Master's thesis, University of Tulsa, 1973.

Knight, Raymond. "The Origin & Development of the Junior High School System in the Tulsa Public Schools." Master's thesis, University of Oklahoma, 1946.

McGill, Kenneth Wayne. "Establishment and Growth of the American Airlines Maintenance and Engineering Center, 1945-1966." Master's thesis, University of Tulsa, 1971.

Miller, Shana Marie. "Race/Age Group Differences in Exposure to Concentrated Urban Poverty." Ph.D. diss., University of Oklahoma, 1993.

Mitchell, James. M. "Politics in a Boom Town: Tulsa from 1906 to 1930." Master's thesis, University of Tulsa, 1950.

Phillips, Anne Elizabeth. "The Merchant's River of Gold: Civic Boosterism and the McClellan-Kerr Navigation System." Master's thesis, University of Tulsa, 1993.

Potter, Bobbye Ruth. "Tulsa, Oklahoma, Properties Listed on the National Register of Historic Places." Master's thesis, University of Tulsa, 1983.

Powell, Richard Hays. "The Oil Industry and the Depression from the Development of Greater Seminole Through the Passage of the Oil Code." Master's thesis, University of Oklahoma, 1968.

Quinten, Bobby Thomas. "The Social Impact of the Great Depression on Metropolitan Tulsa, 1929-1932." Master's thesis, Oklahoma State University, 1963.

Rains, Roy. "The Spavinaw Water Construction Project." Master's thesis, University of Tulsa, 1959.

Roberson, Glen Romaine. "City on the Plains: The History of Tulsa, Oklahoma." Ph.D. diss., Oklahoma State University, 1977.

Roberts, Joe Donald. "An Economic and Geographic History of Cushing, Oklahoma, from its Origins through the Oil Boom Years, 1912-1917." Ph.D. diss., University of Minnesota, 1976.

Robinson, Esther Martin. "A History of the Spartan School of Aeronautics and Spartan Aircraft Company, 1928-1954." Master's thesis, University of Tulsa, 1960.

Smith, Lee Rand. "A Comparative Study of the Achievement of Negro Students Attending Segregated Junior High Schools and Negro Students Attending Desegregated Junior High Schools in the City of Tulsa." Ed.D. diss., University of Tulsa, 1971.

Snider, Jill D. "Flying to Freedom: African-American Visions of Aviation, 1910-1927." Ph.D. diss., University of North Carolina at Chapel Hill, 1995.

Thiele, Karl. "The Racially Changing Community." Master's thesis, University of Oklahoma, 1962.

Turner, Alvin O'Dell. "The Regulation of the Oklahoma Oil Industry." Ph.D. diss., Oklahoma State University, 1977.

Webber, Larry Dean. "A Case Study of Closing Schools in a Large Metropolitan School District Experiencing Declining Enrollment." Ed.D. diss., University of Oklahoma, 1983.

Wilkinson, William R. "A History of Negro Public Education in Tulsa, Oklahoma." Master's thesis, University of Tulsa, 1954.

Young, Gloria Alese. "Powwow Power: Perspectives on Historic and Contemporary Intertribalism." Ph.D. diss., Indiana University, 1981.

JOURNALS AND PERIODICALS

American Scene.

Gilcrease Magazine.

Inside Tulsa.

Lifestyle Tulsa.

Oklahoma Monthly.

Tulsa.

Tulsa Magazine.

Tulsa Spirit.

Tulsa Tribune.

Tulsa World.

FILMS AND VIDEOS

City of Pride. Tulsa Studios, Inc.: Tulsa, Oklahoma.

Holy Tulsa. Vintage Films: Tulsa, Oklahoma.

Goin' Back to T-Town. Washington: Public Broadcasting Service.

Greenwood Blues. KOCO-TV: Oklahoma City, Oklahoma.

Kendall-Whittier: A Neighborhood Renaissance. Tulsa Kendall-Whittier Ministry: Tulsa, Oklahoma.

Let's Go Downtown. Vintage Films: Tulsa, Oklahoma.

Stuff That's Gone. Vintage Films: Tulsa, Oklahoma.

Things Not in Tulsa Anymore. Vintage Films: Tulsa, Oklahoma.

Tulsa's Art Deco. Vintage Films: Tulsa, Oklahoma.

Tulsa: We're Speaking Your Language. Tulsa Chamber of Commerce: Tulsa, Oklahoma.

Tulsa: Building a World around You. The Studios: Tulsa, Oklahoma.

Tulsa Memories. Vintage Films: Tulsa, Oklahoma.

Tulsa's Secret: The Race Riot of 1921. KTUL-TV: Tulsa, Oklahoma.

Tulsa's Uncommon Houses. Vintage Films: Tulsa, Oklahoma.

SOUND RECORDINGS

Junior League of Tulsa. *Historical Preservation Project.*

National Public Radio. *A Conspiracy of Silence: The Tulsa Race Riot of 1921.*

BOOKS

Alexander, Charles C. *The Ku Klux Klan in the Southwest.* Lexington, Kentucky: University of Kentucky Press, 1965.

Allen, Clarence C. *Who's Who in Tulsa 1951.* N. p., 1951.

American Petroleum Institute. *Petroleum Facts and Figures.* New York: J. J. Little and Ives Company, 1928.

_____. *Petroleum Facts and Figures.* Baltimore: Lord Baltimore Press, 1931.

_____. *Petroleum Facts and Figures, 1967.* New York: American Petroleum Institute, 1967.

_____. *Petroleum Facts and Figures, 1963.* New York: American Petroleum Institute, 1963.

American Public Welfare Association. *Welfare and Child Care Services in Tulsa City and County.* N. p., 1947.

American Red Cross. *Report of Tulsa Race Riot Disaster Relief.* N.p., n.d.

Art Work of Tulsa. Chicago: Gravure Illinois Company, 1920.

Arts of Tulsa. *Tulsa Tornados June 8, 1974.* Tulsa, 1974.

Bayne, S. G. *Derricks of Destiny.* New York: Brentano's, 1924.

Bernard, Richard M. *The Poles in Oklahoma.* Newcomers to a New Land Series. Norman: University of Oklahoma Press, 1980.

Bicha, Karel D. *The Czechs in Oklahoma.* Newcomers to a New Land Series. Norman: University of Oklahoma Press, 1980.

Blakey. Ellen S. *Tulsa Spirit.* Tulsa: Continental Heritage Press, 1979.

Blessing, Patrick. *The British and Irish in Oklahoma.* Newcomers to a New Land Series. Norman: University of Oklahoma Press, 1980.

Braunlich, Phyllis. *A History of Gilcrease Hills and Surrounding Landmarks in Near Northeast Tulsa.* Tulsa: Gilcrease Home Owners Association, 1990.

Brossard, E. B. *Petroleum, Politics and Power.* Tulsa: PennWell Books, 1983.

Brown, Kenny L. *The Italians in Oklahoma.* Newcomers to a New Land Series. Norman: University of Oklahoma Press, 1980.

Butler, William James. *Tulsa 75: A History of Tulsa Commissioned by Mayor LaFortune.* Tulsa: Tulsa Metropolitan Chamber of Commerce, 1974.

Chadsey, Charles Ernest. *Report of an Inspection of the Tulsa School System.* Tulsa: Tulsa Board of Education, 1928.

City Demonstration Agency. *Tulsa Model Cities Program: A Comprehensive Demonstration Program to Improve the Quality of Urban Life.* Tulsa: The Agency, 1969.

Clark, J. Stanley. *The Oil Century from the Drake Well to the Conservation Era.* Norman: University of Oklahoma Press, 1958.

Clinton, Fred. *First Oil and Gas Well in Tulsa County.* Oklahoma City: Oklahoma Historical Society, 1952.

Coble, George. *The History of the Tulsa Fire Department, 1905-1973.* Tulsa: Intercollegiate Press, 1973.

Community Service Council of Greater Tulsa. *Tulsa County Data Base Report, 1980-81.* Tulsa: The Council, 1982.

Connelly, W. L. *The Oil Business as I Saw It.* Norman: University of Oklahoma Press, 1954.

Continental Oil Company. *Conoco: The First One Hundred Years.* New York: Dell Publishing Company, 1974.

Corrubin, Paul E. *Tulsa: Oil Capital of the World.* Tulsa: Corrubin, 1937.

Debo, Angie. *Tulsa: From Creek Town to Oil Capital.* Norman: University of Oklahoma Press, 1943.

_____.*The Road to Disappearance: A History of the Creek Indians.* Norman: University of Oklahoma Press, 1941.

Domestic Violence Intervention Services: *A Celebration of Twenty Years of Service, 1976-1996.*

Douglas, Clarence B. *Some Men of Tulsa.* Tulsa: Dexter, 1922.

_____.*The History of Tulsa,* Oklahoma. 3 vols. Chicago: Clarke Press, 1921.

Duncan, Kelley. *Cultural Resources in the Tulsa Urban Study Area.* Tulsa: Archaeological Research Association, 1977.

Duncan, Jean. *A Patchwork of Memories.* Tulsa: J. R. Woods, 1983.

Dunn, Nina Lane. *Tulsa's Magic Roots.* Tulsa: Oklahoma Book Publishing Company, 1979.

Eagleton, Norma. *Charter and Revised Ordinances of the City of Tulsa, 1990.* Tulsa: City of Tulsa, 1990.

Economic Development Information Center. *Tulsa Data Book.* Tulsa: The Center, 1988.

Ellis, William D. *On the Oil Lands with Cities Service.* Tulsa: Cities Service Oil and Gas Corp., 1983.

Ellsworth, Scott. *Death in a Promised Land: The Tulsa Race Riot of 1921.* Baton Rouge: Louisiana State University Press, 1982.

Everly-Douze, Susan. *Tulsa Times: A Pictorial History: The Boom Years.* Tulsa: World Publishing Company, 1987.

Everly-Douze, Susan. *Tulsa Times: A Pictorial History: Coming of Age.* Tulsa: Tulsa World Publishing Company, 1988.

Everly-Douze, Susan. *Tulsa: A Pictorial History: The Early Years.* Tulsa: World Publishing Company, 1986.

Federal Writers Project. *Tulsa: A Guide to the Oil Capital.* Tulsa: Mid-West Printing Co., 1938

Fisher, Ada Lois Sipuel, with Danney Goble. *A Matter of Black and White: The Autobiography of Ada Lois Sipuel Fisher.* Norman: University of Oklahoma Press, 1995.

First Presbyterian Church of Tulsa. *Membership Roll and Parish Plan.* Tulsa: The Church, 1920.

First National Bank and Trust Company. *A Story of a City and Its Bank.* Tulsa: The Bank, 1970.

Foreman, Grant. *Indian Removal: The Emigration of the Five Civilized Tribes of Indians.* Norman: University of Oklahoma Press, 1932.

Fourth National Bank of Tulsa. *Moccasins to Metropolis.* Tulsa: The Bank, 1970.

Franklin, Jimmie Lewis. *The Blacks in Oklahoma.* Newcomers to a New Land Series. Norman: University of Oklahoma Press, 1980.

Franks, Kenny A. *The Oklahoma Petroleum Industry.* Norman: University of Oklahoma Press, 1980.

Galbreath, Frank. *Glenn Pool and a Little Oil Town of Yesteryear.* Tulsa: Galbreath, 1978.

Gardner, James Henry. *Journal of 100 Years Ago in the Region of Tulsa.* Oklahoma City: Oklahoma Historical Society, 1933.

Gilcrease Institute of American History and Art: A National Treasure. N.p., n.d.

Girl Scout Troop 202. *Shadows of the Past: Tombstone Inscriptions in Tulsa County.* Tulsa: Tulsa Genealogical Society, 1986.

Glasscock, Carl B. *Then Came Oil: The Story of the Last Frontier.* New York: Bobbs-Merrill, 1938.

Gordon, Seth K., and W. B. Richards, comps. *The Oklahoma Red Book.* 2 vols. Oklahoma City: Democrat Publishing Company, 1912.

Graham, Thomas E. *The Wedding of Tulsa to the Spavinaw Hills.* Tulsa: Oklahoma Press, 1924.

Gregory, Robert. *Oil in Oklahoma.* Muskogee: Leake Industries, Inc., 1976.

Haddock, Louise. *History of Tulsa Baptist Association.* Tulsa: Allied Printers and Publishers, 1974.

Hale, Douglas. *The Germans from Russia in Oklahoma.* Newcomers to a New Land Series. Norman: University of Oklahoma Press, 1980.

Hall, James M. *The Beginning of Tulsa; First Men; First Events.* Tulsa: Tulsa Tribune, 1928.

Halliburton, R. Jr. *The Tulsa Race War of 1921.* San Francisco: R & E Research Association, 1975.

Harrell, David Edwin Jr. *Oral Roberts: An American Life.* Bloomington: Indiana University Press, 1985.

Hatley, Allen G. Jr., ed. *The Oil Finders: A Collection of Stories about Exploration.* Tulsa: American Association of Petroleum Geologists, 1992.

Hill, Edward Allison. *Story of the Mid-Continent Oil and Gas Field.* Tulsa: Burkhart Printing and Stationery Company, 1914.

Hofsommer, Donovan L., ed. *Railroads in Oklahoma.* Oklahoma City: Oklahoma Historical Society, 1977.

Howlett, Grayle Wallace. *Tulsa Oilers All-time Baseball History.* Tulsa, 1955.

Indian Nations Council of Governments. *Demographic Atlas of Tulsa County.* Tulsa: The Council, 1990.

Inhofe, Marilyn. *Footsteps through Tulsa.* Tulsa: Inhofe, Reeves, Jones, 1984.

Interstate Oil and Compact Commission. *A Study of Conservation of Oil and Gas in the United States.* Oklahoma City: The Commission, 1965.

Ironside, Roberta. *An Adventure Called Skelly: A History of Skelly Oil Company through Fifty Years, 1919-1969.* New York: Appleton-Century-Crofts, 1970.

Joyce, Davis D. *"An Oklahoma I Had Never Seen Before": Alternative Views on Oklahoma History.* Norman: University of Oklahoma Press, 1994.

Junior League of Tulsa. *Tulsa Art Deco, 1925-1942.* Tulsa, 1980.

Kaoata, Ken, and Carol Eames. *Tulsa Zoo: The First Fifty Years.* Tulsa: Tulsa Zoo Development Inc., 1978.

Kennedy, Samuel Grant. *Memoirs of Dr. Samuel Grant Kennedy, 1865-1941.* Tulsa: Joe E. Kennedy, 1985.

Lage, Gerald M., et al. *A Profile of Oklahoma Economic Development, 1950-1975.* Oklahoma City: Frontiers of Science Foundation, 1977.

Lampe, William T., comp. *Tulsa County in the World War.* Tulsa: Tulsa County Historical Society, 1919.

Litton, Gaston. *History of Oklahoma at the Golden Anniversary of Statehood.* 4 vols. New York: Lewis Historical Publishing Company, Inc., 1957.

Logsdon, William G. *The University of Tulsa.* Norman: Oklahoma Heritage Association and the University of Oklahoma Press, 1977.

Markhaw, Mary Ellen. *Tulsa Opera, Inc. Dec 4, 1948-March 17, 1973.* Tulsa: Markhaw, 1974.

Masterson, V. V. *The Katy Railroad and the Last Frontier.* Norman: University of Oklahoma Press, 1952.

Mathews, John J. *The Osages: Children of the Middle Waters.* Norman: University of Oklahoma Press, 1961.

McCloud, Paul. *Profiles of Achievement in Tulsa Public Schools.* Tulsa: Tulsa Public Schools, 1970.

McNabney, Raymond. *War Notes: From the Letters of Sgt. Raymond McNabney, 1942-1945.* Tulsa: Cock-a-Hoop Publishing, 1994.

Metropolitan Human Services Commission. *Tulsa, Today and Tomorrow: Social and Economic Environment, 1986.* Tulsa: The Commission, 1986.

Metropolitan Tulsa Economic Foundation. *Metropolitan Tulsa Five Year Economic Plan.* Tulsa: The Foundation, 1988.

Miner, H. Craig. *The Corporation and the Indian.* Columbia: University of Missouri Press, 1976.

Morgan, Anne Hodges. *Robert S. Kerr: The Senate Years.* Norman: University of Oklahoma Press, 1977.

Morris, Lerona R. *Tulsa: The City Beautiful.* Tulsa: Banknote Printing Co., 1927.

Myers, Fred A. *Thomas Gilcrease and His National Treasures.* Tulsa: Thomas Gilcrease Museum Association, 1987.

Nash, Jay Robert. *Encyclopedia of World Crime.* Wilmett, Illinois, 1990.

National Urban League. *Social and Economic Considerations of the Negro Population of Tulsa.* Washington, D. C.: The League, 1946.

Neither Black Nor White: A History of Integration in the Tulsa Public Schools, 1954-1983. Tulsa: Tulsa Public Schools.

Oklahoma Advisory Committee to the United States Commission on Civil Rights. *School Desegregation in Tulsa, Oklahoma.* Washington: Government Printing Office, 1977.

Oklahoma Center for Urban/Regional Studies. *Tulsa, Oklahoma, Land Use Survey, 1955.* Norman: University of Oklahoma Press, 1956.

Oklahoma State Regents for Higher Education. *The Tulsa Junior College Consultants' Papers on Planning and Establishing a New Urban Junior College.* Oklahoma City: The Regents, 1969.

Parrish, Mary E. Jones. *Events of the Tulsa Disaster.* Tulsa, 1922.

Patton, Ann. *Fifty Years Remembered: The First Fifty Years of the Tulsa District U. S. Army Corps of Engineers.* Tulsa: U. S. Army Corps of Engineers, 1989.

Philbrook Museum of Art. *The Philbrook Museum of Art: A Handbook to the Collections.* Tulsa: The Museum, 1991.

Rister, Carl C. *Oil! Titan of the Southwest.* Norman: University of Oklahoma Press, 1949.

Roberts, Evelyn. *His Darling Wife, Evelyn.* New York: Dial Press, 1976.

Robinson, Wayne. *Oral: The Warm, Intimate, Unauthorized Portrait of a Man of God.* Los Angeles: Acton House, 1976.

Sampson, Anthony. *The Seven Sisters: The Great Oil Companies and the World They Made.* New York: Viking Press, 1975.

Savage, William W. Jr. *Singing Cowboys and All That Jazz.* Norman: University of Oklahoma Press, 1983.

Settle, William A. Jr. *The Dawning: A New Day for the Southwest: A History of the Tulsa District Corps of Engineers, 1939-1971.* Tulsa: U. S. Army Corps of Engineers, Tulsa District, 1975.

Sinclair Oil and Gas Company. *A Great Name in Oil: Sinclair Through Fifty Years.* New York: McGraw-Hill, 1966.

Smith, Michael M. *The Mexicans in Oklahoma.* Newcomers to a New Land Series. Norman: University of Oklahoma Press, 1980.

Snider, L. C. *Oil and Gas in the Mid-Continent Fields.* Oklahoma City: Harlow Publishing Company, 1920.

Southern Hills Country Club. *Southern Hills Country Club: A Forty-two Year History, 1935-1977.* Tulsa: Tulsa Litho, 1977.

Stansberry, Lon R. *The Passing of 3D Ranch.* Tulsa: George W. Henry Printing Co., n.d.

Strickland, Rennard. *The Indians in Oklahoma.* Newcomers to a New Land Series. Norman: University of Oklahoma Press, 1980.

Sullivan, Robert E., ed. *Conservation of Oil and Gas: A Legal History.* Chicago: American Bar Association, Section of Mineral and Natural Resources Law, 1960.

The Tulsa Tribune. *The Tulsa Tribune: Eighty Years of History.* Tulsa: Allied Printers & Publishers, 1980.

The Tulsa Exclusive Register. Tulsa: O. L. Harper, 1933.

Thomas Gilcrease Institute of American History and Art. *Art Treasures of Gilcrease Museum.* Tulsa: Thomas Gilcrease Museum Association, 1982.

Thompson, Mildred. *Tulsa City-County Library, 1912-1991.* Tulsa: The Library, 1992.

Tobias, Henry J. *The Jews in Oklahoma.* Newcomers to a New Land Series. Norman: University of Oklahoma Press, 1980.

Trekell, Ronald L. *History of the Tulsa Police Department 1882-1990.* Tulsa: The Department, 1989.

Tucker, Howard. *A History of Governor Walton's War on the Ku Klux Klan.* Oklahoma City: Southwest Publishing Co., 1924.

Tulsa County Genealogical Society. *Tulsa County Voting Records, 1926-1936.* Tulsa: The Society, 1993.

Tulsa Independent School District. *Our Tulsa Schools: Fifty Years, 1907-1957.* Tulsa: Tulsa Public Schools, 1957.

Tulsa Chamber of Commerce. *Tulsa and the Petroleum Industry.* Tulsa: The Chamber, 1945.

Tulsa Council of Social Agencies. *A Guide for Community Action: A Study on Needs, Resources, and Priorities in Health, Welfare and Recreation.* Tulsa: The Council, 1964.

Tulsa Chamber of Commerce. *Reach the Southwest Market from its Center.* Tulsa: The Chamber, 1945.

Tulsa Chamber of Commerce. *Pictorially Presenting Tulsa.* Tulsa: The Chamber, 1945.

Tulsa Chamber of Commerce. *Facts about Tulsa.* Tulsa: The Chamber, 1915.

Tulsa Museums. Tulsa: Metropolitan Tulsa Chamber of Commerce, n. d.

Tulsa Chamber of Commerce. *1964 Who's Who in Tulsa: Biographical Sketches of Men and Women of Achievement.* San Antonio: American Yearbook Company, 1964.

Tulsa Chamber of Commerce. *Economic Trends in Tulsa, 1978.* Tulsa: The Chamber, 1978.

Tulsa Chamber of Commerce. *Census Data for 1962-1972 and Economic Profile of Tulsa.* Tulsa: The Chamber, 1973.

Tyson, Carl N., James H. Thomas, and Odie B. Faulk. *The McMan: The Lives of Robert M. McFarlin and James A. Chapman.* Norman: Oklahoma Heritage Association and the University of Oklahoma Press, 1977.

Vaughn-Roberson, Courtney Ann and Glen. *City in the Osage Hills: Tulsa, Oklahoma.* Boulder, Colorado: Pruett Publishing Company, 1984.

Wallis, Michael. *Beyond the Hills: The Journey of Waite Phillips.* Trackmaker Series. Oklahoma City: Oklahoma Heritage Association, 1995.

_____. *Pretty Boy: The Life and Times of Charles Arthur Floyd.* New York: St. Martin's Press, 1992.

Winterringer, Clyde M. *Starting of Tulsa.* Tulsa: Winterringers, 1991.

Yergin, Daniel. *The Prize: The Epic Quest for Oil, Money, and Power.* New York: Simon and Schuster, 1991.

Yoch, James J. *A Guide to Villa Philbrook and Its Gardens.* Tulsa: Philbrook Museum, 1991.

PERIODICAL LITERATURE

Beck, W. A. "As Different as Night and Day: Street Sanitation Program." *American City.* October 1953, 92-93.

Bennett, C. F. "Oil Capital of America." *Travel.* January 1945, 19-21.

Billingsley, L. "Oral Roberts Reports a 7-Hour Talk with Jesus, Asks for Money." *Christianity Today.* 18 February 1983, 29.

Bolling, L. R. "Oral Roberts' Impossible Dream." *Saturday Evening Post.* September 1983, 42-45.

Bradshaw, H., and V. Bradshaw. "Tulsa." *Travel/Holiday.* August 1981, 52-55.

Bremser, L. W. "Tulsa Solves a Sewage Problem." *American City.* January 1955, 95-97.

Broad, W. J. "And God Said to Oral: Build a Hospital." *Science.* 18 April 1980, 267-268.

Broeg, H. "Oil Makes the Hurricane Roar: Tulsa University's Coach H. Frnka." *Saturday Evening Post.* 24 November 1945, 20.

Coleman, M. "When the Troops Took Tulsa." *Nation.* 5 September 1923, 239-240.

Eckle, L. G. "Tulsa Puts on Long Pants." *Christian Science Monitor Magazine.* 22 October 1949, 10.

Feis, Herbert. "Tulsa." *Survey.* 1 October 1923, 18-24.

Feldman, N. G. "Pride in Heritage or Resentment? A Sociologist Analyzes Library Staff Reaction." *Wilson Library Bulletin.* January 1972, 436-440.

Firth, M. M. "Education for Home Living: The Daniel Webster and the Will Rogers Senior High Schools." *Journal of Home Economics.* May 1938, 317-318.

Firth, M. M. "Parent Cooperation for the Home Economics Curriculum." *Journal of Home Economics.* September 1935, 438.

French, M. "Parent Education by Radio." *Journal of Home Economics.* March 1932, 239-240.

Gibbons, M. L. "Community Life Helpers: Irving School." *School Arts.* April 1941, 285.

Hambridge, G. "Meals at Six Cents a Day: How Tulsa Feeds Its Unemployed." *Ladies Home Journal.* October 1932, 21.

Hand, I. "Coordinating City and County Planning." *American City.* July 1952, 83-85.

Harrison, E. M. "Tulsa Schools Maintain Classes to Educate Parents for Home Tasks." *School Life.* September 1928, 16-18.

Hickey, M. "League of Women Voters in Tulsa." *Ladies Home Journal.* April 1950, 23.

Holden, W. "How Tulsa Will Expend $6,230,000 to Carry Out its City Plan Commission's Recommendations." *American City.* April 1930, 162-163.

Holway, W. R. "New Water Supply for Tulsa." *American City.* December 1924, 553-555.

Houston, N. "Talk about Tulsa!" *Holiday.* October 1954, 105.

Ingalls, R. W. "Strip Mine Becomes a Sanitary Land Fill." *American City.* January 1955, 11.

Jessen, C. A. "School-Work Programs for High School Youth." *Educational Victory.* 20 April 1945, 9.

Jordan, R. P. "High Flying Tulsa." *National Geographic.* September 1983, 378-403.

Keerdoja, E. "Roberts: The Lord Told Me to Build." *Newsweek.* 10 December 1979, 24.

Klein, K. "On Dealing With Declining Enrollments in Tulsa." *Phi Delta Kappan.* October 1983, 143.

Lyons, T. D. "Trolley to Tulsa: Algeresque Career of a Baltimore Street Car Motorman." *Commonweal.* 8 February 1946, 426-428.

Martin, A. B. "Decision in Tulsa: An Issue of Censorship." *American Librarian.* April 1971, 370-374.

McHenry, R. B. "Vocational Training for Defense Workers: Broadcasting Script." *Independent Arts and Vocational Education.* February 1943, 45-47.

Meyers, H. "Home Planning as a Sixth Grade Art Project: Eugene Field School." *School Arts.* April 1941, 278-279.

Miller, H. G. "Science and Prayer: Keys to the City of Faith." *Saturday Evening Post.* July 1979, 22.

Osborne, B. A. "Tulsa's Internationally Known Petroleum Library." *Wilson Library Bulletin.* December 1943, 344.

Post, C. "Once Called a Musical Sahara, Tulsa Now Boasts an Active Musical Life." *Musical America.* 1 January 1954, 33.

Prunty, M. "Educational Objectives of the Senior High School." *National Education Association Journal.* 1926, 809-817.

Remington, E. "Freedom in Creative Design: Woodrow Wilson Junior High School." *School Arts.* April 1941, 277.

Riggs, C. E. "No Accidents Yet Where Yield Signs Used." *American City.* June 1951, 133.

Shibley, M. C. "Sane and Simple Street Naming and Marking." *American City.* March 1938, 91.

Snider, E. "Tulsa's Big Four: Finances of Religious and Charitable Organizations." *Christian Century.* 25 January 1978, 68.

_____. "Tulsa Reacts to a New Medical Center." *Christian Century.* 1 March 1978, 216-217.

Stout, W. S. "Cities of America." *Saturday Evening Post.* 5 July 1947, 24-25.

Swartz, R. G. "Pride in Heritage: One Library's Approach." *Wilson Library Bulletin.* January 1972, 431-435.

_____. "Community Finds Its Forum." *American Librarian.* June 1970, 554-561.

Teeter, V. A. "Simple Does It: Detention Home for Girls." *Survey.* November 1936, 331.

_____. "Receiving Home for Girls Held by Juvenile Court." *American City.* July 1936, 81.

Thomas, L. "Read Oil Boom in Tulsa's Facades." *Southern Living.* November 1981, 98.

Thomas, L. "In Tulsa, Look Up." *Southern Living.* December 1992, 28.

Vollmer, B. "Tulsa City Commission Takes to the Air." *American City.* October 1941, 97.

Wardle, A. N. "Mohawk Reservoir and Pump Station." *American City.* September 1925, 237-40.

Watson, J. "Tulsa and the Wild West: Exhibition of the Philbrook Art Center." *Magazine of Art.* November 1941, 495.

Wehmeyer, P. "Oral Roberts Opens His Tulsa Hospital." *Christianity Today.* 11 December 1981, 41.

Woodbury, R. "Putting the Brakes on Crime." *Time.* 2 September 1991, 65.

Woodward, K. L. "Appeal to the Flock." *Newsweek.* 10 September 1979, 79.

Wooten, W. R.. "Paving Oklahoma's Busiest Street." *American City.* June 1950, 110-111.

Ziegler, O. A. "Abandoned Water Plant becomes Fine Bathhouse and Pools." *American City.* February 1929, 114-115.

"Bicentennial Salute." *Nation's Business.* September 1975, 57-60.

"Boston Avenue Methodist Episcopal Church South." *Architectural Record.* December 1929, 519-526.

"Danger at Loma Linda." *Newsweek.* 18 October 1954, 28.

"Face of the U. S. A." *Collier's.* 5 February 1949, 24-25.

"Frnka's 4-Fs." *Time.* 13 December 1943, 50.

"Masked Floggers of Tulsa." *Literary Digest.* 22 September 1923, 17.

"Mixed Fare, High Hopes: Tulsa Opera Club." *Christian Science Monitor Magazine.* 8 April 1950, 13.

"Oral Roberts: Faith in the City of Faith." *Christianity Today.* 19 May 1978, 63-64.

"Oral Roberts' Gift Adds to Hospital Glut." *Business Week.* 31 October 1977, 35.

"Patchwork Pioneers: Murals." *Time.* 20 November 1950, 70.

"Pay-As-You-Go Refuse-disposal Service." *American City.* August 1950, 90.

"Prairie City Reaches for the Sky." *U. S. News.* 22 March 1976, 48

"Public Schools as Agencies of Adult Education." *Elementary School Journal.* January 1934, 333-334.

"Red Carpet in Tulsa for Business Users." *Library Journal.* 1 April 1968, 1402.

"Touring Tulsa's Street Department." *American City.* November 1953, 108-109.

"Traveling Museum." *Recreation.* September 1937, 376.

"Tulsa Goes Modern: Mural for First National Bank." *Life.* 5 March 1951, 68-70.

"Tulsa: The City that Studhorse Notes Helped to Build." *Forbes.* 15 November 1977, 148.

"Tulsa Builds Its Second Aqueduct." *American City.* May 1950, 108-109.

"Tulsa to Build New Dam and Pipeline." *American City.* September 1948, 9.

"Tulsa Experiment with Ungraded Schools." *Elementary School Journal.* June 1933, 733.

"Tulsa High Schools are Making Progressive Theories Work." *Life.* 13 April 1942, 79-85.

"Tulsa, Oklahoma, Center Plaza." *Architectural Forum.* May 1971, 28-31.

"Tulsa Deaths Bring to Light a Sordid Tale." *Newsweek.* 22 December 1934, 5-6.

"United for Tulsa." *Business Week.* 24 November 1945, 18-19.

"Update: Greater Tulsa, Inc." *Business Week.* 7 August 1954, 81.

"Welded Water Reservoir Solves Demand Increase." *American City.* July 1942, 58.

"What Progressive Communities are Doing." *National Education Association Journal.* February 1934, 62.

"When God Talks, Oral Listens." *Time.* 16 November 1981, 64.

INDEX

McBride, Don 234, 237

McClellan, John 238

McClellan-Kerr Arkansas River
Navigation System 241

McClure, H.O. 59

McCullough, Grant 107

McCullough, Mrs. Grant R. *103*

McDonnell Douglas 244, 245

McEwen, J.H. 101

McFarlin, Robert 92, 95, 99, 101, 102, 117,
167, 170, 288

McGraw, Joseph R. 254

McIntosh, Colonel James 28

McLaurin, George W. 210

McMan Oil Company 92, 99

Merrill, Maurice 209

Methodist Espiscopal Church 41

Mid-Continent Oil and Gas Producers
Association 137

Mid-Continent Refinery *87, *185

Midland Valley Railroad 58, 123, 255, 273

Mississippi River 13, 15, 57, 108, 236, 238, 249

Missouri, Kansas and Texas (Katy) Railroad
30, 31, 57

Mitchell, John 65, 102

Monroney, A.S. "Mike" 234, 238, 239,
242, 245

Moore, William P. 30

Mowbray, George W. 46, 48, 57

Municipal Rose Garden 164, *164*

Murray, William Henry David ("Alfalfa
Bill") 150

Muskogee, Oklahoma 30, 44, 46, 57, 61, 67,
167, 233, 237

N

Nabritt, James 209

National Association for the Advancement
of Colored People 208, 211, 285, 286

National Child Labor Committee 43

National Housing Board 172

National Register of Historic Places 274-275

National Youth Administration 148

National Urban League 206

nationalism 117

Native American Coalition 288, 290

Native American tribes: Creek 13, 14, 15, 16,
22, 25, 26, 27, 28, 29, 30, 33, 34, 36, 37, 41,
42, 43, 44, 46, 48, 49, 51, 67, 108, 122,
123, 189, 274, 279; Cherokee 25, 28, 31, 34,
44; Chickasaw 25; Choctaw 25; Delaware
31; Osage 34, 37, 38, 42, 57, *94,* 280;
Seminole 25, 26, 44

Neharkey, Moosar 43, 48

Neharkey, Wehiley 48, 273

Neighbor for Neighbor 288, 289, 290

Neodesha, Kansas 89

Neosho River (see Grand River) 28

New Deal 148, 150, 170, 171, 242, 250

New Fox Hotel 120

New York City 58, 59, 82, 135, 142, 143,
184, 230

New York Stock Exchange 168

Newblock, H. F. 259

Nichols, Jesse Claude 188

North American Aviation 244, 245

North Greenwood Church of God in
Christ 209

Norton, Ruth 201

Norvell, George 259

O

Odd Fellows 123

Office of Price Administration and Contract
Distribution 173

Office of Priorities 173

Oil and Gas Journal 89

Oil Capital of the World 80, 83, 92, 108, 140,
143, 148, 163, 169, 230, 246, 276

Oklahoma Eagle 263

Oklahoma Natural Gas 257

Oklahoma Planning and Resources Board 234

Oklahoma Sun 123

Oklahoma, University of 209, 210, 228

Opothle Yahola 13, 14, 15, 27, 28, 29, 34,
276

Organization of Petroleum Exporting Countries
(OPEC) 247

Owen, Aunt Jane 21, 30

Owen, Chauncey A. 30, 31, 38

P

Page, Charles 102, 170

Page, Sarah 114, 124, 129

Parent-Teacher Association 195, 213

Parker, Judge Isaac 38, 44

Partridge, Kipsee 29

Partridge, Noah 29, 31, 33

Patterson, N.R. 237